# Survival From the Skies

# Survival From the Skies

## Airmen who Fell, Floated, and Walked from Adversity in the Second World War

Colin Pateman

AIR WORLD

First published in Great Britain in 2024 by
Air World Books
An imprint of
Pen & Sword Books Ltd
Yorkshire - Philadelphia

Copyright © Colin Pateman, 2024

ISBN: 978 1 03611 577 7

The right of the Colin Pateman to be identified as author of this work has been asserted by him in accordance with the Copyright, Designs and Patents Act 1988.

A CIP catalogue record for this book is available from the British Library
All rights reserved.

No part of this book may be reproduced or transmitted in any form or by any means, electronic or mechanical including photocopying, recording or by any information storage and retrieval system, without permission from the Publisher in writing.

Typeset in INDIA by IMPEC eSolutions
Printed and bound in the England by CPI

Pen & Sword Books Ltd incorporates the imprints of Pen & Sword Archaeology, Air World Books, Atlas, Aviation, Battleground, Discovery, Family History, History, Maritime, Military, Naval, Politics, Social History, Transport, True Crime, Claymore Press, Frontline Books, Praetorian Press, Seaforth Publishing and White Owl

For a complete list of Pen & Sword titles please contact:

PEN & SWORD BOOKS LTD
47 Church Street, Barnsley, South Yorkshire, S70 2AS, UK.
E-mail: enquiries@pen-and-sword.co.uk
Website: www.pen-and-sword.co.uk

or

PEN AND SWORD BOOKS,
1950 Lawrence Road, Havertown, PA 19083, USA
E-mail: Uspen-and-sword@casematepublishers.com
Website: www.penandswordbooks.com

# Contents

| | | |
|---|---|---|
| Acknowledgements | | vii |
| Foreword | | viii |
| Introduction | | xi |
| **Chapter 1** | Parachutes | 1 |
| **Chapter 2** | The Caterpillar Club | 9 |
| **Chapter 3** | Warrant Officer Bailes – The British Parachute Company | 19 |
| **Chapter 4** | Flight Lieutenant Charles Woodbine Parish – Swam 7 Miles | 25 |
| **Chapter 5** | Sergeant Kenneth Board – Caterpillar Club Evader | 33 |
| **Chapter 6** | Sergeant Percival Miller – Caterpillar Club | 47 |
| **Chapter 7** | Flight Sergeant Cecil Lockwood – Caterpillar Club, Japanese Prisoner of War | 54 |
| **Chapter 8** | The Goldfish Club – Ditching | 65 |
| **Chapter 9** | Pilot Officer Roger Osborn DFC – Goldfish Club | 73 |
| **Chapter 10** | An Extraordinary Goldfish Crew | 87 |
| **Chapter 11** | Sergeant Brian Beecroft – Goldfish Club Twice and Prisoner of War | 92 |
| **Chapter 12** | Sergeant Frederick Price – Goldfish Club, Adrift for Six Days, Prisoner of War | 102 |

| | | |
|---|---|---|
| Chapter 13 | Flight Sergeant Victor Jarvis DFM – Air-Sea Rescue | 111 |
| Chapter 14 | Sergeant James Burness – Caterpillar Club, Dinghy Dropping | 123 |
| Chapter 15 | Warrant Officer Robert Rawlins – Goldfish Club Endorsed Member | 128 |
| Chapter 16 | Flight Sergeant Alexander Sutherland DFC – Goldfish Club | 137 |
| Chapter 17 | Sub-Lieutenant Reginald Singleton, Fleet Air Arm – Goldfish Club | 147 |
| Chapter 18 | The Late Arrivals Club | 157 |
| Chapter 19 | Sergeant Henry Rolph – Late Arrivals Club | 161 |
| Chapter 20 | Flight Sergeant Thomas Docherty – Caterpillar Club and Late Arrivals Club | 173 |
| Chapter 21 | Major Robert Morrison DFC – Late Arrivals Club | 180 |
| Chapter 22 | Guinea Pigs | 190 |
| Chapter 23 | Sergeant Dennis Taylor – Guinea Pig and Goldfish Club | 197 |
| Chapter 24 | Pilot Officer William Batson DFM – Caterpillar Club, Captured | 205 |
| Chapter 25 | Sergeant Cecil Room – Goldfish Club, Adrift for Three Days, Rescued by the Luftwaffe | 216 |
| Chapter 26 | Sergeant John Lord – Caterpillar Club, Killed in Error as Prisoner of War | 234 |
| Chapter 27 | The Importance of the Written Word | 241 |
| References | | 251 |
| Index | | 254 |

# Acknowledgements

The author would like to recognise the original compilers of the flying logbooks and associated material that have been used to assemble the foundation to this work. The terms of the Open Government Licence facilitate the use of historic material from the National Archives, while other material, particularly photographic work, sits within the public domain created by the Government prior to 1957. If not credited otherwise, the images originate from the author's collection; other contributors have been duly accredited where possible.

Jason Phillips, Bob Marchant, Colin Bain, David Room, Steve Palmer, Jason Warr, Andy Saunders and Matthew Poole deserve recognition for their willingness to share information. The publishers who willingly saw the merits in creating this testimony of bravery against adversity in the Second World War are likewise thanked by the author.

Finally, I would like to acknowledge the assistance of my wife, Sarah-Jane, who endeavours to support my passion for collecting, researching, and writing.

# Foreword

During the years of the German occupation of territories across Europe between 1939 and 1944, every aircraft that flew offensively into Europe flew over the English Channel, the North Sea or the Mediterranean. Those waters were responsible for taking the lives of many airmen within the RAF's Bomber, Fighter and Coastal Commands. Aircrew and pilots parachuted out of stricken aircraft for many varied enforced reasons. These men also ditched on to the waters, but lives could be lost swiftly, trapped inside a sinking aircraft. The Bomber Command air-sea rescue summary for 1943 indicates the total of rescues in home waters for that year was 1,679. Most of those rescues would only have been made possible by a rubber dinghy known as the yellow doughnut to the serviceman or a life preserver universally referred to as a Mae West.

Morale was boosted by exclusive clubs that celebrated the survival of these airmen. The manufacturers of parachutes and rubber dinghy products formed these clubs and encouraged membership with advertised messages in *Flight* magazine. The clubs issued membership cards and badges to the applicants. Each individual story of rescue or survival against the odds was acknowledged and celebrated by several manufacturers of survival products. The application for membership often surrounded the tragic circumstances of crew members who had not survived.

These survivor clubs were outside of official service recognition. However, by example, the tiny gold caterpillar pins from the Irvin parachute company were worn openly on uniforms, and little if any redress was made against recipients by those who enforced dress regulations with discipline. The woven Goldfish badge awarded after a sea rescue was on occasions sewn openly on to battledress tunics or more frequently underneath a tunic lapel. In North Africa, the metal flying boot for those who survived the desert expanses on foot was often worn completely unhindered in all respects. It was the only club formed that had a direct connection to a serving officer within the Royal Air Force.

Gallantry medals were awarded and accolades were written from within theatres of operation across the world. However, within Bomber Command alone 55,573 men became fatal casualties. The Commonwealth War Graves Commission has registered 347,151 recovered casualties from all services in the Second World War. An additional 232,931 personnel are registered as missing, with no known grave. These casualties are commemorated by individually inscribed names upon many memorials across the world. The principal air force memorials recording these losses are at Alamein, Singapore, Malta and the Runnymede memorial in Surrey, England.

These young men and women did more than anyone could have asked of them. On 11 March 1943, in the House of Commons, the Right Honourable Robert Boothby MP engaged in a reply to a question on the bombing of Germany. He said:

> It is an arresting thought that when we carry out one of our big raids over a German town there may be anything from 3,500 to 4,500 young men in the air, about three miles above the target. When we staged our big raid on Cologne, no fewer than 7,000 young men were in the air over that town together at a given moment. These bomber crews display a quality of cold courage which has never been matched and which is quite unparalleled in the annals of war.

The stories I have researched within this book are those from men that had a chance to cling to life and survive. These are the men from all walks of life who served across Europe and beyond. Behind the membership of these exclusive clubs of the Second World War, there are thousands of accounts that have been lost for all time. All deserve recognition and these are a few of the many.

Colin Pateman

# Introduction

During the Second World War, the aviation industry made considerable efforts to develop and expand all aspects of efficiency in saving the lives of Allied aircrews from emergency situations in the air. Certain aspects involved the development of both individual and entire aircrew safety products. This book expands upon the evolution of exclusive clubs connected to that industry and the men whose lives were saved by the use of equipment manufactured and supplied for the Air Ministry.

Among others, this book explores the silk parachute and rubberised dinghies deployed throughout the Royal Air Force. Those men who claimed the use of that specific life-saving equipment often carried membership cards and wore club badges with pride. The existence of these exclusive clubs without doubt boosted morale in the dark and terrible times of war.

These survival clubs were personal arrangements communicated between the airmen and the manufacturing company. Each club required an application with the facts of survival. Accounts of training incidents and operational deployments across all commands within the Allied air forces were welcomed.

Any recipient of the Late Arrivals Club became a member through sheer determination to return back to Allied lines in the Western Desert through whatever means possible. This club had no connection to any particular survival products supplied to airmen. Likewise for the Guinea Pig Club, where membership was reserved to airmen who were operated on by the legendary plastic surgeon

Archibald McIndoe. There were individuals that achieved eligibility to a combination of clubs through one incident alone. An airman who used a parachute to save his life from a burning aircraft with subsequent medical treatment by McIndoe potentially made him a member of both the Caterpillar and Guinea Pig Clubs. The dinghy and Mae West manufacturers often differentiated between a man's life saved by the Mae West life jacket or the yellow doughnut dinghy.

There were a significant number of manufacturers engaged in the production of equipment designed to save the lives of those who served in the air. PAK Parachutes in Mitcham, Surrey, had patents upon their own parachute designs, yet they made and supplied many parachutes under licence for other parachute manufacturers. Stoke Road in Guildford Surrey was home to several factories including the RFD Company, who produced parachute harnesses, and the GQ Parachute Company, who designed and produced their own parachutes. They became a significant rival to the well-established Irvin parachute company. Both GQ and Irvin parachutes established a membership club for the men who had their lives saved using their products. These were by no means the only companies engaged in the production of such equipment. They are, however, some of the more significant of that time.

Each company engaged in the manufacturing of survival equipment were required to provide the Air Ministry with quality-controlled products. In respect of parachutes, the Royal Air Force issued individual record cards, forms 1507. These documents recorded the store's reference number, the contract number, supplier's reference, the parachute's personal identification number and any modifications undertaken to the parachute. An inspection date record was noted against the authorising officer's signature, which was confirmation and an endorsement that the item was serviceable.

The same procedure was followed with Mae West life jackets. Several officers, particularly within Fighter Command, personalised these with painted charms or mascot images. No doubt they were regarded as personal issue by those pilots and treated in the same way as their flying helmets and oxygen masks, which became the personal responsibility of individual recipients. Each item was given a unique serial number, enabling every Mae West life jacket, parachute, harness or dinghy to be identifiable.

It would be remiss to not acknowledge that on the commencement of the Second World War, the Women's Auxiliary Air Force registered a strength of 1,734. In 1943, when the force was at the height of its strength, 181,909 women wore the Royal Air Force uniform. By the end of the war, women served in more than eighty trades, including those of flight mechanic, fitter, electrician, radar mechanic and wireless mechanic. The morale boost, company and friendship they provided probably outweighed everything else that they undertook during the Second World War. It was more often than not that an airman's parachute had been packed and handed to him for operations by a member of the Women's Auxiliary Air Force.

*Chapter 1*

# Parachutes

Flight safety was a high priority for research and development for all aircrew within the Royal Air Force and Henlow in Bedfordshire had a direct connection to the research and development of silk technology. Parachutes had been tested at Henlow since 1925, the same year in which the Irvin Air Chute became standard equipment employed within the Royal Air Force. Towards the end of 1940, Henlow employed up to 300 men and women in the repair and packing sections, with more than 200 parachutes being processed each week. The growth in parachute training saw the development of Number 1 Parachute Training School at Ringway, in effect a further extension of the parachute test unit that also included a unit called the Special Parachute Equipment Section. This had special responsibilities for supply dropping and, additionally, Special Operations Executive parachute requirements, all of which originated at Henlow's research and development offices.

Before taking over as Commander in Chief within Bomber Command, Arthur Harris had voiced his concerns over the loss of aircrew and pilots in circumstances where he felt it may well have been possible to escape from a stricken aircraft sooner. Harris mooted that pilots should assess a situation in relation to saving lives and not attempt to force-land an aircraft unless there was a 75 per cent chance of succeeding. In addition, the pilot should not retain his crew on board an aircraft unless he assessed the circumstances as being 99 per cent certain of being successful. Clearly this last statistic indicates that aircrew personnel were to be ordered to jump from the aircraft more frequently than had been previously experienced. Harris took the view that the pilots and crews were far more valuable than the actual aircraft and although the risk of an abandoned aircraft killing civilians was a concern, it was regarded as remote enough to be acceptable. There appears little doubt that this reasoning explains the many accounts of pilots instructing aircrew to parachute out of a stricken aircraft while the pilot later engaged in a sole attempt to land. There were obviously many differing circumstances during the Second World War where pilots or aircrew leapt from an aircraft and entrusted their lives to the parachute. Each one was, however, regarded as an emergency escape.

During the immediate war years, the development of a synthetic substitute material to replace silk grew expeditiously. Initial tests indicated that nylon, invented by DuPont in 1938, would not only serve as an acceptable substitute but that it had several characteristics that made it superior to the traditional best grade of Japanese silk. Silk would forever be associated with parachutes, but nylon effectively took hold and efforts were made to improve the quality and to increase the quantity available for parachute material. By the autumn of 1941, a survey of production capability revealed that approximately sixteen thousand nylon parachutes could be produced each month at that time.

The design of material panels required precision stitching and they had to be examined carefully for flaws. The canopy consumed 56 square yards of material and was 24ft in diameter. The parachute pack had two rings known as the D rings attached. The right ring had a run of twelve rigging lines up the right side of the canopy and down the left side, which fastened onto the left ring. These lines measured 52ft a piece and totalled 700ft. The canopy and lines were folded precisely into a small pack 11in by 16in. The handling and folding of such a large quantity of material and lines in a small space required skill, without distraction. The weight of the parachute complete with harness was about 25lb.

Even with a fully functioning and correctly deployed parachute, safety was not guaranteed to those men forced to use one. Initially, fighter pilots engaged with aircraft as their sole target. That philosophy changed, extending to the pilot and in some instances the parachute itself.

The parachute was an important life-saving mechanism and the Air Council responsible for its progressive development was credited in *Flight* magazine in April 1943:

> Few decisions of the Air Council can have had more far-reaching effects on the morale, economy of manpower and operating efficiency of the Royal Air Force than the adoption of the Irvin Air chute for flying personnel.

The parachute was without question the saviour of countless lives, but it was not, however, infallible. The device operated with a sequence of events that would normally lead to the successful parachute deployment to suspend the airman and allow a safe descent. The inability to operate the rip cord as a result of injury or incapacity of the wearer inevitably created fatal consequences and any deployment of the parachute canopy in circumstances where the device was prevented from inflating properly by severely tangled lines was also most likely to prove fatal.

Unexplained parachute malfunctions also occurred. Pilot Officer Martyn King, flying over Southampton during the Battle of Britain, was forced to bail out from his Hurricane as a result of damage inflicted during the air battle. The parachute inflated correctly but then inexplicably collapsed during descent, resulting in Pilot Officer King falling to his death. The statement frequently seen upon archive documents, 'died as a result of a parachute malfunction', provides little explanation of the personal circumstances involved in such cases.

Squadron Leader Ahrens, a Typhoon pilot, attacked enemy transport on the roads in France on 16 July 1944, during which his aircraft sustained damage. He gained sufficient height and was forced to parachute out from the fighter-bomber near Caen. He fell away safely from the cockpit and pulled the ripcord. The parachute streamed out above him but failed to open. The pilot fell to his death due to the parachute malfunction. On that same operation and flying with Squadron Leader Ahrens was fellow Typhoon pilot Flight Sergeant Ewen. His Typhoon suffered engine failure and he parachuted out in an identical way. Having pulled the ripcord, his parachute streamed out and inflated correctly. Both pilots had drawn their respective parachutes from the same parachute stores on the same squadron.

Sergeant George Motts, who flew with Bomber Command over Nuremburg on 30 March 1944, befell a tragic demise after the starboard wing of his Handley Page Halifax suffered ruptured fuel lines and an eruption of flames. It was the second occasion that fire had broken out in the aircraft during that flight, but a final night fighter attack induced a critical situation, forcing an emergency escape for the entire crew. Sergeant Motts' parachute had suffered damage from the flames, and it malfunctioned as he dropped to earth. Three days later, his body was found entangled in a tree. The burnt remains of his parachute were draped about his lifeless body.

Luck and misfortune often mixed together to create circumstances that shaped many lives. Flying Officer Frederick Watts was attacking Stettin on 17 August 1944 when his Avro Lancaster also suffered significant flak damage. He made for Sweden, where he ordered the crew to parachute out anticipating internment as safety. Unfortunately, unlike his crew who landed safely, he became entangled in a tree and the parachute shroud lines caused strangulation, which took his life.

These are by no means exceptional examples. Squadron diaries and official operational records, particularly within Fighter Command, hold many reports and incidents that had been witnessed in daylight. Parachute failures after initial deployment were frequently referred to as 'Roman Candles', a nickname that still exists. Aircrew who parachuted into the sea were at significant risk. If the parachute should be affected by wind or heavy sea swell and fill with water it had the capability to drown the unfortunate individual still attached to the harness.

Pilots sat on their parachute when in the cockpit and their harness strapped the pilot into his seat. The Sutton harness was fitted with a quick release buckle, which meant that in the event of an emergency the pilot could quickly negotiate his way from the seat while still retaining the actual parachute and its own harness.

Aircrew personnel were issued with 'observer'-type parachutes. These were stowed in the aircraft according to the position and duties of the individual crew members. The parachute harness was worn at all times and, if ordered by the pilot to 'prepare to abandon aircraft', the parachute was simply clipped on via two stout hooks situated at the front of the harness. The parachute itself rested on the chest of the wearer. Abandoning an aircraft was a well-practised drill, additionally practised in darkness, requiring the crew to locate and fit the parachute in replicated operational conditions. Heavy bomber crews were primarily involved in night operations and in the event of needing to abandon an aircraft, the aircrew would await the order to 'jump', pull off their helmet with the attached oxygen mask and microphone leads, and then exit from the aircraft. All aircraft had different escape hatches to engage with. Those positions with no line of sight to the pilot were expected to advise of their leaving. This enabled the pilot to manage his own escape once all crew had left.

Survivors often provided evidence of explosions occurring and fires originating from fuel tanks and oil leaking from hydraulic lines.

The emergency evacuation procedure in the Lancaster specified that the bomb aimer, flight engineer, navigator and wireless operator should escape through the front hatch and that they escaped in that sequence. The mid-upper air gunner and rear gunner had instructions to leave through the rear starboard door in that order. The pilot was inevitably the last member of the crew to leave the aircraft via the front hatch. It was possible for the pilot and other crew members to use the escape panel above the cockpit as an auxiliary emergency exit, but this was mainly used after having ditched into the sea or in a forced landing situation where the aircraft collapsed on to runways or other terrain.

The Lancaster had a front emergency escape hatch in the bomb aimer's compartment that would be released by retaining catches, which then lifted up and jettisoned into the open hatch void. The hatch was only 22in wide and 26in deep, the barest minimum dimensions for escaping through. It was not unknown for the hatch cover to jam into the void as it was discarded. The force of air rushing through the opening was intense and all too often the hatch needed to be kicked free. Using this escape while wearing full flying gear and a chest-mounted parachute must have been daunting, with men mentally assessing if they were able to get through the opening safely while avoiding all the equipment fitted within the enclosed area. The escape route at the rear starboard door was simpler in that the doorway was a large opening. The slipstream, however, made it difficult to open and the men who used this escape could suffer traumatic injuries sustained when they were deflected into the tailplane configuration that was immediately behind the doorway.

The construction of the Halifax involved two large metal wing spars crossing the fuselage at a height of about 2ft above floor level and 12ft apart. These had to be climbed over to reach the deep step in the floor at the rear of the bomb bays. This area also had the mid-upper gun turret, which hung down and was prime for collision with their heads. At night all of these features had to be negotiated in almost complete darkness.

The Lancaster parachute exit hatch in the floor of the nose section was initially designed to be released by securing clips that when lifted inwards allowed the hatch to be jettisoned. A later modification resulted in the hatch being enlarged and refined, opened by a handle arrangement fitted at the port side. The hatch opened inwards and was secured by a clip that held the hatch open on the starboard side. This modification was a most important improvement and would have assisted the crews who were forced to use them in emergencies.

Within the Lancaster, hand-operated fire extinguishers were available at several positions, one positioned in the nose on the right side of the bomb aimer's compartment and one within the cockpit situated on the left side of the pilot's seat. There was one on the right side forward of the front spar, another further down the fuselage, aft of the mid-upper turret, and finally one at the left side of the rear turret. The Halifax was equipped with additional fire extinguisher stations to the Lancaster. One was positioned in the navigator's station, one on the lower panel of the flight engineer station, one within the reach of the pilot, three at positions within the fuselage and the final position accessible to the rear gunner.

The men who flew in the heavy bombers knew that fire was always likely to place the crew in imminent danger and if at all possible, efforts to quell the flames were fundamental to their survival. However, if unsuccessful then all hopes rested with an emergency parachute.

The Operational Research Section concluded from the gathered intelligence that the respective heavy bomber aircraft designs appeared to have had a direct connection to survivability in emergency escapes. Moreover, they deduced that the differing crew positions also had correlated survivability statistics, and these were connected directly to the escape locations used within the heavy bombers.

In November 1945, *The Aeroplane* magazine printed an advertising statement that 99.9 per cent of all life-saving parachutes used by British and Allied forces had been manufactured to Irving Air Chutes designs.

*Chapter 2*

# The Caterpillar Club

Leslie Irvin was the first person to demonstrate a successful free fall parachute drop from an aircraft, in 1919, having constructed the 'chute himself. Safety experts were impressed with the demonstration and both the US Army Air Force and the Royal Air Force engaged in the use of the parachute as essential safety equipment.

Irvin opened production factories for parachutes in the United States and England. An early brochure of the Irvin Parachute Company acknowledges William O'Connor, who on 24 August 1920 at McCook Field near Dayton, Ohio, became the first person to be saved by the emergency use of an Irvin 'chute. This was followed on 20 October 1922 by Lieutenant Harold R. Harris at the McCook Field Flying Station, who jumped from a failing monoplane fighter. Reporters from the *Dayton Herald* newspaper suggested that a club should be formed for these life-saving events. Thereafter, any person who jumped from a disabled aircraft with a parachute to save their life was entitled to become a member of the Caterpillar Club.

The name of the club is related to the caterpillar's silk threads that were used to make the original parachutes. In the 1940s, when the switch to nylon occurred, it did not spark a change of name. 'Life depends on a silken thread', is the club's motto.

In 1922, Irvin agreed to give a gold pin to every person whose life was saved by one of his parachutes. The Irvin Golden Caterpillar originally had amethyst eyes. To gain membership to the Caterpillar Club, prospective members were required to produce documentation of the life-saving incident to the parachute manufacturer. Often, applications were able to identify individual parachutes by serial numbers and model types. Those details were often checked against the factories' production information. Many letters to Irvins were incredibly detailed as the requirements for receiving a gold pin and membership were stringent.

Pilot Officer Penfold became the first Royal Air Force pilot to apply for membership into the Caterpillar Club. In his account of 17 June 1926, he said his Avro developed aileron control difficulties that forced him to bail out over a golf course. Within a matter of weeks, two flight sergeants, H. Steanes and W. Frost, were to become the first non-commissioned officers to be accepted. On 20 July 1926, the pilots collided in their Fairey Fox aircraft over Andover, Hampshire. Between June 1926 and June 1930, the Caterpillar Club enrolled a total of forty-seven Royal Air Force applicants.

There were other parachute manufacturers who issued an insignia for successful survival jumps. GQ Parachutes formed their Gold Club in 1940 and issued an engraved lapel pin and an impressively large, illuminated certificate. The Switlik Parachute Company of Trenton, New Jersey, issued both gold and silver caterpillar pins and the Pioneer Parachute Company in Skokie, Illinois, presented plaques to people who packed the parachutes that saved lives.

In addition to the membership pin, Irvins issued a membership card. At least three variants exist. One of these is the European Division, which has an illustration of a large caterpillar on the card. The more commonly seen membership card depicts two parachutes. All variants were hand signed by Leslie Irvin and heat sealed within plastic. A number of examples exist where Mrs Leslie Irvin applied the signature instead of her husband.

By 1939, membership of the Caterpillar Club had risen to four thousand and the total grew steadily throughout the Second World War. When victory in Europe was declared in May 1945, membership had reached 20,952. When the final Allied victory was attained in September 1945, the figure had reached 23,797. The following month an expeditious application for membership arrived, with Irvin accepting 6,203 applications. In early 1945, the combined camp registration undertaken by the Germans indicated that approximately 169,000 officers and men of the British Dominions and other Allied forces were imprisoned across these European camps. With victory achieved, by the end of October 1945 the total membership of the Caterpillar Club had reached thirty thousand. Many late applications originated from repatriated Allied airmen who had been prisoners of war, imprisoned in Stalag Luft camps across Europe.

During the war Leslie Irvin became proficient at processing the applications received from prison camps received via the *Kriegsgefangenenpost* prisoner of war postal system. This censored mail was always replied to by Leslie, his wife, or a member of his staff. Frequent instructions were received from the airmen to send the membership card and caterpillar pin to a wife or family member. In 1944, the club commenced writing to new members advising that the membership cards would be forwarded as requested, but it was proving impossible to keep up with the supply of the gold caterpillar pins. Many applicants from the 1944–45 period did not receive their membership pin until well after the war. Many others received the economy issue caterpillar pin, but regardless of type all were engraved to the recipient.

During the war, eligible aircrew would wear the tiny caterpillar on their uniform, or the pin would be attached to any medal ribbon, typically the Distinguished Flying Cross or the Distinguished Flying Medal. The pins were frequently lost and post-war years saw requests to the club for replacements. As a service to members who had experienced the loss of their original gold pin, Irvin supplied replacement silver pins. For this reason, other variations of the pin exist. Early-issue pins were engraved 'Pres [Presented] by Irvin', with the recipient's rank and name below. Later-issue pins included only the recipient details. The minute chisel engraving was masterful in detail.

In February 1945 Irvin Air Chutes published a special request to all of its members:

> The Caterpillar Club is a properly constituted organisation open to all who save their lives in emergency with an air chute of Irvin design, regardless of the manufacture. There is no entrance fee or charge of any kind. Those who qualify are enrolled as soon as authenticated applications have been scrutinised. A membership card is sent immediately to a newly elected member and, shortly afterwards, follows the Club badge, the little golden caterpillar, with his name engraved on the back. This genuine gold pin is the only approved badge of the Club. Members are particularly asked not to wear any other unofficial insignia and to discourage others from purchasing or wearing any imitation or unapproved substitute such as the embroidered fabric badges which are being sold by apparently misguided traders.

The Switlik Parachute Company evolved within the same time period as Irvins. A pilot called Harold Harris jumped to safety using his Switlik parachute in late 1922. Harris was employed as a test pilot at the engineering division at Dayton, Ohio, in the United States. During the investigation of the aircraft accident, it was suggested the parachute escape should herald the start of an exclusive club. Various names including the Skyhookers Club were suggested, however it also became known as the Caterpillar Club. In 1925, Walter Lees of the Packard Motor Car Company suggested some sort of emblem for the members. He had a vested interest in the club as he had recently become a founding member. A pin in the shape of a caterpillar worm, with the word Caterpillar Club boldly emblazoned across its back, was designed by Milton St Clair, who worked in the military engineering division at Ohio. This was a larger, bolder badge, quite different from the subtle and small gold pin created by Irvins. At that time there was no formal connection to any parachute manufacturer. Any person whose life was saved by the use of a parachute in an emergency jump from an aeroplane was eligible for membership of the Ohio-based Caterpillar Club.

The Caterpillar Club name and badge design was technically held under the control of St Clair, who later left the United States Army Air Corps engineering division and gained employment with Switlik. As a result of the boom in aviation, Polish immigrant Stanley Switlik had begun manufacturing parachutes in the 1930s and had been responsible for the development of the company that carried his name. In 1941, the War Department directed Switlik to increase production to a most significant scale. They became one of the US's most efficient and effective suppliers of parachutes during the war. On 18 June 1943, St Clair sold the Caterpillar name and design to Switlik for just one dollar. St Clair stayed with the company as an engineer for more than twenty years.

Even though the Switlik Caterpillar Club had a large membership, only twenty-five members of the Royal Canadian Air Force and the Royal Air Force satisfied the stringent requirements to gain admittance during the war. Many Commonwealth pilots and aircrew were trained at airfields across both Canada and the United States, and therefore these twenty-five Switlik members most probably joined as a result of training incidents involving emergency escapes. Switlik Parachute Company continues to develop and manufacture survival equipment for the military and civil aviation industry today. The Switlik Caterpillar Club archives are held within the company's repository, and among them are the exclusive members from the Second World War.

The Dominion Parachute Company was another parachute manufacturer and based in Sydney, Australia. It was a significant manufacturer of parachutes for the Allied Far East campaign during the war. Their parachutes carried the identification label 'Dominion Parachute' with the company logo of a kangaroo depicted descending upon an inflated chute. The factory commenced major production in early 1941, and the design was primarily to the standard set by Irvin. As with Irvin, the company decided to allow any Dominion Parachute user whose life was saved to join a club administered from their factory. This Roo Club was represented by a parachuting kangaroo.

Dominion acknowledged events over Buckingham Palace in London on Friday, 13 September 1940. The presentation of a special Dominion parachute seat pack assembly was made to the Hurricane pilot who shot down a Luftwaffe bomber that dropped several high-explosive bombs into the quadrangle and forecourt of the Palace. Three staff and a warden were slightly injured as a result of the attack. The damage was not particularly serious, but the incident drew much media interest. Photographs of the bomb damage to the iron railings breaching the security to the palace created a strong physical image in the newspapers. The King and Queen were resident in the palace at the time of the raid.

*Blitz: Then and Now* (After the Battle, 1987) provides the following quote from His Majesty King George VI:

> We went to London from Windsor and found an air raid in progress. The day was very cloudy and it was raining hard. The Queen and I went upstairs to a small sitting room overlooking the quadrangle. All of a sudden, we heard the zooming noise of a diving aircraft getting louder, and louder, and then saw two bombs falling past the opposite side of Buckingham Palace into the quadrangle. We saw the flashes

and heard the detonations as they burst about eighty yards away. The blast blew in the windows opposite to us, and two great craters had appeared in the quadrangle. From one of these craters water from a burst main was pouring out and flowing into the passage through the broken windows. The whole thing happened in a matter of seconds, and we were very quickly out into the passage.

In all, five bombs had been dropped. Sergeant Ginger Lacey, of 501 Squadron from Kenley, was vectored on to an area of sky covered in deep cloud in difficult flying conditions. Managing to maintain contact with the Luftwaffe bomber, Lacey attempted to shoot it down. His Hurricane was in turn struck by the bomber's defensive guns, resulting in a fire in the aircraft's engine. Undeterred, Lacey continued to fire, which caused both engines of the bomber to erupt in flames. Lacey needed to escape from his cockpit as the flames had entered the footwell and his trousers were alight. He was about to experience bailing out and parachuting to safety for the first time. Lacey then saw his Hurricane, P2793, plunge into the ground near Maidstone, Kent.

Air Vice-Marshal Sir Quintin Brand KBE DSO MC, Air Officer Commanding 10 Group RAF, presented Sergeant Lacey with the specially made Dominion parachute at Chilbolton in July 1941. It became a treasured possession of Lacey, who had received the Distinguished Flying Medal and bar while in the non-commissioned ranks. Later commissioned and promoted, he is regarded as one of the great 'Ace' pilots of the Battle of France and Battle of Britain. At the end of the war, Lacey had destroyed a total of twenty-eight enemy aircraft, with five probables and nine others damaged.

Ginger Lacey died in 1989 and the presentation Dominion parachute that he had kept and treasured was later handed over into the care of 501 Squadron. It is now regarded as a most important piece of history for this famous Battle of Britain fighter squadron. The special parachute is referred to as the 'Royal Parachute' due to the connection with the Buckingham Palace raid. The metal quick release box was engraved: 'For Gallant Service Over Buckingham Palace, Presented by Staff of Light Aircraft Pty Ltd. Sydney Australia'.

Returning to the renowned Irvin Caterpillar Club, the scrutiny of the entitlement to membership was carried out rigorously. The identification of a particular parachute that had saved an airman's life was always sought but not always possible. This is shown by an incident involving 159 Squadron Liberator AL531 in which the captain ordered his crew and passengers to jump from the aircraft over Karachi aerodrome, India, on 4 November 1942. The Liberator was carrying an unusually high number of men and eleven consisting of the crew and some groundcrew passengers took to their parachutes. The captain and second pilot decided to attempt to salvage the aircraft by carrying out a forced landing on defective landing gear, which they achieved although the Liberator was badly damaged.

On 10 November 1942, a letter was sent from India to Irvin Air Chutes in England asking for those who had jumped to be admitted into the Caterpillar Club. The letter was signed by Flying Officer J. Evans, as witness and captain of the aircraft. Each man was identified to 159 Squadron via a personal home address, although the men were operationally from Headquarters India. The application detailed each individual Irvin parachute used in the emergency escape. Without doubt, the ground crew on this transit flight were not trained in any respect for emergency parachute jumps and it would have been a traumatic experience. This was a highly unusual application and possibly unique as it featured eleven men making an application to join the club having jumped from the same aircraft:

Sergeant Rockett. Parachute number A94896
Sergeant Nightingale. Parachute number A110360

Aircraftsman Barker-Read. Parachute number A18798
Sergeant Dunlop. Parachute number A29715
Flight Sergeant Clegg. Parachute number A110348
Flight Sergeant Hughes. Parachute number A94830
Sergeant Corrie. Parachute number A94747
Sergeant Collins. Parachute number A110487
Sergeant Cheshire. Parachute number A87142
Sergeant Fleming. Parachute number A15286
Leading Aircraftsman Wilson. Parachute number A94718

Leslie Irvin replied on 1 March 1943, addressing his letter to Wing Commander Keegan in India. The application had been accepted and also wished the eleven airmen the very best of luck on behalf of the club.

Wing Commander Keegan received a further letter with enclosures from Leslie Irvin on 28 April 1943.

Dear Wing Commander Keegan.

Further to my letter of 1 March, I am pleased to say that Caterpillar Pins and membership cards have now been received for Sgts. Rickett, Nightingale, Aircraftsman Baker-Read, Sgt. Dunlop, F/Sgt. Clegg and Hughes, Sgts. Corrie, Collins, Cheshire, Fleming and Leading Aircraftsman Wilson.

I have much pleasure in sending to you herewith the eleven membership cards for the above and have today sent their Caterpillars to the addresses given in your letter of November 10, 1942.

Thanking you in anticipation.

Yours Sincerely.
Leslie L. Irvin.

In 1944 Irvin published an important notice to dispel any misunderstandings in regard to eligibility for membership to the original Caterpillar Club founded in 1922:

> Anyone who saves his life in emergency by using an Irvin-type air chute automatically qualifies for membership to the Caterpillar Club and, on making duly authenticated application, will be enrolled. In wartime the demands for Irvin air chutes far exceeds the capacity of even greatly augmented Irvin factories and, to meet the requirements of the services, air chutes of Irvin design and identical in every respect those of Irvin manufacture are made by many other firms. The factory name on the chute can therefore be disregarded and applications for membership should be sent direct to the Honorary Secretary, The Caterpillar Club, Letchworth, Hertfordshire.

*Chapter 3*

# Warrant Officer Bailes – The British Parachute Company

Flight Sergeant Alan Bailes was a pre-war wireless operator/air gunner who saw service with several units. He was involved in the early radar trials before other postings that saw him eventually serve in the North African desert. A subsequent posting to India with 113 Squadron followed, where in March 1942 he underwent additional training before flying to Burma to fight the advancing Japanese.

On 24 April 1942, Flight Sergeant Bailes was at Lashio, a northern Burma airfield. He was briefed for an operation involving four Blenheim crews that took off in pairs to attack Japanese concentrations along the Hopong–Loilem road. Each aircraft carried four 250lb general-purpose bombs with eleven-second delay fuses, intended to be dropped from a low level. Flight Sergeant Bailes was in Blenheim Z9831 flown by Flight Sergeant W. T. Hind and the observer was Warrant Officer Aitken.

The first pair of aircraft attacked successfully, and they were followed by the second pair, although their bombing run did not go to plan. The lead Blenheim of the pairing had attained a greater distance ahead than was desirable. As Hind followed, he dived over the Japanese column at the required low altitude. Flight Sergeant Bailes was firing his Browning machine guns when there was an explosion on the ground below them from the leading aircraft's bombs. The Blenheim climbed away having released its bomb load, but the starboard engine had been damaged, most probably by the explosion.

The crew of the damaged Blenheim immediately attempted to gain sufficient height for an emergency escape but Bailes was the only crew member to jump successfully before it crashed. With barely sufficient height for a safe parachute descent, he came down among a scattered tree area. Aircrew in Burma were not uniformly equipped with flying gear in 1942 and Bailes was wearing a khaki bush-shirt and trousers with unsubstantial footwear. He had no escape pack, compass or map of any description. Good fortune and a functioning parachute had saved his life but he was in a precarious position. However, knowing his escape route was northwards, he set off walking using the sun for bearings. He came to a remote village, where he rested before progressing north the following day. He crossed a river before once again seeking shelter for nightfall.

On the third day, and with both of his feet in a worsening condition, he heard rifle fire ahead of him. He took cover for some considerable time before moving. The Japanese were either ahead of him or not very far behind. An hour or so later he came across a small group of Chinese soldiers, so he approached them with great caution and told them as best he could that he wanted to get back to his airfield, Lashio. This proved successful as he was taken there in a truck, arriving in the early evening of the third day after the crash. At Lashio Group Captain Singer, the officer who had briefed Bailes' crew on his ill-fated operation, greeted him and ensured medical attention was given to his feet. However, Lashio was soon to be overwhelmed by the Japanese and efforts were under way to withdraw. Bailes was flown in one of the withdrawing aircraft to Loiwing on the China–Burma frontier. On 29 April 1942, the last aircraft departed Lashio, and all usable materials were destroyed. That day, Japanese forces occupied the base and cut the Burma Road. Mandalay fell to Japanese forces on 1 May and Allied forces focused on establishing themselves in India. Bailes was then based at Dum Dum airfield in Calcutta.

The bodies of Warrant Officers Aitken and Hind, the other crew of Blenheim Z9831, were never found. Both men are commemorated on the Singapore Memorial.

Flight Sergeant Bailes had a remarkable escape from both the aircraft and the advancing Japanese forces. Once fully recovered he underwent training for duties in heavy bombers, eventually flying from India in Liberator bombers with 355 Squadron, Royal Air Force South-East Asia Command, in 1944. He was unlucky to be involved in another emergency escape, at 0605 hours on 16 September 1944. Liberator EV902 took off from Salbani in Bengal to attack railway targets in the Maymyo–Mandalay area of central Burma. Now a warrant officer, Bailes was the senior wireless operator/air gunner in that aircraft. His crew consisted of Flight Lieutenant P. J. Gray as first pilot; Warrant Officer Green, second pilot; Warrant Officer R. W. Stephens, navigator/bomb aimer; Flight Sergeant L. J. Lewis, flight engineer; Pilot Officer F. H. Blackman, second wireless operator/air gunner; Flying Officer J. B. FitzGerald, rear gunner; Flight Sergeant P. H. Dexter, mid-upper gunner; Sergeant D. J. Drake, front gunner; with Sergeant R. Kelsall in the under ball turret.

The crew was experienced with more than twenty operations completed in Liberators. They were briefed to fly in formation alongside several Liberators from 356 Squadron. This was an unusual formation and things began to go wrong as soon as all the aircraft joined up. The pilot and captain of Warrant Officer Bailes' Liberator took up position astern and below of the rearmost 356 Squadron aircraft. However, it proved difficult to maintain that station because of the slipstream from the six aircraft ahead, which forced it to adopt a loose formation starboard of the lower Liberators in the formation.

Three hours into the flight, and getting near the target area, Bailes sighted a number of fighter aircraft, and his pilot tightened the formation to avoid being a straggler in the event of attack. Almost immediately, his Liberator collided with another. A gale hurtled into the flight deck through a huge, ripped hole in the fuselage. The pilot and his seat had simply disappeared through the gaping hole of torn metal. Bailes grabbed his parachute pack from its stowage low down on the starboard side. Instinctively knowing there would be no time to reach an escape hatch, he made for the gaping hole. One shoe became entangled in the wreckage, but he managed to get free, plunge through the hole and pull the parachute rip cord. The parachute inflated well, but only one clip was attached to his harness, putting immense pressure on the one securing point. Bailes had no doubt missed the second attachment in the panic before escaping but it was now impossible to rectify. The strap held and as he descended he witnessed the tragic sight of the two Liberators crashing to the ground in flames and smoke. He only saw one other parachute as he descended.

The second parachute was that of Flight Sergeant Peter Dexter from Bailes' Liberator. He had somehow escaped from the stricken aircraft but landed unconscious with his parachute almost shrouding him. Bailes managed to get to him despite a nasty gash on his own leg inflicted by the wreckage as he escaped the aircraft. Using the first aid dressing from his battledress, he applied it to his wound. He roused his crew member and they found refuge for the night. Both men knew the distance to reach India or Assam from their position was too great and eventual capture by the Japanese was imminent. The following morning two Japanese soldiers armed with rifles found them and immediately tied their hands behind their backs. They were taken in a bullock cart back to the two mangled bombers, where the mutilated bodies of the crew were awaiting burial. Taken away, they were later locked up in a small wooden cage too low to stand up in. Already inside the cage was Warrant Officer Ralph Stephens, another member of EV902 who had also escaped by parachute.

The three aircrew were moved to a Japanese Air Force base at Meiktila and interrogated before being taken to Rangoon jail. Conditions on the way were poor and Rangoon was reached on 29

September 1944. As newly captured men, further interrogation took place. There was a Beaufighter navigator in the next cell to Bailes and another Beaufighter navigator, Flying Officer Bernard Brodie Mearns of 211 Squadron, was in a cell not far away. In the Far East, the vast majority of Royal Air Force prisoners of war were ground crew. Actual aircrew were treated with contempt.

Squadron Leader Bradley and Flying Officer Jeffery of 159 Squadron also occupied cells in Rangoon. Their crew had parachuted from Liberator BZ938, which crashed in Burma as a result of engine failure. Their wireless operator, Flight Sergeant Woodbridge, along with four other members of his crew had been captured by the Japanese. That crew was collectively taken by truck to Rangoon jail and separated. The four sergeants were then taken to a nearby forest, where the Japanese selected Woodbridge, whom they identified as the wireless operator, as being in a position to give them information about secret wireless equipment, codes and wavelengths. They subjected him to a period of the most brutal torture. The prisoners had been made to dig their own grave trench and then ordered to stand in line before it. The Japanese officer, Lieutenant Matsui, invited his soldiers to abuse the prisoners with violence. The airmen were then brought to the immediate edge of the trench, then blindfolded and forced to squat. Matsui ordered two of the airmen to be beheaded by sword and then ordered a corporal under his command to undertake the beheading of the third airman. All the bodies were additionally subjected to bayoneting. Woodbridge was forced to witness the beheading of his three fellow crew mates. His final interrogation was then undertaken at the place of execution. Woodbridge would have been in absolutely no doubt that if he refused to talk he would likewise be beheaded. When all efforts to make him speak proved futile, the exceptionally brave young airman was decapitated by a Japanese officer's sword. The sword had been yielded by the Japanese officer Lieutenant Okami.

The remains of Flight Sergeants Leslie Bellingan, Robert James Snelling, John Derek Woodage and Stanley James Woodbridge were located after the war. They were exhumed and reburied in Rangoon War Cemetery, Burma. The seventeen airmen of 355 and 356 Squadrons who lost their lives in the collision on Saturday, 16 September 1944 are buried in collective graves in Taukkyan War Cemetery, Burma.

Warrant Officer Bailes, although a wireless operator, appears to have escaped any such brutal attempt by the Japanese to secure radio intelligence. After his liberation and recuperation from his time in Rangoon jail, Bailes contacted the British Parachute Company in Cardiff, part of Elliot Equipment Limited. He reported that his second emergency parachute escape over Burma had been undertaken by a parachute made by them. Additionally, and assumed from memory, he said that the parachute used was serial number 6797. The British Parachute Company replied, congratulating him on his life-saving jump and presented a small signed certificate recording the details of event. The company later presented a silver engraved goblet to Bailes, the engraving recognising the date and details of his use of their company's parachute. The Elliot Equipment Company itself also presented engraved goblets commemorating emergency descents with an Elliot parachute. The certificates and goblets are rare items, although the Imperial War Museum in London has an example of the latter gifted to them for display.

In September 1948 Flight Sergeant Woodbridge was posthumously awarded the George Cross for his fortitude, loyalty to his country and complete disregard for his own safety.

*Chapter 4*

# Flight Lieutenant Charles Woodbine Parish – Swam 7 Miles

Charles Woodbine Parish was a Royal Air Force pilot who flew with 149 Squadron and later 7 Squadron. He was born on 12 April 1915 at Upton on Severn, Worcestershire, the son of Clement Woodbine Parish and Elsie Mary Bonham Christie. *The London Gazette* holds an announcement on 5 November 1943 that he had been awarded the Distinguished Flying Cross with effect from 14 March 1943, but he had since died. The Distinguished Flying Cross could not be awarded posthumously so in this instance the recommendation and authorisation to award had been administered before his death.

Interestingly, during the war years Charles had been resident at Batemans, the home of Rudyard Kipling, in Burwash, Sussex. The church at Burwash now has a memorial bell in the bell tower as Clement Parish, Flight Lieutenant Parish's father, had gifted a set of bells to commemorate the men of Burwash who lost their lives during the Second World War. Both of the new bells was inscribed with a dedication. One carries the words: 'Hearing me remember well, Burwash men who fought and fell', and the names of fourteen Burwash men who lost their lives. The other bell commemorates his son, Flight Lieutenant Charles Woodbine Parish, who was lost over Germany on his fifty-seventh bombing raid: 'For memory I peal or toll of one beloved Christian soul.' His mother, Elsie, privately published a book about her son's life, simply titled *Charles Woodbine Parish DFC RAF*, which was printed by The Medici Society

Limited, London. This route to publish was not readily available to the many, proving again the status and position in society held by Parish's family.

No doubt many incidents of note occurred during the accumulation of operations flown by Parish. One in particular on 9 September 1940 demonstrates his will to fight and endure during the greatest of misfortune. Pilot Officer Parish was acting as second pilot in Wellington P9245 operating to Boulogne. Squadron Leader L. V. Andrews was the pilot when the aircraft was hit by flak over the target area. Inclement weather conditions caused icing and the port engine failed and caught fire after a lightning strike. The second engine then failed, causing the pilot to order his crew to bail out at a time when they were over water in the English Channel. From the crew of six men, only one man survived, Pilot Officer Parish. He had inflated his life jacket and swam for several hours using the stars as navigation, covering approximately 7 miles of tidal water. His crew of five all perished, presumed drowned.

The following story was published in the *Daily Mail* on 21 September 1940 under the headline 'Pilot jumps and swims seven miles'. The article incorrectly reported the bomber was returning from Germany:

> Here is one of the most amazing stories of the war. It was told to me yesterday by a young Pilot Officer, sole survivor of the crew of a heavy bomber that crashed into the Channel when returning from a raid on Germany last week.
>
> The machine was struck by lightning, one engine caught fire and the other failed. The pilot officer saved himself by swimming seven miles in darkness, in his Mae West flying jacket, to the English coast. This is his story in his own words.
>
> We were flying at 6,000 feet when we ran into a storm, thunder and lightning. We went up to 9,000 feet and turned

on the de-icers. Suddenly there was a terrific clap of thunder right over us, and for a few seconds we were completely out of control. The aircraft was badly iced up, and we began losing height at the rate of 2,000 feet a minute, though the nose was up. Because of the thickness of the ice on the windscreen we were flying blind, and just as we turned course to head for home, the port engine packed up. We tried the de-icers, but without effect. The rear gunner then reported that the engine was on fire, but this did not worry us much, and we went on until we saw searchlights, which meant the coast of England.

At this moment the other engine conked out. We were flying at 7,000 feet. The captain decided we'd get over the coast and then jump. Soon, he asked the rear gunner if he thought we were over land and both the rear gunner and the navigator agreed we were, though we were still flying blind. The captain then ordered the crew to abandon the aircraft.

We were now down to 4,000 feet. The ice had gone and I saw searchlights about five to ten miles away on the starboard side. The compass was quite hopeless and no earthly use. I thought we were flying south along the coast. The captain ordered me to jump. We wished each other Good Luck and just before I jumped, I yelled to him, Turn Right. The parachute opened alright and going down I could see the searchlights about seven miles away.

When I landed in the sea, I must have gone down a pretty good depth, and came up with a terrific rush. In fact, I practically took off, as my parachute dragged me along at a terrific speed. I lay flat on my tummy and planed across the rough water. I jettisoned the chute and flying boots and began to swim. The searchlights had gone out, so I tried to guide myself by the North Star. I kept it on my right and swam towards the coast. My Mae West was very useful.

After about an hour the searchlights came on again, and I swam towards them. I swam for a long time. Twice I almost gave up but something kept me going. When dawn came, I saw that I was about three-quarters of a mile from shore. I took off my trousers and made a last effort, as I was about all in. I reached the shore opposite a pillbox. I was too weak to pull myself out of the water and was rolling about half in and half out of the sea. I shouted several times, and at last some soldiers rushed out of the pillbox and picked me up. The soldiers were very good to me. I am sorry to say my five colleagues were lost.

Wellington P9245 had taken off at 0014 hours from Mildenhall on 8 September 1940. One hundred and thirty-three aircraft from Bomber Command had been tasked with bombing the ports and barge stocks accumulated for the Nazis' planned invasion of the United Kingdom. The Wellington had been allocated the target of Boulogne. The threat of invasion at that time was very real. A German wireless broadcast on 7 September 1940, uttered by Hermann Göring, announced that Adolf Hitler had ordered a mighty blow to be struck against the capital of the British Empire and he had assumed control of the attack.

Sunday, 8 September was to become a significant day for Pilot Officer Parish and for the thousands of civilians of London. For many Londoners, this had been the first time that they had experienced the effects of saturation bombing. It had been a sleepless night for most as the bombing attacks that commenced during the afternoon of the previous day carried on through the night. Anderson shelters rocked as each bomb exploded. After almost twelve hours of non-stop continuous bombing, people emerged from shelters, basements and underground railway stations. Many had heard on the radio fleeting reports of German forces reported to have landed on the south coast of England. In the early morning news broadcasts, it was confirmed that no enemy paratrooper sightings had been made, nor had any German ships or barges crossed the Channel during the night. It had been a night of terror and by the early morning of 9 September, after the last of the enemy bombers had returned back to their bases, little did the population of London know that they would now come under heavy bombardment for fifty-seven consecutive nights.

Five crew members from Wellington P9245 failed to return from the operation to bomb the invasion barges. Amongst the casualties were four families who would be denied the opportunity to grieve with a grave. The sea kept the bodies of Squadron Leader L. V. Andrews, Sergeant N. J. Bull of Sydney, New South Wales, Australia, Sergeant D. M. Payne and Pilot Officer W. G. Searles. They are commemorated upon the Runnymede Memorial in Surrey. The body of Sergeant J. L. Brown was recovered and he was later buried by family request at Colchester cemetery.

The incredible survival of Pilot Officer Parish was without doubt achieved initially by his parachute and then by his Mae West life preserver providing buoyancy in the English Channel. No. 149 Squadron records state that Parish came ashore at Clacton beach and he was uninjured. Within ten days he was flying operationally again and took part in an additional four raids on Germany, including the capital Berlin, before the end of September 1940. Eventually he was rested from operations, having completed a full tour, and he was later promoted to flight lieutenant.

It is unlikely that Parish ever communicated with the maker of the life jacket, P.B. Cow, about his survival. The company were yet to advertise widely in a drive for recognition of their life-saving products. No doubt the publication of Parish's survival in a national newspaper brought him much recognition. Parish was entitled to apply to the Caterpillar Club, his life saved by parachute. Many membership applications were administered retrospectively long after the date of incident. However, he would be denied that opportunity by virtue of circumstance.

Flight Lieutenant Parish flew in the large Stirling heavy bomber on his second tour of operations. In November 1942, he found himself assisting in the conversion training of 75 Squadron crews from the Wellington onto the Stirling. That squadron became operational towards the end of November and on 20 November four Stirling crews were tasked with bombing Turin, Italy. On 28 November, as the conversion training progressed, an entire crew were killed on a training flight at Oakington. That night another Stirling was lost crashing at Newmarket returning from operations while low on fuel. Two of the crew were fortunate to survive, parachuting from the stricken aircraft at less than 600ft. Other losses followed.

On 17 December 1942, five Stirling crews were briefed to attack Fallersleben in the Ruhr, part of a small bomber force targeting the Opel works. Four crews failed to return, among them Stirling BK620, which had become impossible to control through flak damage. The pilot, Flight Sergeant Dunmall, ordered his crew to parachute out over Holland. The bomb aimer in that aircraft was Pilot Officer Eric Williams. He and the entire crew were captured, becoming prisoners of war. Williams later became legendary for his remarkable escape in the famous wooden horse escape tunnel from Stalag Luft III. He returned to England, where he was awarded the Military Cross.

Stirling training and operations continued into 1943 with a depleted strength of aircraft. Flight Lieutenant Parish flew infrequently on operations during this period. His last operation with 75 Squadron was on 14 January and he then joined 7 Squadron. On the night of 21 April 1943, he took off from Oakington airfield at 2100 hours flying Stirling R9261. The target was Stettin and they had been briefed to locate the target area and mark it with incendiaries as a guide for the rest of the bombing force, an operation that required accuracy. There was an extra crew member on board; Squadron

Leader Blake, a Canadian pilot who was new to the squadron and accompanying them for an operational experience flight. Over Stettin, one of the engines was hit by flak and they left the target area on a north-westerly course navigated to take the aircraft across the island of Falster. Parish spotted a vessel and fearing it to be a flak ship, he diverted the Stirling over the island of Zealand, Denmark. The crew spotted a Luftwaffe Bf 110 night fighter and shouted on the intercom for the pilot to take evasive action. At that same moment, the Stirling came under fire from the Luftwaffe aircraft. Parish gave orders for an emergency escape, but the circumstances were unsurprisingly difficult bearing in mind the lack of power from the damaged engine combined with the fact that rear gunner Sergeant Lees was still firing. Only one crew member managed to escape by parachute: the Canadian flight engineer Sergeant Donald Smith who witnessed the Stirling crashing and exploding into flames north-west of Kelstrup near Slagelse, on Zealand. Smith safely landed in a field a short distance to the south of the crash site. Hiding his parachute, he commenced a most incredible escape assisted by the underground, who eventually smuggled him into neutral Sweden by rowing boat. Smith became the first airman from Bomber Command to successfully evade and escape from Danish territory, something that featured predominately in the award of the Distinguished Flying Medal that he later received.

The remains of the crew of Stirling R9261 were laid to rest at a cemetery in Southern Zealand, overlooking Dybsø Fjord. The churchyard at Svinø contains a Commonwealth plot of sixty-two burials, all of which are airmen. Eight of those brave men were unable to be positively identified. It was on 24 April 1943 when the remains of Flight Lieutenant Parish and his crew were interred. The headstone for Parish celebrates the award of his Distinguished Flying Cross medal, confirmation of his bravery and his determination in the face of adversity.

Donald Smith, the survivor from the crew, died in Ontario, Canada, in October 1998. His last wish was to rest among his crew on Svinø cemetery. A ceremony was held on 4 May 1999, when his urn was set down next to the grave of Flight Lieutenant Charles Woodbine Parish and the crew who perished in April 1943.

*Chapter 5*

# Sergeant Kenneth Board – Caterpillar Club Evader

In 1936 the Air Council sent a memorandum to the Treasury on the formation of the Royal Air Force Volunteer Reserve. It was seeking both approval and funding for a growth plan to expand the RAF through the training of reserve pilots, with an anticipated growth of 800 men in 1936, 1937 and 1938. Further plans were developed for a reserve of men to train as observers.

In 1938, as part of this expansion and with the threat of an impending war, the Air Defence Cadet Corps was formed under the guidance of the Air League of the British Empire. The first squadron of volunteers was formed at Leicester in July 1938 with an ambition to train young boys between fourteen and eighteen in all matters connected with aviation. A squadron consisted of 100 boys, divided into flights of twenty-five. It proved to be very popular and by the end of 1938, forty-one squadrons had been formed.

During 1939, in excess of 16,000 boys and 700 officers were members of the Air Defence Cadet Corps. The General Secretary and head of the organisation was Air Commodore Chamier, who had been Secretary of the Air League of the British Empire between the war period. The RAF was soon to embrace the advantage of having young men who had received basic training in matters connected with aviation as a pool of potential recruits for aircrew.

By 1940, the Air Defence Cadet Corps was making a direct contribution to the recruitment for the RAF and the War Cabinet positively engaged in providing pre-entry training for candidates for aircrew and technical duties for both the RAF and the Fleet Air Arm. In September 1940, the Air Training Corps evolved from this establishment of more than 18,000 cadets. Those established units that were close to aerodromes became frequent visitors and naturally any opportunity to go up on air experience flights was sought eagerly.

The dangers of flying were not often recognised during the short opportunities that existed. However, according to the Commonwealth War Graves Commission data, forty-four boys under eighteen years of age lost their lives in accidents while in the Air Training Corps during the Second World War. Cadet Peter Bond is the youngest name to be remembered, at just fourteen years old. He along with Cadet Desmond Fox and Cadet 1st Class Ernest Hall, both aged seventeen, lost their lives on 8 September 1943. Lancaster JB153 of 103 Squadron was due for a cross-country air test and the three cadets were allowed on board to experience a flight in a heavy bomber. It was ultimately an opportunity to reward the boys, who had helped to raise money for the Wings for Victory campaign. All were members of the Chapel-en-le-Firth Flight of 1180 Buxton Squadron. The Lancaster took off and was flying circuits of the aerodrome at a height of approximately 400ft. Something caused the aircraft to go into a spin and it began tumbling violently before it collided with a tree and burst into flames, crashing south-east of Wymeswold airfield, Leicestershire, with no survivors. The three cadets had a joint funeral and were interred in a communal grave at Chapel-en-le-Frith Churchyard at St Thomas Becket Church, High Peak, Derbyshire. Teenage cadets as young as fourteen losing their lives in uniform in wartime are deserving of commemoration.

In 1943, Kenneth Board, a cadet with ambitions to join the RAF, volunteered directly from the Air Training Corps. Enlisting in May 1943, he attended an Initial Training Wing in October 1943, as aircrew under training. In June 1943, the RAF had announced

## Sergeant Kenneth Board – Caterpillar Club Evader

in order A538/1943 that it would accept direct entry candidates for the position of aircrew flight engineers. Volunteers who responded to this entry undertook an assessment at an Aviation Candidates Selection Board. It is unknown if Kenneth Board took this route into service but he most certainly volunteered to become a flight engineer, possibly having seen the Air Ministry pamphlet titled 'Your place in the Air Crew Team'. This pamphlet explained individual aircrew duties including the position of flight engineer. It related:

> The Flight Engineer is the member of the crew most concerned with the care and maintenance of the aircraft as a whole. When he is not flying, the Flight Engineer in a Squadron is the link between the captain of the aircraft and the ground servicing party. He takes a close interest in their work, each day he carries out for himself an inspection of a different part of the aircraft, and when the aircraft is being prepared to fly, supervises such work as refuelling, filling oil and coolant tanks and applying de-icing paste to the wings.
>
> Just before the flight, the Flight Engineer does an engineering check of the aircraft, both outside and in, and then he helps the Pilot to start up and records the gauge readings during the ground test. During take-off he operates some of the engine controls, watches to see that engine running limitations are not exceeded and, in some cases, raises the undercarriage and retracts the flaps on instructions from the Pilot. During flight, he is responsible to the captain for the engines. He operates such controls as the air intake shutters, cooling gills and fuel cocks and advises the Pilot how to handle the engines to fly the greatest distance for the amount of fuel carried.

After selection, volunteers arrived at an aircrew reception facility and the volunteers were formed into flights, normally consisting of sixty men. They were subjected to dental checks and inoculations against diphtheria, typhoid and smallpox. Every student commenced service wearing the fibre board identity tags around their neck that identified every man, his religion and his personal service number. Daily routines included instruction on service law, signal skill, use of weapons, mathematics, swimming, training drills and lectures, all of which were endorsed with aptitude tests. Swimming lessons were put in place for any volunteer who was unable to swim.

More formal training then took place in an Initial Training Wing. Six weeks' training was designed to instil discipline, improve physical fitness and provide a sound basic knowledge of RAF structure. The Initial Training Wing syllabus included understanding the principles of flight, augmented by additional mathematics, aircraft recognition, and meteorology. Individual aptitude tests and combined tests between students often required apparatus manipulation. These were designed to test the speed of learning. The understanding of mechanical problems and the ability to apply eye, hand and foot co-ordination was significantly important. Aptitude tests were strictly pass or fail, with no second test facilitation permitted. During the Initial Training Wing course, the tangible connection with flying became a reality with the issue of flying clothing. These items were personal issue and, in keeping with common practice, the service numbers or other means of identity were applied to each item, which included a flying helmet, with oxygen and communication mask, flying goggles, a flying suit – either one piece or separate Irvin jacket and trousers, a pair of leather gauntlets, a pair of inner silk gloves, flying socks and boots, a Mae West life jacket and a parachute harness.

All flight engineers wore an observer's parachute harness. This was a somewhat cumbersome item when first seen but it actually fitted well and would ultimately be responsible for saving many hundreds of lives. The harness was manufactured in webbing material with bright plated alloy buckles and clips. The four main straps located into a quick release buckle, which would be positioned on the lower chest position. In order that the harness straps did not twist, they passed through a rear back pad, making it as comfortable as possible. The parachute pack itself was a rectangular shape with a canvas exterior fitted with four carrying handles, one to each side. The metal D ring or ripcord connected directly to the parachute canopy. Fitted to the reverse was a pair of metal buckles with spring clips for attaching onto the hooks that fitted to the observer's parachute assembly harness. Once attached the parachute sat upon the wearer's chest. If the parachute was deployed, the harness strapping would be torn away from its stitching when the parachute inflated rapidly. This assembly was well liked by the vast majority of personnel and in any emergency the parachute could be attached with no regard to its position. Either way up, the ring or rip cord could be pulled by the left or right hand. The personal harness was worn at all times while in the air, normally without a parachute attached. The parachute pack would be stowed and accessible at all times. It was simple to clip the parachute pack onto the harness hooks. Sergeant Board at that time had no idea that this equipment would save his life and ultimately allow him to become a member of the coveted Caterpillar Club.

Manoeuvrability within an aircraft was of utmost importance to flight engineers and the Irvin flying jacket was an ideal garment for their use. Designed by the parachute pioneer Leslie Irvin, the first examples went into production in 1931. These were manufactured with undivided one-piece body panels requiring only the minimum of necessary seams. Although this facilitated easier assembly, it consumed large quantities of sheep fleece material. As the demand for jackets increased, a more economic method of manufacture was devised. Smaller panels of sheepskin were used that naturally increased the number of seams, creating almost patchwork results. Flight engineers therefore inevitably wore the multiple-panelled Irving jackets. The Irvin jacket has become an item strongly associated with airmen of the Second World War.

The successful completion of the Initial Training Course involved constant assessment and examinations, all of which had to be passed in order to progress. Those successfully qualifying from the Initial Training Wing were awarded seven days' leave and provided with a free travel warrant to their chosen leave address.

The School of Technical Training was where aircrew flight engineers received their technical training. All student flight engineers within the RAF were instructed at St Athan. A memorial board was hung in one of the aircraft hangars there that recorded:

> In this workshop between the years 1941 and 1951, 22,599 flight engineers received their ab initio training.

Ab initio is a Latin term meaning 'from the beginning'. The memorial board survives and is now on display at the Newark Air Museum. A total of 17,885 RAF flight engineers passed through St Athan between 1941 and 1945.

Kenneth Board was one of those young men and he then joined a heavy bomber crew of predominantly New Zealanders. Board was the last position to be occupied on that crew at the heavy conversion unit where bomber crews were posted for a six-week period of conversion instruction. The crew had flow together in training but it was here that the flight engineer himself finally gained experience in the air. In June 1944, Board achieved his ambition to become an integral part of a crew in Bomber Command at just nineteen years of age.

The pilot, Flying Officer Godfrey Brunton, along with two New Zealanders, wireless operator Pilot Officer Elliotte and Navigator

Flying Officer Wilkinson, had joined together at the Operational Training Unit at Upper Heyford. They would be joined by their air gunners, Sergeant Hall and Sergeant Hayler, both British, and a further New Zealander, Flying Officer Baker, the air bomber, before moving to the Operational Training Unit at Chipping Warden in March 1944. Board joined the Brunton crew just before its operational posting to 75 Squadron. It was no coincidence that 75 Squadron was the destiny for this crew. The squadron had been initially equipped by the New Zealand government and held a large contingent of New Zealanders.

On 5 August 1944, the operational briefing disclosed to the crews the first operational target to be oil storage facilities at Bassens in Bordeaux, a target for which the River Gironde would assist the bomb aimer significantly. The crew were allocated Lancaster HK593, with the identification letter H and known as Hell's Angel. Eighteen aircraft were detailed to attack the target, all of which successfully identified and bombed it visually and a very concentrated raid was reported. Several large explosions and much smoke was seen on leaving the target. Anti-aircraft opposition was very slight.

On 7 August, the crew's second operational briefing saw them selected for an attack against an enemy stronghold in northern France. Seventeen of the squadron's Lancasters were part of a force of more than 1,000 aircraft attacking tactical targets in the Normandy battle area. The crew were allocated Lancaster HK567. The specific target was enemy troop concentrations and armoured vehicles at Mare de Magne. The target was selected to support the Allied armies' advance in the Caen area. All seventeen aircraft took off and dropped their bombs with the aid of markers. Anti-aircraft opposition was very slight, but enemy fighters were active across the area. The crew had taken off in Lancaster HK567 at 2200 hours for what should have been a relatively short operation. However, the aircraft was attacked by a Ju 88, the port outer engine was set ablaze and this proved impossible to extinguish. The starboard outer engine had also been set alight during the attack. With little chance of surviving the situation, the pilot gave the order to abandon the aircraft before it inevitably crashed in the target area. Five of the crew escaped by parachute while two of the air gunners failed to escape. It is possible they had died in the German attack but this was never substantiated. The escaping crew landed across the rural district of Normandy. Some carried injuries but despite that four of them including Sergeant Board successfully evaded capture. A number of surviving debriefing reports provide first-hand accounts.

Sergeant Kenneth Birt Board 3030159 flight engineer, MI9 (S/PG 2192):

> My flight and experiences are the same as Flying Officer Brunton up to the time that I baled out. I landed north-east of St. Sxlyestae Le Co about 03:00 hrs on the 8 of Aug 1944. I hid my harness, mae west and parachute, and then lay up in some thick brambles on the hillside nearby. A few hours later I came down from the hillside and sat on a fence near a farmhouse. Shortly afterwards a young girl came up to me and told me that F/O Brunton was sheltering in the farmhouse. She took me to meet Flying Officer Brunton and from this point my story is the same as his.

Flying Officer Brunton, MI9 (/S/PG 2154):

> I was pilot of a Lancaster which left RAF MEPAL to bomb a tank concentration in a wood near CAEN (France, 1:250,000 Sheet 8, U 06) at 2200 hrs. on 7 Aug 44. We had dropped our bombs when we were attacked by a JU.88, which set the starboard outer engine on fire, we failed to extinguish the fire. I then gave the order to abandon aircraft. I baled out

and landed near a farm five miles West of CORMEILLES (NW EUROPE 1:250,000, sheet 7, Q6598). This was about midnight. I sprained my ankle on landing and had previously been deafened by the explosions.

As soon as I landed a farmer came running up to me and told me to come with him to his house, where he gave me food and drink and civilian clothing. He then went back to the field and collected my parachute, harness and mae west, which he hid in a loft and subsequently, I think, burnt. I spent that night there.

The following morning the farmer came in with Sgt. Board MI9 (S/PG2192). The farmer said that he and his daughter were going to CORMEILLES to try to contact the Maquis. The daughter came back about 1100 hrs. and told us that the Gestapo were looking for us, and that they had shot ten Frenchmen in CORMEILLES in reprisal for their having shot two Germans. She said that her father had been taken by them but he was released about 1500 hrs. the same day. We left the farm and hid in a ditch in the bottom of a nearby valley.

About 1900 hrs. another Frenchman appeared and told us to come with him to another farm just East of CORMEILLES, where we spent the night in a barn. This barn appeared to be the local hide-out for the Maquis. Here we were questioned very thoroughly. Next morning (9 Aug) at about 0300 hrs. the farmer's son guided us to a little shack on the outskirts of ST. SYLVESTRE-DE-CORMEILLES about 2 kms. East of CORMEILLES. There was a member of the Maquis living there with his wife, and sheltering two members of the 9th Parachute Div., Sgt. Smith, E., and Cpl. WILSON, G., and F/Sgt. CHARTERIS, 57 Sqn., RAF. We stayed in this shack for about three days. The head of the local resistance group fed us during this time, bringing the food up from his house. We spent the nights hidden in the surrounding woods merely going into the shack for meals.

On 12 August the whole resistance group, with their wives, families, and belongings mustered at the shack, because we had been betrayed to the Gestapo by a woman collaborator in return for the freedom of her son. I do not know whether she gave them our names or not. We all left that night and walked about 7 or 8 kms. through the woods in an Easterly direction, having an armed guard and patrols out to watch for Germans. We arrived at the barn where we stayed for the remainder of that night and the following day. The next night we moved on to another barn about ½ km. away where we stayed for nearly a week.

On the night of 19 Aug, when I was on patrol, I came across a German tank crew who were repairing their tank in the wood. On the following Monday (21 Aug) some German artillery officers came and sited a gun close to us in the wood, so we decided to move back to the shack near ST. SYLVESTRE. We moved that night, travelling across country. It was raining very hard so we spent the remainder of the night in the shack. The next morning (22 Aug) a German battalion moved into the village, so we took to the woods again. During the day a captain of the Maquis came and told us that we had better give ourselves up as he thought we could not get through, and the resistance group were dispersing. I, being the only one who spoke French, went to the head of the resistance group and told him we would try and walk to the British lines by ourselves. He would not hear of it and said that he and his family and another young couple would continue to look after us.

The young couple took us to a barn where we stayed for about an hour, when the head of the resistance group came rushing up to say that there were some German troops coming up the valley towards us from ST. SYLVESTRE. We crept out to his house on the outskirts of the village, where he hid us in a secret loft which communicated with his bedroom. On 23 Aug the Germans retreated from ST. SYLVESTRE, leaving a mortar platoon with their gun about 100 yards below the house. We spent that day and the following night in the loft. The next day (Aug 24) we crept out into the woods and I spent the following night in a dry cattle [drinking] pond on top of a hill. Meanwhile the battle was taking place all round us. The next day (25 Aug) we walked down into CORMEILLES and found it had been taken by British troops.

Flying Officer Wilkinson's MI.9 debrief:

After baling out well behind enemy lines Flying Officer Wilkinson went into hiding for the best part of a day to avoid the search parties combing the vicinity of the crash. Then, estimating his position from his own navigation in flight, he began to move westwards, walking across country by night and sleeping in hedgerows by day. Travel was difficult as German troops were everywhere. Near St. Aubin he almost walked into a stationary truck full of German soldiers and shortly after he was forced to 'go to ground' in a drainpipe. On another occasion he found himself in a German camp and had to worm himself out on his stomach. Eventually gun flashes indicated the direction to the front line but the way was barred by a river and sentries patrolling the bridges. Undaunted he swam across, picked his way through the swamps on the other side and reached the shelter of some woods. This was on his sixth night and he was soaked, cold and very hungry. As he moved, he nearly stumbled on some

Germans lying in a forward observation post. Fortunately, one of the Germans coughed when he was only a few yards away and on hearing a rifle bolt being pushed home he hit the earth quickly and crawled slowly away making for the far side of the field. Later, feeling badly in need of a drink he crept into a bomb crater to find some water. On lifting his head he saw two rifles pointing at him and he put up his hands and crawled out. To his great relief the men behind the rifles were members of the Durham Light Infantry.

Flight Lieutenant Jack MacGregor Elliotte evaded and returned on 25 August 1944. No report has been traced.

Flying Officer Bernard Charles Baker was a prisoner of war at Stalags XIIA and Luft I. He was repatriated on 14 May 1945.

Sergeant Thomas John Hall, mid-upper gunner, was killed, aged nineteen. Son of Thomas Patrick and Ada Alice Hall, of Ilford, Essex, he was buried in St-Valery-en-Caux Cemetery in a joint grave, B 23-24.

Sergeant Edwin John Hayler, rear gunner, was killed age nineteen. Son of Frank and Alice Rose Hayler, of Burpham, Sussex, he was buried in St-Valery-en-Caux Cemetery in the joint grave with Sergeant Hall.

On 17 December 1946, Kenneth Board wrote to Irvin Air Chutes in Letchworth applying to join the Caterpillar Club. The company replied on 20 December 1946, congratulating him on his life being saved by an Irvin chute and on his escape and return home. His membership card and Caterpillar pin were placed on order and the company requested details of where he had landed for their records. On 24 January 1947, Irving Air Chutes posted the membership card and Caterpillar pin to Sergeant Board to his home address, 33 Connaught Avenue, Enfield. Board initially kept in touch with Madame Simone Piron, a young French woman who had played such a significant part in his survival in Normandy. Kenneth married in 1952 and was employed at Southend airport as a draughtsman, losing touch with Simone.

In the early 1970s, Kenneth Board and his wife went to France in an attempt to locate Simone. It was an unsuccessful journey but eventually a connection was made and Simone sent a letter to Kenneth. After thirty years, the French Maquis underground operative reconnected with Kenneth. Simone travelled to England and visited him and his wife. She brought with her a small section of parachute silk that had been recovered from where Kenneth had hidden it in 1944. A Madame Quibel had made some garments from it and later gave pieces of the silk to her Maquis associates for safe keeping. This remarkable reunion revealed that Kenneth had landed by parachute near a farmhouse in Trouville, miles behind the German lines.

Simone was twenty-six when he dropped into her life, and she was married with children. Her home was a safe house for resistance fighters and evading airmen, who were hidden in her attic. In 1944, two British paratroopers were in hiding along with an evading airman from Scotland and Sergeant Board. With so many people needing food, Simone was forced to buy bread in the town bakery. A mistress of a German officer worked there and she passed on to him her suspicions that airmen were being sheltered. However, by good fortune this was overheard and a desperate case of evacuation and escape was put in place before the house was searched. Immediately the British escapers were guided by the Maquis and everyone fled the house. It was a terrible situation for Simone, carrying a young child and little else. They needed to pass through a wooded junction where Germans were known to be entrenched. The escaping party walked across the road in bare feet, one at a time. Simone carried her six-month-old baby, followed by Kenneth Board with Simone's eight-year-old son Claud. Then, moving from barn to barn for sanctuary, they eventually reached the Allied front but not before encountering a frightening mortar bomb barrage. British troops secured the escapers and brought them to safety behind the Allied lines.

Simone endured a sad life in the immediate post-war years. Her husband Marcel, who had bravely resisted the German forces, died of cancer. She remarried and moved to Paris, only to be widowed for a second time. In 1974, Simone set out to contact the men she had helped in 1944. She sought the help of the RAF along with the BBC, which broadcast an appeal by Charlie Chester and this brought success. Eventually a reunion took place in England and Simone was hosted by Kenneth's pilot, Godfrey Brunton, at his home in Kent. Simone's son Claud brought his son to accompany his grandmother to the reunion. The group reminisced and the magazine *Woman's Realm* published the incredible story in November 1975. The piece of parachute that had supported Sergeant Board's emergency escape became a most treasured item for him alongside his Caterpillar Club memorabilia.

*Chapter 6*

# Sergeant Percival Miller – Caterpillar Club

The early Second World War radar apparatus known as ground control interception was capable of showing the position of aircraft within its range of detection upon a fluorescent screen display. It became crucial to develop and refine the ability to fight the Luftwaffe in the night sky over England. The pressure to develop these capabilities was intense, primarily to create airborne interception and thus enable night fighter crews to search the skies independently and at will having been directed by the ground controllers on to targets located on their electronic systems.

The first ground control interception capability became operational at Sopley in Hampshire in January 1941. Five additional sites became operational by the end of that month and later extended across the south coast and upwards along the lower east coast of England. With the help of the chain of stations, improvements in the manufacture and delivery of night fighter aircraft, predominantly the Bristol Beaufighter, which was equipped with radar sets, and combined with better-trained night fighter crews from the operational training units, the capability in night fighting improved significantly. Tactics were developed by controllers and in the air the night fighter crews grew in confidence as they responded to directions and hunted for close-quarter interceptions.

The Mk IV Airborne Interception equipment was the first successful interception radar. The equipment could detect targets from a maximum range of 20,000ft down to a minimum range of 400ft. This equipment quickly became the standard fit in night fighters and was installed just in time to take part in the defence of Britain during the Blitz in 1941.

Sergeant Percival Miller was an operator of this equipment, but it was not until the sets were refined to enable men such as him to place their pilot behind the Luftwaffe target that the night fighter force began to offer anything close to real offensive resistance to enemy bombers. Sergeant Miller experienced the ongoing developments and saw operational service with his regular pilot, Sergeant Harling Walter Watson. As with any night fighting team, both men had challenging circumstances to overcome before the inevitable success of shooting down an enemy aircraft was achieved.

Twin-engine aircraft like the Beaufighter equipped with Airborne Interception and operating under ground control interception control within a small number of specialised squadrons created the main defence against the Luftwaffe night raiding offensive. The system limitations meant that controllers were only able to direct one fighter at a time towards any possible interception, a distinct limitation when the Luftwaffe's mass attacks were being undertaken against England. The controller communicated with the fighter pilot by issuing a flow of instructions concerning the movements detected on the raiders flight path. This would often lead to a crossover of incoherent information. It was eventually decided that the pilot should announce immediately the moment any contact had been achieved. The controller could then leave the crew to pursue their contact without interference from ground control.

Sergeant Miller was in effect an observer, navigator and radar operator when flying in a Beaufighter. He would sit facing forwards towards the pilot in his Perspex dome situated in the central fuselage, enabling him to see the pilot but little else. He was responsible for tracking the target in order for the pilot to identify and engage should it be an enemy aircraft. By March 1941, the Airborne Interception-equipped fighter had become the established form for night fighter defence. It was subsequently deployed for offensive night fighter operations over occupied Europe and further afield.

Airborne Interception training was a necessity for crews. It could be precarious and training accidents were not uncommon. For example, a collision occurred between two Beaufighters of 219 Squadron on the afternoon of 30 April 1941 when they were flying over Brighton, Sussex. Both crews were engaged in training prior to becoming operational at night, practising ground control interception techniques. Beaufighter R2127 was crewed by Sergeant Harry Twidale and Sergeant Thomas Forster, and Beaufighter R2083 by Pilot Officer Richard Holman and Pilot Officer Alexander Black.

In the file, AIR 81/6161 at the National Archives, there is a letter from Wing Commander Pike, the Officer Commanding, 219 Squadron, sent to RAF Tangmere, in which he gives his thoughts on the accident:

> At the time of the accident the two aircraft were carrying out a GCI. Interception, one acting as bomber and the other as fighter. The stage was reached where Pilot Officer Holman was instructed to act as bomber and Sergeant Twidale as fighter. At this time Sergeant Twidale was flying on a steady course and Pilot Officer Holman behind him at a safe distance, and not in formation. Pilot Officer Holman then told Sergeant Twidale on the radio transmission that he was about to overtake him and go in front. In carrying out this manoeuvre, for some unexplained reason Holman's aircraft collided with the machine in front. Visibility at this height was good and the only possible explanation that I can think of is that Pilot Officer Holman endeavoured to overtake the leading aircraft by flying above him instead of below him and to one side. If he did in fact do this, Twidale's aircraft would be invisible for most of this manoeuvre owing to the natural blind spot when looking down.

This opinion could only have originated from the airfield controller, however, no evidence appears to exist of that, or any other source. The actual collision was witnessed from the ground, but no real evidence exists that Pilot Officer Holman had carried out the manoeuvre as stated. Group Captain Woodhall, at Tangmere, sent the information to the Air Ministry, concurring with Wing Commander Pike's remarks and stated that in his opinion no court of inquiry was necessary.

Police Constable Lawrence Holford was on patrol in the Lewes Road area of Brighton at the time of the accident. At approximately 1500 hours, Constable Holford had called in on the gatekeeper of the Allan West factory. One aircraft disintegrated over the factory, with one engine smashing down, killing Constable Holford and the gatekeeper, Mr Dyer, instantly. Another engine landed on allotments in Roedale Road, while one of the crew fell through the roof of a house in Roedale Road. Pieces of the destroyed aircraft were scattered over a large area of central Brighton.

Sergeant Twidale was the only survivor, having parachuted from a relatively low height. Flying Officer Black and Pilot Officer Holman were both later buried at the churchyard in Tangmere, while Sergeant Forster's body was taken to his home and buried in Northumberland.

Returning to Sergeants Miller and Watson, they also joined 219 Squadron and were operationally ready for night fighter duties from 1 July 1942. They undertook training sorties, night flight testing and interception practice. Just four days after arriving, they witnessed another crew's emergency with an erupting engine fire shortly after take-off. The pilot, Flying Officer Carroll, gained height and escaped by parachute, while navigator Sergeant Hobdey somehow became entangled in his escape attempt and remained in the aircraft, which crashed. Remarkably, Hobdey suffered only a broken leg and minor injuries in what were most remarkable circumstances of good fortune.

Sergeants Miller and Watson flew dusk landing exercises among other flying assessments into August 1942. Squadron records then details the reason why Miller joined the Caterpillar Club.

The crew were airborne in the afternoon of 11 August and found the port tailplane elevator unresponsive. After lengthy discussion, the pilot in charge of the Beaufighter instructed navigator Sergeant Miller to bale out as any landing attempt was likely to be difficult and dangerous. The parachute deployed safely and Miller descended on to the aerodrome safely. Watson decided to attempt a landing, controlling the aircraft by the use of trim. He executed a safe and excellent landing, saving the aircraft. Watson was promoted to flight sergeant, while his navigator hoped that his promotion would follow. Both men were unexpectedly posted to North Africa for night fighter operations in Beaufighters with 600 Squadron.

Troublesome mosquitoes, basic amenities, sand and heat greeted the new arrivals. Flying from cleared areas of ground with planking for ground stability were challenging conditions. However, Flight Sergeant Watson and Sergeant Miller were well trained and experienced. They embraced the challenges and flew many ground control interception sorties but success against enemy aircraft continuously eluded them. Aerial chases took place but none developed into confirmed combat. The month of May 1943 saw 600 Squadron claim ten enemy aircraft as attacked and destroyed. The North African conflict was regarded as won.

No. 600 Squadron relocated to Malta to cover the invasion of Sicily, and this proved to be a very active posting for the ground-controlled night fighters. Malta in the darkness was problematic for the night fighters. The flarepath was lit but very dim and it was dowsed quickly after an aircraft had landed. The aircrew were split between two flights, which were on duty every alternate night. Patrols were flown throughout the night, one aircraft relieving the other. The basic procedure deployed using airborne interception aircraft by ground control interception was to fly patrol lines and obtain occasional fixes of position by means of voice fixing. This provided sufficient reassurances of location and patrol courses, and times would be worked out before taking off and be noted on the recognition card carried by each pilot. The sector controller would instruct aircraft individually from the patrol line to the interception by giving the pilots vectors that would bring them to a point for the controller to take over and direct according to the equipment readings. Only with co-operation could effective use be made of fighters in the air.

The period when hostile aircraft were in the area of the ground control interception would be limited, so between them the sector controller and the ground controller endeavoured to secure the maximum number of airborne interception contacts during that short period available to them. The ground controller put the fighter into airborne interception contact with an incoming raid as quickly as possible. The aircraft's radar operator needed to inform the pilot once a good contract had been established. The pilot would give notice of contact and the ground controller would then take on another fighter that had been fed to him by the sector controller. Once in airborne contact the pilot would endeavour to close and engage the enemy as directed by his navigator sitting behind him. If contact should be lost the pilot called the sector controller, who fixed his position and gave instructions whether to return to the patrol line or to land. If after an interception chase the crew should find themselves out of transmission range or they became lost, the pilot would make use of the Inter Sector Emergency Control system to gain directions.

Sergeant Miller was by now wearing the radio operator's half wing worn by airborne interceptor operators. It had become a rather prestigious wing to be worn in the Royal Air Force. No. 600 Squadron was delivering cover for the invasion of Italy when Flight

Sergeant Watson received a commission as an officer and Sergeant Miller stepped up to flight sergeant. On 7 August 1943, Pilot Officer Watson and Flight Sergeant Miller, having flown a four-hour patrol searching the skies, suffered a hydraulic failure of their aircraft. A crash-landing occurred at Cassibile in Sicily, resulting in a few minor injuries for the pilot, while Miller escaped the carnage unhurt. Both men regarded themselves as fortunate and remained together flying endless sorties directed to contacts. Despite Miller's expert interpretation of his equipment, contacts were lost through electronic interference, distractions or frequent identification of non-hostile aircraft. It was later established that around this time the Luftwaffe had for the first time started dropping foil strips known by the British as Window to confuse night interception radar.

Flight Sergeant Miller had worn the tiny Caterpillar pin on his uniform and his laminated membership card was a well-kept possession throughout his life. Maybe it was good fortune that came to him on the two sorties that he survived – the parachuting out over his aerodrome and the subsequent crash-landing after the hydraulics failures – both of which he escaped from unscathed. His last recorded operation undertaken in 600 Squadron came at the end of February 1944. The hours and operations he had flown were more than enough or expected in order for him to have completed a tour of operations, entitling him to be withdrawn from operational flying.

*Chapter 7*

# Flight Sergeant Cecil Lockwood – Caterpillar Club, Japanese Prisoner of War

During the Second World War airmen trusted their lives to parachutes in all theatres of war, however, it would be a fair observation that Caterpillar Club membership in the Far East air war is seen infrequently, and opportunities to explore the survival of these men is rarely encountered.

Flight Sergeant Cecil Harry Lockwood was born on 16 October 1918. He lived in Lower Station Road, Chivenor, Oxfordshire. Throughout his life, he preferred to be known by his middle name, Harry. Aged eighteen, he enlisted in the RAF and after his initial training he volunteered for aircrew duties and undertook the lengthy observer training structure in place at that time. The developing instabilities across the world influenced the British Government to introduce a rearmament programme in March 1938. Flying training schools were increased and at that time the Royal Air Force Volunteer Reserve had accepted over a thousand men for pilot training. Sergeant Lockwood was posted as an observer to the Far East, to serve in Singapore with 36 Squadron.

By 1938, Japan had occupied a vast area of the Chinese coastline in an attempt to establish Japanese primacy in Asia and incorporate China. On 27 September 1940, Japan signed the Tripartite Pact with Germany and Italy, binding the three countries to provide each other with mutual support. Unexpectedly however, the Russian intervention alliance to Germany came as a disturbing development to the Japanese. A Japanese–Russian non-aggression pact was subsequently negotiated by Japan's foreign minister in 1941. Russia would eventually break the terms of that agreement. American intelligence infiltrated Japanese diplomatic ciphers and acted decisively with economic warfare, placing embargoes on Western trade with Japan. Japan responded with negotiations while they deliberated over war but with the deadline for accepting American concessions set at 25 November 1941, shortly after Japan declared war against the Allies, on 7 December.

Since the outbreak of war with Japan, 36 Squadron and 100 Squadron had been undertaking night reconnaissance operations over Japanese-held airfields and camps up and down the Malay Peninsula. In early December 1941, Singapore had been heartened by the arrival of Churchill's promised consolidation of battleships, HMS *Prince of Wales* and HMS *Repulse* along with their destroyer escort. The elation was to be short-lived. Offensive Japanese actions had already commenced upon Malaya and in the early hours of 8 December 1941 a reconnaissance pilot found a significant Japanese naval warship convoy heading south-west from Saigon. The pilot photographed the ships from high altitude in his Beaufort. It was located some 30 miles offshore, and photographs were taken when the Beaufort crew thought they saw Japanese Zero fighters taking off from an aircraft carrier within the fleet below them. The Beaufort pilot was Flight Lieutenant Mitchell. Suddenly, he came under attack from Japanese fighter aircraft that were protecting the invasion forces. The Beaufort's port engine was hit by gunfire, causing the aircraft to go into a spin from which Mitchell managed to recover and thereafter headed for cloud cover. The air gunner, Sergeant Barcroft, was injured during the fight, but later reported that he had in turn hit one of the attacking fighters, which he thought he had shot down. The wireless operator Sergeant Gibson also received slight wounds to his thigh. The pilot managed to land the Beaufort at Kota Bharu in northern Malaya despite a Japanese strafing attack upon the landing field at that time. Mitchell managed to get the photographic evidence back to Seletar by flying in an airworthy Brewster Buffalo. Attempts to repair the damaged Beaufort were thwarted by the Japanese air attacks and eventually the aircraft caught fire and was destroyed.

The first Japanese air raid on Singapore came on 8 December, with bombs falling on Seletar airfield along with reports of landings in Thailand and northern Malaya. The unexpected raid on Singapore caused minor damage. Five Beaufort aircraft remained at Seletar, all of them minus bomb or torpedo racks, and guns, and all suffering various technical deficiencies such as inadequate fuel feed lines, airscrew problems and inefficient brakes. It was clear that these aircraft needed much work before they would be fit for combat, and it was decided that they should be returned to Australia to prevent them falling into enemy hands. On 19 December 1941, four of the five Beauforts took off for the first leg to Surabaya Java under the command of Wing Commander McKern. The Far East Command was split into three areas of command: Northern Malaya, Central and Southern Malaya and Singapore.

The aircraft complement to defend Singapore was no more than a few Vickers Vildebeests, Fairey Albacores and Lockheed Hudson aircraft, with a few Hawker Hurricanes as fighter cover. The Vildebeests were too vulnerable for use in daylight attacks, so these rather lumbering biplanes were held in reserve, while the more modern Albacore biplanes were sent north to Kuantan in central Malaya to join 36 Squadron along with the available twin-engine Hudsons.

The Japanese attacked Kuantan on 10 December. Little damage was caused to the airfield, although one Vildebeest was lost, and Kuantan managed to hold out for two weeks. The next day, 11 December, disaster struck when the British battleships *Prince of Wales* and *Repulse* sailed to intercept the Japanese invasion fleet. Without air cover, the ships came under attack from escorting

Japanese submarines. With both battleships damaged, they were then attacked from the air and sunk. The tragedy was immense, with the loss of more than eight hundred men, making it one of the worst disasters in British naval history. The sinking of the two battleships sent shock waves through the country. The early days of war with Japan were tumultuous and chaotic, made more so by the failing communication ability within Far East Command, something that had contributed to the loss of the two battleships because of the lack of aerial protection.

The Japanese came ashore in a three-pronged attack at Singara, Kron and Kota Bharu on the north-east coast of Malaya. By the end of 1941, the Japanese invading forces had occupied much of the western coast of Malaya. Due to the lack of fighter cover, the slow-flying Vildebeests were restricted to making night attacks only, and throughout December Allied ground forces were obliged to make a series of withdrawals. The Japanese advance continued and they captured Singara, Kota Bharu, Alor Star, Georgetown, Butterworth, Penang, Taiping, and Ipoh. Kampar fell on 2 January 1942. The Slim River had been crossed, and Kuala Lumpur was taken on 11 January 1942. On 20 January, eleven Vildebeests of 100 Squadron attacked Kuantan, destroying six Japanese aircraft. On 24 January accompanied by three Albacores, they destroyed a vital rail bridge at Labis and on the night of 25 January, the squadron took part in action to cover the evacuation of an Australian battalion trapped near Bata Bahat.

On 26 January, a Japanese convoy was sighted heading for a landing at Endau on the east coast of central Malaya. The Vildebeest and Albacore bombers of 36 and 100 Squadrons based at Seletar in Singapore were thrust into the attack at Endau in broad daylight, a dire situation for those aircrew taking part. Two Royal Australian Air Force Hudson crews had spotted the Japanese convoy early that morning, but their radio messages were jammed and the information did not get back to base in Singapore until they landed shortly after 0900 hours. Both Vildebeest squadrons had flown operations the night before, therefore it was not until the early afternoon when the first wave took off for Endau. Twelve Vildebeests and nine Hudson bombers, with a fighter escort composed of twelve Brewster Buffalos and nine Hawker Hurricanes, flew towards the enemy. The Japanese landings on Endau had been in progress for more than four hours by the time the aircraft arrived. The Japanese naval force had upwards of twenty aircraft for aerial protection. Despite this, two shipping transport targets carrying Japanese troops were bombed, and men and equipment on the beach were strafed. Five Vildebeests were lost in the attack, including the commanding officer of 100 Squadron.

The second wave consisting of seven biplane Vildebeests and three Albacores of 36 Squadron and two Vildebeests of 100 Squadron took off at 1615 hours. This attack was led by Squadron Leader Markham. Flying on his wing would be Flight Sergeant G. B. Peck, his observer Flight Sergeant C. H. Lockwood and their Australian air gunner Sergeant H. A. Kelly in Albacore T9184. Although the twelve aircraft arrived over Endau at 1730 hours, their escort of seven Hurricanes and four Buffalos were late and the biplanes were attacked by twelve Japanese fighters before their escorts could reach them. The attacking force took substantial losses, with five Vildebeests, two Albacores and one Hurricane shot down. The operation had effectively been a disaster.

Flight Sergeant Peck recalls in the book *Bloody Shambles* by Chris Shores:

> I remember that as we neared Endau, we had a clear sky with Markham away out in front and Flemming (RNZAF) lagging far behind. We were engaged by a Jap fighter. On the second pass George (F/Sgt Peck) took evasive action whilst I was firing and I was thrown onto the floor of the machine

and knocked out. When I came around, the supposedly self-sealing petrol tank was holed and petrol was gushing into the back cabin. My leg was cut slightly, I think from metal bits off the machine. The intercom was smashed so we couldn't speak to George. The machine was diving steeply so Harry (F/Sgt Lockwood) the observer baled out and I followed. I must have passed out again or hit something going out as all I can remember of the fall was leaving the aircraft. I can't even remember pulling the cord. My next recollection was standing on the ground amongst tall timbers with my parachute around me.

Flight Sergeant Lockwood also recalls in *Bloody Shambles*:

Before baling out we were at about 10,000 feet. Our formation of Vildebeests and Albacores broke and it was each man for himself. I saw at least three aircraft falling in flames in the first two minutes over the target. I saw two or three aircraft get their bombs away but I don't think they had much time to do much conventional bomb aiming. Then a Jap latched onto us, he was right on our tail, so close that I swear I could see his spectacles behind his flying goggles. Alex Kelly's bullets I could see were bouncing off the Japs engine cylinders and cowling. At the same time another Jap came up underneath us and his cannon shells ripped through the floor of our aircraft and split open the fuel tank between myself and George Peck. The tear must have been about three feet long from the floor to the centre of the tank. Fuel spilled out into the cabin from the aircraft like a stream of steam. I tried to stop the flow with our gas masks that we carried, but they both fell inside the tank, so big was the split. The aircraft was in a steep spiral dive, radio was out, and I think we both thought

(Kelly and I) that we were going in. We couldn't contact anyone by radio, even George, so at about 3,000 feet I took my chute and opened the door and baled out. After a few seconds I saw Alex behind me. A few things concerned me as I left the aircraft. Firstly, my skin was smarting agonisingly from my petrol soaked clothing, and splinter wounds on my legs were painful, and thirdly, I got a terrific crack on the forehead as the hook on my chute harness passed my head as the chute opened. A particularly nasty Jap in a Zero followed me down so closely firing his front guns that I instinctively drew up my legs as he flew under me, and I remember feeling more apprehensive of being incinerated by his tracer than being hit by a bullet.

In the meantime, Flight Sergeant Peck regained control and managed to fly the badly damaged Albacore back to Seletar, where he was surprised to discover his crew had baled out. Albacore T9184 was the only Albacore to return.

Of the seventy-two aircrew from 36 and 100 Squadrons who participated in the raids, thirty-eight were missing. Eight survivors including Lockwood would eventually return back to Singapore, while two others were captured. In the third wave, six Hudsons of 62 Squadron at Palembang attacked the Endau, during which two were shot down. A fourth raid, consisting of five Palembang-based Bristol Blenheims of 27 Squadron, was aborted when darkness fell before they reached the target. Despite claims to have scored a number of hits on both transports and a cruiser by the gallant crews, neither the transports nor any of their escorts had been seriously damaged. Many lives had been lost in ill-advised operations being undertaken in drastic circumstances flying outdated aircraft.

In response to the Japanese naval forces approaching the mouth of the Endau River on the east coast of Malaya on 26 January 1942, the Australian destroyer HMAS *Vampire* with the British destroyer HMS *Thanet* had sailed in company to intercept the enemy and frustrate the troop landings. *Thanet* was sunk on 27 January 1942 by the Japanese destroyers *Fubuki*, *Asagiri*, *Yugiri* and *Shirayuki* off Endau while attempting to attack Japanese transport ships. *Vampire* had attempted to lay a smokescreen around the hapless *Thanet* as the crew were abandoning ship. Still illuminated by searchlights, the Japanese continued firing at the survivors. *Vampire* was unable to rescue any survivors and was forced to make an escape. *Thanet* sank at 0420 hours. Some of the survivors, including the commanding officer and his engineering officer, managed to board lifeboats and others grasped the small Carley cork floats to make their way as best possible to the shore.

Flight Sergeant Lockwood recalls in *Bloody Shambles*:

> I had come down in a tree one mile inland. My back was injured but I escaped capture and headed south, later joining forces with six British sailors, survivors from HMS Vampire and Thanet.

The survivors from *Thanet* had reached Mersing at the mouth of the Mersing River on a life raft. Lockwood recalled:

> Leaving the party on the beach, I walked across the tennis courts and up to the foyer of the Rest House. At the top of the steps, I opened the door and to my horror saw a group of Jap Officers sitting around a table in the foyer. I don't know who was most surprised. Of course, I took off down the steps and through the gates of the tennis courts to cross to the beach. As I ran the Japs were following me firing their small arms and I rather stupidly was firing back over my shoulder, haphazardly, with my revolver upside down.

Anyway, why I don't know, but while I went through the gates of the courts, they ran around the outside, which was further, so I widened the gap and shouted to the boys on the raft to push off, which they did when they saw what was happening. They were in about ten feet of water when they dragged me on board. Shots were fired after us but no one was hit. I think the surprise confused them.

I found that was hard to live down with the others as I was so sure and they trusted in me that the Aussies were there. Anyway, they weren't and that was that.

Lockwood and the sailors sailed on in the life raft for several days until they were picked up by the cargo vessel *Lee Sang* near the Limas Islands. Suffering from the experience, they were taken to hospital in Singapore. Endau was one of several disastrous operations conducted during the Japanese offensive. The Endau action by *Vampire* and *Thanet* was considered to be the last aggressive naval operation undertaken by Allied warships before the evacuation and surrender of Singapore on 15 February 1942.

Three Distinguished Flying Medals were awarded to surviving participants of that battle and two posthumous Mentions in Dispatches for both of the squadron commanders who were both killed. Without doubt, in differing circumstances many other awards would have been given for such outstanding bravery in the air. Flight Sergeant Lockwood's survival was quite remarkable but ultimately unrecognised other than his personal but belated membership of the Caterpillar Club several years after the event.

Towards the end of January 1942, the Vildebeests of 100 and 36 Squadrons loaded up with torpedoes and whatever spares that could be carried in preparation for evacuation to Java under the command of Squadron Leader J. T. Wilkins of 36 Squadron. The final days of the fighting in Singapore and Java were confused and chaotic, and it appears that the remaining Vildebeests left Singapore for Tijikampok in northern Java on 8 February 1942, with Lockwood among the aircrew. On 15 February, the aircraft and aircrew were joined by the ground crews, but much of their equipment had been lost in the transit between Singapore and Java via Sumatra. All the squadron records were also lost in the chaos and turmoil of the evacuation from Singapore. That loss is likely to be the major factor in the total lack of decorations awarded to the gallant crews who had taken part in the Battle for Endau.

There had been twelve remaining Vildebeests, but due to lack of spares one aircraft was sacrificed to supply parts for the remainder. On 27 February the Vildebeests were ordered to Mandeong in preparation for an attack on a significant Japanese convoy off the north-east coast of Java. At Mandeong, the aircraft met up with a US B-17 Flying Fortress squadron, and all were briefed to attack the Japanese convoy. Eight Vildebeests and one Albacore made up the RAF contingent.

The Japanese made landings on the north coast of Java the following day some 60 miles from Mandeong. The base was ordered to evacuate and destroy any item of military use in preparation for a proposed evacuation to Australia. On 7 March, the Dutch surrendered in Java and Lockwood was captured by Japanese forces the following day. He was held between March and June at Poernokerto in Java, a camp led by Squadron Leader Harrison, and then at Bandoeng Camp from June to October 1943 under Wing Commander Nicholls. The camp at Bandoeng housed a multinational mix of British, Dutch, Australian, New Zealand, and Canadian servicemen.

Lockwood was part of number nineteen Java party prisoner transportation on the ship *France Maru*, which sailed on 7 November 1943. He was initially allocated prisoner of war number JI 489, which was changed to LL number 6959 on his arrival and processing in Sumatra. During imprisonment a promotion to warrant officer occurred and official documents reflected his rank accordingly. Lockwood was held at Palembang between October 1943 and September 1945. He was interviewed after repatriation. His MI9 Prisoner of War repatriation report WO344/388/2 disclosed his statement:

> Small acts of sabotage were carried out by prisoners of war wherever possible at Bandung [West Java]. Four hundred drums of oil had sand inserted, tyres of transport punctured. Bad workmanship on transport caused breakdowns very often.

The most tangible item of Warrant Officer Lockwood's war service was his Caterpillar Club Membership pin, which he attached to the medal ribbon of his Pacific Star Medal. His Pacific Star was supported by the 1939-1945 Star and British War Medal to reflect the nine years of service and hardship endured. His name engraved upon the precious Caterpillar pin is testament to the dangers he overcame in the torrid Far East campaign against the tenacious and highly motivated Japanese forces. It is a rare example of an emergency parachute escape and survival in extreme circumstances.

*Chapter 8*

# The Goldfish Club – Ditching

The Goldfish Club was formed in November 1942 by Charles Robertson, the Chief Draftsman at P. B. Cow & Co., which was at that time one of the world's largest manufacturer of air-sea rescue equipment. After hearing of the experiences of airmen who had survived a ditching at sea, Robertson decided to form an exclusive club for the pilots and aircrew who owed their lives to the company's life jackets and dinghies. The Air Ministry had previously vetoed an earlier attempt by Reginald Foster Dagnall of R. F. D. Ltd to create a similar organisation named the Silverfish Club. At that time his company was actively engaged in manufacturing rubber life rafts of similar design to those of P. B. Cow. An interesting point to note is that the Goldfish Club was created in the month that Dagnall died.

With P. B. Cow's backing, and tacit consent from the Air Ministry, the club was duly named the Goldfish Club – Gold for the value of life, and fish for the water. RAF and other Allied airmen who escaped from their distressed aircraft over the sea and used an emergency dinghy manufactured by P. B. Cow were invited to become life members of the club. Each member was presented with a heat-sealed, waterproof membership card, an innovative concept for that period in time, and an embroidered badge.

Charles Robertson's original badge design consisted of bound wire thread to make it hard-wearing, upon a dark cloth background. There were initial problems in obtaining the required wire in sufficient quantity. In fact, due to wartime regulations, the production of metallic-embroidered badges became prohibited and all cloth products were severely rationed. These problems were overcome with silk embroidery substituted for wire upon a more obtainable black cloth. However, the obstacle as to the requirement of coupons for the supply of cloth was an issue that needed to be resolved. Robertson's colleagues in the drawing office resolved this issue by volunteering to surrender their dress suits. That material was subsequently used for the initial badges and an appeal by columnist William Hickey of the *London Daily Express* resulted in a substantial amount of old evening dress suits being sent in by readers to the P. B. Cow factory. From that point onwards the production of Goldfish badges had been resolved.

Official uniform dress regulations prohibited the wearing of the Goldfish Club badge on British and American uniforms. Fleet Air Arm aircrew generally wore it on their Mae Wests, whereas many RAF aircrew wore the badge under the flap of their left-hand uniform pocket. The Goldfish badge was also frequently sewn on the central pleat on battledress jackets. Although it was an unofficial award, it was respected by the senior ranks and allowed to be worn openly in many instances. News of the club spread rapidly and in January 1943 the BBC broadcast an interview by Wynford Vaughan-Thomas with Charles Robertson and two new members of the club at the P. B. Cow factory. The interview was conducted sitting in a dinghy surrounded by numerous inflated life rafts and an illustrated air-sea rescue launch as a backdrop. Sergeants Albert Ricketts and Ron Thompson sat next to Robertson and described their ditching returning from a daylight bombing raid on the Phillips Radio Works in the Netherlands on 6 December 1942. Returning to base, their 21 Squadron Lockheed Ventura ditched into the sea about 7 miles off Felixstowe. The immersion switch operated correctly, inflating the dinghy, and the crew were able to climb into it. Within an hour an air-sea rescue launch came alongside and took the crew to Felixstowe.

In April 1943, the correspondence section within the popular *Flight* magazine carried an article titled 'The Goldfish Club. Membership conditions too narrow':

> Some publicity has been given to the formation of the Goldfish Club open to those who have saved their lives by using their rubber dinghies. So far as I can say no provision has been made for those who avoided a watery end by other means. Sometimes, for various reasons, the dinghy didn't work and the crews did it the hard way, hanging on to a piece of aircraft that might sink at any moment. My crew had nearly an hour of this tingling expectancy before the Navy turned up. Fortunately, a cruiser saw us go in. The Goldfish Club, if open to only dinghy users in its present form, is not representative of those who have ditched. Per Ardua Ad Mare.

Charles Robertson replied to the letter on 6 May 1943:

> The letter from 'Per Ardua ad Mare' (Anonymous) expresses the opinion that the qualifications necessary to join the Goldfish Club are too limited. Since I have from time to time received letters from airmen with similar views, it may be of interest generally to explain that the club was originally formed to grant recognition to those airmen who had been through the ordeal of using an emergency dinghy, and thereby saving their lives. The policy of the club was mainly dominated by letters received from aircrews that were exceedingly enthusiastic concerning the formation of a club of this nature. Thus, it will be appreciated that the club qualifications' dependence on the use of an emergency dinghy was introduced by popular consent and confirmed

during the club's inauguration by broadcast in 1942. I do occasionally receive letters from airmen who have saved their lives by the use of a Mae West life jacket, or even by clinging onto aircraft wreckage, and on these occasions, membership is invariably granted, the membership card being endorsed to cover this in an appropriate manner. It should be emphasised that a life saved is the main factor and it is this we really wish to commemorate. While I have the opportunity, I feel sure members will be interested to know that the club badge and illustrated membership card have been accepted as official exhibits in the Imperial War Museum.

C.A. Robertson. Hon Secretary. Goldfish Club

Robertson designed the Goldfish Club membership card himself. His skills as an architect were reflected in the quality of the design, with his own artwork used on the reverse of the card. Examination of a card reveals that the design has stood the test of time as a contemporary piece of art, combining the elements of not only the dinghy produced by P. B. Cow, but impressive illustrations of aircraft, pilot and pertinent elements relative to the club. The front of the card recorded the incident date. All membership cards were personally signed by Robertson and identified to the recipient.

No. 294 Squadron, operating in the Eastern Mediterranean undertaking air-sea rescue, had been formed at Berka, Libya, on 24 September 1943. With its detachment flights it had been successful in rescuing many pilots and airmen. In 1944, it added a further detachment in Greece and became proactive in promoting the Goldfish Club. No. 294 Squadron was instrumental in reiterating to wireless operators in particular the crucial requirement of clear position information in any ditching. In August 1944, the squadron stated it had rescued more than 360 airmen and if wireless operators gave them the correct information they too could wear the Goldfish badge. The squadron would provide all details required to become a member, adding the sobering statement that it was virtually impossible for one man to haul a sodden, possibly unconscious, airman out of the drink on his own.

The lengths to which air-sea rescue personnel endured their duty regardless of danger cannot be better exemplified than by the circumstances surrounding Wellington W5733 of 172 Squadron, Coastal Command, which ditched in the Bay of Biscay at 0645 hours on 20 June 1942. Various distress calls were received reporting engine troubles while on an anti-submarine patrol. Aircraft from 172, 51, 502, 58 and 10 Squadrons were dispatched at different times to search the estimated position of loss across the extensive waters of the Bay of Biscay. Surface craft from Falmouth and Penzance also departed for the search area.

One of the air-sea rescue Whitleys, identified as an aircraft from 51 Squadron, developed a glycol leak in the port engine as it made for the search area and was forced to ditch at 1040 hours. The aircraft was approximately 37 miles south of the Isles of Scilly. The crew successfully boarded their dinghy and were picked up by one of the attending surface launches. Another 58 Squadron Whitley acted as protection for the launch. The survivors were landed safely at St Mary's on the Isles of Scilly later that day and the 58 Squadron Whitley returned to base.

Wellington W5733 remained missing. At 1100 hours Short Sunderland W3999 of 10 Squadron took off from Mount Batten Naval Air Station in Plymouth Bay to join the search. Whitley Z9442 of 58 Squadron took off at 1525 hours and flew to the search area off Brittany, south-west of the Isles of Scilly. Whitley Z9225 from 51 Squadron spotted a dinghy at 1125 hours with survivors on board. The Whitley dropped a Thornaby survival bag containing water and food. At 1744 hours the Whitley crew experienced difficulty in maintaining contact with the dinghy and its position was lost. At 1854 hours the dinghy was located once again and constant observations were successful. At 1920 hours the Sunderland flew over the dinghy, assessing the strength of the swelling seas. The Sunderland remained in the air so it could indicate the position of the dinghy to the oncoming air-sea rescue launch. While maintaining position the Sunderland detected an approaching enemy aircraft and the remaining Whitley likewise made contact, identifying a Luftwaffe aircraft at 2030 hours that subsequently attacked the Whitley from behind. The German seaplane also targeted the Sunderland, which was hit several times, and smoke billowed from its right inboard engine. The aircraft lost altitude and the pilot was forced to make a water landing. The landing, despite moderately high seas, was successful, however within no time the Sunderland aircraft exploded and disappeared, leaving debris strewn on the water. The crew of the Whitley witnessed the tragedy. The Whitley's rear gunner, Sergeant Mchugh, had returned fire against the German attacker but in doing so suffered a head injury. The Whitley's tail section had been damaged and therefore it made for the clouds and returned to St Eval, where it landed at 2215 hours.

The following day the rescue launch located the dinghy using the bearings given from the previous day and took the survivors on board at 2200 hours. Flight Sergeant Virgo, Flight Sergeant Marshall, Flight Sergeant Norton, Sergeant Deacon, Sergeant Bellaby and Sergeant Vardy were taken to St Mary's in the Isles of Scilly for medical attention. They were later taken by sea to Falmouth and then to Chivenor by ambulance on 24 June 1942. There were no serious injuries. The squadron records do mention some mental stress was present in varying degrees. All men were given fourteen days' sick leave and privilege leave of an additional fourteen days before being required to return to flying duties.

The crew of Wellington W5733 undoubtably owe their lives to the many men who sought to rescue them. The rescue operation saw the tragic loss of eleven men, on board the Sunderland. Their bodies were never recovered and remain lost at sea with no known grave. Approximately 200 hours were spent in the air by the RAF search and rescue crews. This rescue was achieved by immense perseverance and bravery.

By the end of the war, the Goldfish Club had 9,000 members from all branches of the Allied Forces. Robertson attempted to end the granting of membership, but with applications continuing to arrive, this continued. Evidence exists in the form of club postcard correspondence to enquiries stating that membership had reached 10,000 and the club was full. Despite resigning from P. B. Cow in 1947, Robertson continued to act as the membership secretary, retaining the club records and operating it at his own expense.

An article in the Royal Air Force Association Journal *Airmail* in January 1951 brought renewed interest in the Goldfish Club, and following a successful and well-attended reunion dinner, it was reorganised on a more formal basis in March 1953 to become subscription based. All members were required to rejoin on an annual basis, providing basic details of their ditching and submitting five shillings a year as the fees due. Reunions have been held annually ever since at various venues with many distinguished guests. In response to a message of greetings sent to her, Mae West made it clear that she took great pride in the fact that members of the RAF had adopted her name for their life jackets. Aircrew who joined the Goldfish Club having had their life saved by the use of a Mae West had the membership card marked 'Endorsed Membership' typed in red advising that it was as a result of the Mae West.

Charles Robertson eventually settled in the market town of Hailsham, East Sussex, where he ran a successful toy shop for many years. The author had the privilege to meet his family during his attempt to locate and secure any Goldfish Club records of administration. Sadly, due to the passing years, and with no reason to think otherwise, the original Goldfish Club records regarded as personal to Robertson were destroyed, hence they are no longer in existence.

Members of the Goldfish Club have since included aviators from many other aspects of aviation, both military and civilian. Many of the older club members have passed on but new members continue to keep the club in existence.

*Chapter 9*

# Pilot Officer Roger Osborn DFC – Goldfish Club

Pilot Officer Roger William Osborn was an officer in the RAF equipment branch who volunteered to fly in Bomber Command. He was selected for duties as an observer, commonly referred to as a navigator. His service took him into a world of electronic offensive and defensive measures that saw immeasurable development throughout the Second World War. It was in October 1935 that the Secretary of State for Air expressed concern about the development of radio research work in the RAF. There was a research facility at Bawdsey, Suffolk, directly responsible for the conduct of research and development work on the detection and location of aircraft. In February 1936 the Air Ministry give permission for a War Office team to work at Bawdsey, in conjunction with its experimental team. This provides a little insight into the immediate pre-war stages that were evolving. In spite of Air Ministry opposition, the War Office moved their team from Bawdsey to the Air Defence Experimental Establishment at Christchurch in August 1939.

Pilot Officer Osborn was to fly within 100 Bomber Support Group as a navigator and radio operator flying night fighter and intruder operations in Beaufighters and Mosquitoes. He undertook specialist skilled work, for which in 1945 he was rewarded with the Distinguished Flying Cross. Moreover, he became a member of the Goldfish Club after surviving a traumatic ditching in the English Channel.

No. 100 Bomber Support Group, under Command of Air Commodore E. B. Addison, was formed on 3 December 1943. The development of radar and radio as weapons of war induced the associated deployment of electronic countermeasures, which became very important to both the RAF and the Luftwaffe. Close liaison with the operational staff and operational commands was required for this important structure to deliver the specific duties imposed upon it. The work was so important and secretive that policy, planning and direction had to be delivered at an unusually high level. The group was under the administrative and operational control of Headquarters Bomber Command and subject to its general technical control. The reason for the formation of 100 Group was the progression from defensive to offensive radio countermeasures. The main purpose of the group was to reduce the escalating losses of RAF heavy bombers. It had two objectives: to effectively cancel out the Luftwaffe electronic eyes and ears that penetrated the dark skies, and secondly to destroy the formidable defending Luftwaffe night fighter force. Within 100 Group, both bomber and fighter activities were blended successfully under the same command.

Before mid-1941, men were allowed to voluntarily enlist for immediate training as wireless operators, with the ability to progress straight through the entire training requirements. The wireless course itself was split into two, the initial training at Blackpool, purely ground training, then training for air operating. By the middle of 1941, it was established that wireless operators who had completed their aircrew wireless training could not be absorbed into the gunnery schools at the rate at which they were being passed out by the signals schools. Additionally, improvements in the standard of wireless training of the wireless operator/air gunner were identified. It was therefore decided that all wireless operators and under-training air gunners should follow their wireless training with a minimum of three months' employment at an operational unit in order to gain general signals experience. This policy adversely affected morale because of long waiting periods between courses. Therefore, in 1942 a straight-through training system for wireless operators/air gunner developed and became operative in 1943. With the advent of the two-seater long-range fighter, a new type of aircrew category became necessary and in July 1941 the radio observer wing appeared on the navigators' tunics. In September 1942, there was an official change of title from observer to navigator, marked by the introduction of the N brevet. There was initial resistance from the men who carried the O brevet, many significantly delaying an exchange from one to the other.

Flying Officer Osborn qualified as an observer radio operator at 62 Operational Training Unit towards the end of 1942, additionally passing his observer's navigation course at Staverton, Gloucestershire. He gained experience in the Beaufighter aircraft at Woodvale with 256 Squadron before moving to Charter Hall and the satellite station Winfield, in Scotland. Here he flew consistently with his pilot, Flight Lieutenant Ferguson, together learning the skills of night fighting. In the summer of 1943, Osborn and Ferguson were posted to 141 Squadron at Wittering, Stamford. At the time of joining, the unit was commanded by the night fighter ace Wing Commander, later Group Captain, John Randall Daniel Braham. During the war, he would become the most highly decorated fighter pilot in the Royal and Commonwealth Air Forces. Osborn had flown a local test flight as the navigator to Cunningham, who would go on to become the highest-scoring British night fighter ace of the war. Osborn was in esteemed company and the assessment of his proficiency confirmed he was ready for operational duty in the trade of night fighting. Unbeknown to him, the squadron would shortly be transferred into 100 Group.

On 15 September 1943, orders were received for seven Beaufighter crews to fly to the airfield at Ford near Chichester in Sussex. Wing Commander Braham with Flight Lieutenant Jacobs were the first crew that left for the south coast, with intruder operations ordered for all seven crews that night. Osborn and Ferguson took off from Ford at 2215 hours. Once in the air, the English Channel was immediately visible in the available light. They made for central France and undertook an uneventful patrol. Upon their return flight, navigation was set making for the Sussex coast. At 0057 hours, Ferguson radioed, reporting one engine unserviceable and oil pressure issues were present with the other engine. Wing Commander Braham responded and instructed the crew to bale out if they had sufficient height. Ferguson acknowledged the communication but thereafter nothing was received and the crew failed to arrive in Sussex.

Ferguson and Osborn were recorded on the operational record as officially missing, having failed to return from operations. The six 141 Squadron Beaufighter crews who had returned to Ford safely subsequently returned to Wittering.

Later that evening, the 16th, a dinghy was sighted in the Channel by an RAF Typhoon of 486 Squadron. The sighting was in the approximate area where the missing Beaufighter might have been, raising hopes. Operations continued for 141 Squadron, with six Beaufighters departing Wittering for West Malling to fly intruder operations that night. A telegram was sent to Flying Officer Osborn's address at Bowran Manor, St Clement, Truro, Cornwall. His father read, 'Deeply regret to inform you that your son Flying Officer R W Osborn (62203) failed to return from an operation flight last night please accept my deepest sympathy, letter to follow.' His father set off to personally find some news of his son and arrived at Wittering on 17 September. Mr Osborn senior was met by Wing Commander Braham. It was during their meeting that air-sea rescue flights were deployed following the dinghy sighting and they brought forth news to Wittering that a 277 Squadron Walrus had located the dinghy and Osborn was found in it. He was suffering from exposure and a few cuts and bruises but was now in safe hands. This ditching incident was well documented by Osborn during his recuperation. It is rare to have such a detailed first-hand experience of becoming a Goldfish, and Osborn's handwritten account of his ditching experience reads as follows:

> On the night of September 15/16, I was navigator in a Beaufighter on Intruder Patrol in France. The port engine failed when we were about 30 miles inland in France and we commenced to lose height rapidly. At the same time excessive vibration developed and in fact became so bad that my pilot, F/L R.W. Ferguson, found it almost impossible to read his instruments. It soon was obvious that unless the port airscrew, now windmilling uselessly and dragging us down, fell off we had little chance of reaching the Channel and still less of reaching the British Coast. Ferguson, who had already spent two years in a French internment camp, told me to bale out if I liked, but that he intended trying to ditch the aircraft in the Channel. Although a Beaufighter is a very bad machine to ditch, I told him I would stay with him and busied myself establishing our position. We passed out over the French coast at about 500 ft., somewhere north of Le Havre, and as we were then too low to bale out, I removed my parachute and inflated my Mae West. There was almost a full moon and I could see the sea shining down below. Suddenly, less than two minutes after crossing the coast, my pilot said 'Christ, look at that.' I looked out and saw the port wing go right down and I think the engine itself was breaking loose. I threw off my helmet, threw back the cockpit cover, and the next thing I knew I found myself in the sea with no sign of the aircraft or wreckage. I looked around and there was the aircraft dinghy (H Type) floating right way up about 40 or 50 yards away. I swam over, and climbed in with some

difficulty as my own K type dinghy was still attached to me. The sea was choppy and the dinghy was beginning to fill with water. I blew my whistle and looked round for my pilot, but there was no sign of him. I had had a severe crack on the head and I think I lost consciousness at intervals during the night – the rest of the time I spent baling hectically as the dinghy was shipping water. Dawn seemed a long time coming, but shortly after daylight a Spitfire passed overhead very low and very fast – heading for England. I gave him a Red signal but he didn't see me. I now had a chance to examine the dinghy and myself more closely. The full emergency pack was there with Very pistol, distress cartridges, fluorescent dye, Everhot water bottle, two emergency ration packs for two, 8-pint tins of water. and a flag. The dinghy itself was as sound as a bell, and as tight as a drum in spite of the crash, and the emergency immersion switch had obviously worked perfectly. The sea had now abated so I baled it out as dry as I could and had a good look around. It was only then I realised how close to shore I was. I could see it plainly as I sat on the bottom of the dinghy and cannot have been more than five miles out. I myself was wet and cold, and severely bruised and knocked about, but apart from one knee which I could not bend and a pain in the back was in pretty good shape. I was desperately thirsty but not hungry and I decided to ration myself to about half a pint of water a day and 6 Horlicks Tablets. With this I reckoned I should be good for 14 days. The weather improved as the day went on, and the afternoon blazing hot and flat calm. I therefore removed my cloths and boots and wrung them out and hung them up to dry. I was keeping an anxious eye out for aircraft. I was if anything further off from the shore which cheered me up a bit, I saw no aircraft until about 1800 hrs.

Osborn's account ends there. He had been spotted by a Typhoon flown by Wing Commander Scott of 486 (New Zealand) Squadron. It was based at Tangmere, close to Ford. Following his rescue, Squadron Leader J. D. Waddy of 486 Squadron wrote to Osborn telling him how pleased they were to hear that he had not suffered very much from the long spell in the sea. He advised him that Wing Commander Scott was now in command of the Typhoon wing and that a body was seen floating in the sea on the day of his rescue about 10 miles from his position and was thought to have had no clothes on, the implication being that it may have been that of his pilot. The squadron leader passed on his unit's best wishes and said that the one regret was that he could not have been picked up on the night that they first saw him. Scott, who sighted the dinghy on the evening of 16 September 1943, had returned to that area on 17 September. He was accompanied with his flight of Typhoons to search for the dinghy. Only later in the day did he relocate the dinghy and an air-sea rescue Walrus flying boat later landed on the sea nearby, rescuing Osborn.

Osborn's entry in his logbook notes that he was a passenger in a Walrus flown by a Sergeant Fletcher and that he was flown from the rescue location to Ford after a journey of one hour. He recorded that he had been adrift in the dinghy for forty-eight hours. The following day when news of his rescue spread, 141 Squadron sent him a telegram of congratulations. He had been born in Battle not far from Hastings and recuperated at Littlehampton. He had an appreciation for the efforts that had taken place in his rescue but the personal sorrow of knowing his pilot's life was taken in the ditching was difficult to bear.

The air-sea rescue pilot, Sergeant Fletcher, was a recipient of the Distinguished Flying Medal and Bar. He had left Shoreham airfield at 1110 hours on 17 September in a Walrus seaplane escorted by two Spitfires in the attempt to rescue the then unknown occupant of the rubber dinghy from the sea off Dieppe. The dinghy was sighted several miles due south of Beachy Head. The body of Osborn's pilot, Flight Lieutenant Ronald William Ferguson, may or may not have been the one spotted floating some 10 miles from Osborn's dinghy on the evening of 16 September. His body was never found or recovered. Having no known grave, his life is commemorated by name on the Runnymede Memorial. Aged twenty-six at the time of his death, he was the son of Alexander and Beatrice D. Ferguson, of Peterhead, Aberdeenshire. According to Osborn's account, his pilot had opted not to bale out over France, owing to his previous experience of being held in internment for two years by the French. It appears that the then-Pilot Officer R. W. Ferguson had been interned by the Vichy French along with Sergeant W. G. Stephens and Sergeant E. G. A. Hart. They were the crew of a Blenheim that had force-landed when ferrying across Tunis, North Africa, on 16 September 1940. It is ironic that this incident took place on the exact same date when he ditched and lost his life three years later.

Osborn returned to flying duties with Flying Officer William Boylson, an Australian pilot who had been awarded the Distinguished Flying Cross on two occasions in 1943. The new pairing flew together several times during October and November 1943.

During March 1944, Osborn converted on to the Mosquito with the larger Serrate transmitting aerials, with which they hoped for better reliability in their quest to find the enemy in the dark hours probing the skies. The day 24 March 1944 developed into a one that almost took the lives of both Osborn and Boylson. In preparation for a patrol that evening, a Mosquito Osborn recorded as '911' required a night flight test. While in the air, a violent vibration occurred and an emergency landing was required but the brakes failed. The Mosquito slewed and overshot at speed, missing a hangar by the narrowest margin.

March had, however, been a good month for the Serrate crews on 141 Squadron, with several Luftwaffe aircraft shot down. It did, though, witness the tragic results of the Nuremberg operation on 30 March, when a staggering ninety-five heavy bombers from across the strength of Bomber Command failed to return. The intelligence officers reported that the Luftwaffe night fighters were being controlled and diverted in anticipation of Bomber Command's intended targets. The combination of Luftwaffe Bf 110 and Bf 109 night fighters had shown how lethal and effective they could be defending capital targets over central Germany.

Towards the end of April 1944, Flying Officers Osborn and Boylson separated as a crew. Osborn switched pilots and commenced flying with Flight Lieutenant Lucien Leboutte, a Belgian pilot who had concealed his real age. He had served in the First World War and had more reason to be an aggressive and offensive night fighter than most. He knew Osborn as Leboutte had been with 141 Squadron since August 1942. In 1944 he had been awarded the Distinguished Flying Cross, with the following citation:

> This officer has participated in thirty-two combat missions during which he has destroyed one Junkers 88 and seriously damaged three others. By his enthusiasm and his courage, he succeeded in obtaining precious intelligence for the missions in which he was engaged. During his operational tour he has shown courage and energy and has by this fact been a magnificent example to his squadron.

Osborn and Leboutte only flew together on four occasions. On 26 April 1944, they were briefed upon the heavy bomber raid to Essen. The inevitable heavy anti-aircraft flak, searchlights and night fighter presence must have been a daunting prospect for everyone involved. In the air, the new pairing had two Serrate indications where bearings were taken but then lost. Orbiting the Ruhr, three further Serrate connections resulted in a chase before their quarry was lost. The loss of personnel was sobering, with seven entire crews failing to return, and 141 Squadron also lost the experienced crew of Squadron Leader Forshaw and Pilot Officer Folly that night.

In May 1944, Osborn became ill and the station medical officer diagnosed an inflamed appendix, which resulted in his immediate removal from flying duties. He returned to operations the following month at West Raynham, crewed with Flight Lieutenant Anderson. The recent Allied invasion on the French beaches was foremost on the minds of everyone and operational flying was intense. On the night of 12 June, Osborn was again in for a close call while participating in a sortie to Gelsenkirchen. He noted in the logbook 'port engine burst into flames forty miles off Southwold. Fire extinguisher failed, but flames died down and Andy executed a masterly landing with one engine.'

On 5 July 1944, an intruder sortie to northern France escalated the excitement for Anderson and Osborn. They were flying Mosquito DZ303, which had become a regular aircraft for them. Crossing the French coast, an airborne interception contact registered at maximum range allowed them to close to a visual sighting to see the enemy aircraft climbing to 17,500ft, when it turned hard, returning head on and close enough that the day camouflage could be seen and easily identified as an Fw 190. The Mosquito deviated to prevent the Fw 190 from taking up an attacking option and a dogfight between the two aircraft then took place for some thirty minutes. At 10,000ft, the Fw 190 suddenly dived away to the west. The Mosquito was unable to catch the escaping fighter, which disappeared in the darkness. It had been an extraordinary long chase. The following day, Anderson's promotion to squadron leader was confirmed.

On 28 July, Anderson and Osborn flew protection for a Bomber Command operation to Stuttgart. Nearing the target area, the rearward airborne interception registered a contact immediately behind the Mosquito and closed at speed. Anderson turned hard port and attempted to get in behind the contact. Climbing and closing on the target, it took evasive action before a visual sighting became possible. Closing to 1,000ft, the target opened fire from two rearward-firing guns at the top of the fuselage. The two aircraft exchanged positions constantly in the dogfight, which endured for more than thirteen minutes before the German disappeared within the heavy bomber stream and contact was lost. Osborn's operation of the radar equipment was never in doubt, but yet again he was denied the opportunity of registering a victory in the night fighting battles over occupied Europe and Germany.

At the end of August 1944, the 141 Squadron navigation leader endorsed Osborn's flying logbook as having completed a full tour of operations. Thirty operations had been completed but the comment 'No Huns Destroyed' was not what Osborn wanted to read.

On 17 December 1944, the squadron commander put newly promoted Flight Lieutenant Osborn forward for the award of the Distinguished Flying Cross. The recommendation was as follows:

Flight Lieutenant Osborn joined No.141 (Straits Settlements) Squadron on 7 July 1943, for his first tour of operations. On the return journey from his sixth Sortie, on 15 September 1943, his aircraft was hit by flak and crashed into the sea, when the port engine cut, approximately 5 miles off the French coast. Flight Lieutenant Osborn spent 36 hours in the dinghy before being picked up by an Air Sea Rescue aircraft. Although he had been slightly wounded in the shoulder, Flight Lieutenant Osborn speedily returned to his unit, and resumed flying again, on 18 October 1943. Flight Lieutenant Osborn has now completed 42 Sorties and a total of 164 operational flying hours. Although on his first tour, he had not the slightest hesitation in volunteering to continue it. He has flown on operations with no less than four different pilots throughout his tour, which also suffered a further interruption by his admission to hospital, in May 1944, with appendicitis. Although he has not a large number of claims to his credit, he has, nevertheless, assisted his pilot in the damaging of a locomotive and goods train. His skill as a Navigator/Radio, however, has always been of the highest order, and has enabled his pilot to place complete reliance on his operator, at all times.

Osborn's station commander would further note on 19 December:

He has been a great asset to his squadron where his personality, sound sense and example has exerted an excellent influence over younger and less experienced crews. He has not flagged throughout his long tour in his persistence both on the ground in preparation, or in the air on operations, to engage the enemy. I recommend his non-immediate award of the Distinguished Flying Cross.

The No. 100 Group commander would also note that:

This navigator has set a fine standard of persistence and devotion to duty. I recommend him for the non-immediate award of the Distinguished Flying Cross.

Osborn participated in his forty-third operational sortie on 7 January 1945, when he flew in close support of a raid on Munich, patrolling via Stuttgart and Augsburg. On 14 January the tailwheel of his Mosquito was damaged in a heavy landing. The ground crew immediately worked on his aircraft and readied it for operations that night. That ground crew were awarded a squadron 'Weekly Brown Mark' in the station routine orders. The officer in charge of that ground crew reported to the Station Administrative Officer to receive the award and Osborn pasted a copy of it into his logbook. This speedy repair allowed Anderson and Osborn to participate in a raid on the Merseburg-Leuna synthetic oil works at Leipzig. Flying as close escort to the bombers, they remained in the target area for more than forty minutes. On their return, they were diverted to Ford having completed the longest sortie by the squadron to date: six hours and thirty-five minutes. This was Osborn's forty-fourth and final operational sortie. Osborn's award was published in *The London Gazette* on 23 March 1945.

There are two important remaining matters of note to mention. The first being the award of a 'Green Endorsement' or Air Officer Commanding commendation awarded to Flight Lieutenant Osborn. This rather unusual group award was signed by the squadron commander, the group captain commanding West Raynham, and the air officer commanding 100 Group. It reads:

For Meritorious Service and good airmanship, in that a full operational tour has been completed without having been involved in any accident or ever having an unnecessary cancellation or abandonment of an operational sortie.

The final matter of importance is the record of a flight taken after hostilities had ended on 9 June 1945. Squadron Leader White took Flight Lieutenant Osborn from West Raynham in a 141 Squadron Mosquito. The weather was clear and he viewed the Normandy invasion beaches and spent a long time at the location where Flight Lieutenant Ferguson lost his life when they ditched together on 16 September 1943. His Beaufighter aircraft and the remains of his pilot were beneath the waters he overflew. Becoming a member of the Goldfish Club acknowledged that his life had been saved and his rescue was successful. His service in the air thereafter was dedicated and rightly rewarded with his Distinguished Flying Cross at a time when the Second World War drew to a victory for the Allied forces.

Remaining with the Royal Air Force Reserve after the war, Flight Lieutenant Osborn eventually relinquished his commission on 28 August 1955.

*Chapter 10*

# An Extraordinary Goldfish Crew

No. 217 Squadron, Coastal Command, served in maritime patrol along the Atlantic's Western Approaches and later in an anti-shipping role in the English Channel before it was ordered to Gibraltar and thence Malta in 1942. The squadron was retained in Malta from 10 June through to July 1942 for offensive anti-shipping duties against the Italian and German convoys in the Mediterranean. It was equipped with nine Beauforts capable of carrying torpedoes. Beaufort L9820 was flown by South African pilot Lieutenant Edward Strever. The navigator was British Pilot Officer William Dunsmore and the remaining two crew members were Sergeants John Wilkinson and Alexander Brown, both from New Zealand. The two New Zealand crew members had trained as wireless operators in Canada in 1941. This crew operated from Malta with two other Beaufort squadrons, 39 and 86. Supported by Beaufighter aircraft, they combined in strength to attack Axis convoys, primarily Italian shipping. Lieutenant Strever stood out among the crews. He wore the brown tunic of the South African Air Force, and his two New Zealand wireless operators added to the unusual crew configuration with their broad Kiwi accents. The crew witnessed a rather dramatic anti-shipping operation on 21 June 1942 when Italian gunners shot down an entire formation of Beauforts on a low approach to drop their torpedoes. Nine Beauforts had formed up in groups of three abreast against a heavily defended convoy bound for Tripoli, Libya. The first section of three Beauforts were all struck by accurate gunfire, with one crashing into the sea and the remaining two, unable to maintain height, ditched. Two additional Beauforts were also damaged, however, the attack was successful in that their torpedoes sank the German merchant vessel *Reichenfels*. The remaining aircraft returned safely to Malta. The following day, 22 June 1942, Germany announced the taking of Tobruk and that the Allied troops in North Africa had suffered a very serious defeat. General Rommel was rewarded by Hitler with a promotion to field marshal.

No. 217 Squadron suffered further losses during operations on 23 June and 3 July 1942. Operations in July saw differing tactics deployed in an attempt to reduce the significant attrition rate. Due to the weight of the Beaufort, a steep diving approach was not possible and in order for the torpedo to be released successfully, a low angle of entry into the water was essential. A torpedo attack approach commenced at a relatively low, flat attitude quite some distance from the target. These were predictable circumstances and the enemy gunners needed to be surprised with attacks from opposite directions that diverted concentrated anti-aircraft gunfire. This tactic proved successful on 22 July when the Italian vessel *Vettor Pisani* was destroyed by the Malta Beauforts.

On 28 July 1942, Lieutenant Strever's crew left Malta to attack a large merchant ship escorted by two destroyers south-west of Greece. They were accompanied by an additional eight Beauforts, six of which carried torpedoes and three carried general-purpose bombs, another new tactic. Six Beaufighters provided protection and engaged the vessel's gunners with cannon fire, however, two Beauforts fell to the vessel's gunners on their torpedo runs. One of these, Beaufort L9820, was being flown by Lieutenant Strever. His aircraft was badly damaged to such an extent that a ditching was inevitable. They were relatively close to the Greek island of Sapienza as the Beaufort struck the sea with an initial glancing motion. It was followed by a substantial crash into the water in a nose-heavy trajectory. The navigator, Pilot Officer Dunsmore, was thrown towards the nose section of the aircraft, inflicting a nasty gash wound to his right arm. The two New Zealand sergeants, who were towards the central fuselage area, ensured the dinghy had inflated properly and with it being positioned in close proximity they both clambered into it without issue. The nose section of the aircraft had taken in water and was immersed, with the tail section having now broken away completely.

The pilot and navigator experienced a less pleasant experience in escaping from the front section but they eventually joined the occupants in the dinghy. The contact line attached to the dinghy was cut, freeing it from the aircraft, and the crew commenced paddling towards the shore as the larger section of the Beaufort sank. The initial thoughts of the four crew were to make towards Greece and escape capture. An Italian Cant seaplane appeared overhead an hour or so into their journey and its crew observed the yellow dinghy beneath them. Having circled and lost height, they landed on the water intent on investigating and rescuing the survivors.

This was to be the start of an epic situation that would lead to the award of gallantry medals to all four crew members. The survivors were taken on board the seaplane, which took them into the harbour on the island of Corfu. The treatment of the crew as prisoners of war was impeccable, with food, drink and accommodation provided. The following day after breakfast, the four prisoners became aware that they were to be taken in the seaplane to an Italian mainland destination and onward to a prisoner of war camp. The Italian crew of the Cant made preparations for the departure, scuppering the intentions of the Beaufort crew. They had anticipated a more traditional route into a prisoner of war camp whereby they might have been presented with opportunities for escape overland. An additional armed guard was to join the Italian crew and they boarded for the flight to Italy. It took off at 0915 hours on 29 July and headed westwards making for Taranto. The prisoners hatched a plan to overpower the Italian crew and take control of the seaplane but if it was to take place it was going to have to be spontaneous, led by Lieutenant Strever.

After they had been airborne for forty minutes, Strever indicated to Sergeant Wilkinson, who pointed to the window and shouted 'Spitfire', which caused an immediate reaction of all the Italians on board. A sudden melee of bodies erupted, with the Beaufort crew tackling the Italian crew and managing to disarm them and secure their positions. Strever had felt confident that he could fly the floatplane, although the fuel controls would be challenging. The Cant turned away from its original bearings towards Italy and adopted an assumed course to try and find Malta. Strever chose to fly as low as possible with fuel consumption a serious cause of concern. They had committed to the escape plan fully aware that an Italian Cant floatplane approaching Malta would be of grave concern to its defenders. A decision took place to gain the assistance of the Italian second pilot. He was released from his bindings and gave tacit compliance, resulting in good progression towards Malta. As expected, the Italian floatplane was met in Malta's airspace with predictable aggression, RAF fighters peppering it with cannon fire. The Italian needed little inducement to land the floatplane on the sea to signal surrender and to confirm that they posed no threat. The air-sea rescue launch from Kalafrana, Malta, came out to them and took the Italian aircraft in tow to St Paul's Bay on the island's northern coastline. The launch crew were duly astonished to see four Allied aircrew in the Italian aircraft.

The Beaufort crew had survived a ditching and become prisoners of war but had escaped by executing an audacious and dangerous plan to overpower an Italian aircrew and then fly the enemy aircraft to Malta. In doing so they regained their own freedom from the Italians. The Beaufort crew replicated the hospitable treatment they had received as prisoners of war under Italian control by ensuring the best possible treatment took place for the Italian rescuers, who had themselves now become prisoners of war under British control.

*The London Gazette* dated Friday, 4 September 1942 announced that the entire crew had received awards:

> Lieutenant Edward Theodore Strever, South African Air Force and Pilot Officer William Dunsmore, Royal Air Force. Distinguished Flying Cross recipients.
> Sergeant John A. Wilkinson, Royal New Zealand Air Force and Sergeant Alexander R. Brown, Royal New Zealand Air Force. Distinguished Flying Medal recipients.

The joint citation for these awards read:

> Lieutenant Strever, Pilot Officer Dunsmore, and Sergeants Brown and Wilkinson were the crew of an aircraft which operated from Malta in June and July 1942. During this period, they performed excellent work in attacking enemy merchant vessels and naval forces, and all displayed initiative, courage and devotion to duty of the highest order.

Membership of the Goldfish Club added to the recognition of the remarkable events that took place on 28 and 29 July 1942. In all probability the Goldfish Club's secretary, Charles Robertson, would have been unaware of the full story surrounding this particular Beaufort crew when he signed their individual membership cards. Sometime known as the 'Kipper Fleet', Coastal Command has at times received less attention than Fighter Command or Bomber Command but, as this account fittingly discloses, the work it undertook was equally hazardous and demanding.

*Chapter 11*

# Sergeant Brian Beecroft – Goldfish Club Twice and Prisoner of War

Brian Beecroft attended 11 Air Observers Navigation School, Hamble, between March and June 1940. He was in company with many young men who had volunteered in the hopes of flying in the RAF. The progression from basic training to flight training was without issue for him. The flying logbook that was issued to him provides detailed evidence and begins with training flights in Avro Ansons followed by Fairey Battles and Hawker Demons while at 9 Air Observers School at Penrhos in west Wales, where he undertook a bombing and gunnery course. By September 1940, he had been posted to 15 Operational Training Unit at Harwell, Oxfordshire, for training mainly as a navigator and bomb aimer on Wellingtons. The training was preparing Beecroft for war duties with pace and competency. He remained at Harwell until early November 1940, then he was briefly posted to 214 Squadron and following that 75 Squadron at Feltwell at the close of that month.

In early December, Beecroft was posted to the Photographic Reconnaissance Unit at Oakington, Cambridgeshire. This appears to be an uncommon occurrence as very few bomber aircraft carried dedicated camera and flash bomb illuminators to photograph bombing operations in the early war years. In fact, in November 1940 just three cameras were spread across nine squadrons flying in 5 Group. Around this time the photographic interpretation officers examined one hundred and fifty photographs taken on operations to numerous targets. Just twenty-one actually defined the correct target and others evidenced the bombs dropped many miles from the intended target. There was a surge to improve matters, all driven by photographic evidence. Twelve aircrew were posted from 75 Squadron to Oakington along with six aircrew from 149 Squadron, and these formed No. 3 Photographic Reconnaissance Unit. Flight Lieutenant H. P. Elliott joined from 75 Squadron and led 'B' (Wellington) Flight, with 'A' Flight flying Spitfires. The intelligence officer was Pilot Officer Constance Babington Smith, an assistant section officer in the Women's Auxiliary Air Force, who set up the interpretation section. By 1943, she was heading a large department analysing photographs taken by high-altitude photo-reconnaissance Mosquitoes and Spitfires, identifying developments in secret German technology. Sergeant Beecroft was fortunate to be involved in this early but most import area of work.

Operational duties commenced for Wellington Flight on 4 February 1941. The target was Brest docks, where they were to drop their general-purpose bombs and take reconnaissance photographs. Flight Lieutenant Elliott took off at 1805 hours and the crew, including Beecroft, were over the target two hours later. They made three runs over the docks at 11,000ft and dropped four 500lb bombs onto fires started by 99 Squadron. A second and third run across the target allowed for a series of flash illuminators to be dropped and photographs taken. As the German anti-aircraft fire became increasingly determined, Elliott headed his aircraft for home on a bearing provided by Sergeant Beecroft. However, Beecroft recalled that it was not the last time they were fired upon that night. As they approached the Devon coast they were fired on by ack-ack from Torquay. Beecroft fired off the cartridge colours of the day that identified them as friendly, but these were completely ignored.

Three similar operations to Hanover, the Ruhr Valley and Düsseldorf followed during the same month. These operations were in Wellington T2706 and Beecroft was undertaking both the navigator and bomb aimer duties with Elliott his pilot. The pressure was immense knowing that the accuracy of all his work was subsequently going to be scrutinised by Pilot Officer Babington Smith as she interpreted the images.

On 18 March 1941, the crew flew to Bremen but failed to reach the target. The air time was not wasted for Beecroft, who took photographs over Holland. Later the same day, they flew between Abingdon and their base in Wellington T2707 and for an unknown reason had to force-land.

Beecroft's crew was also involved in testing other types of photographic equipment. The supply of cameras was a problem, especially those suitable for detailed high-altitude reconnaissance. Salvaged German Zeiss cameras from crashed enemy reconnaissance aircraft were used in the flight's aircraft. On the night of 6 April 1941, they undertook a most challenging sortie visiting the heavily defended Kiel German Navy base to photograph it from differing directions. Effectively crossing the target several times, the briefings for these dangerous operations must have been lively with comments. Flight Lieutenant Elliott's aircraft was fitted with two cine cameras, equipment in which a long strip of film moves past the lens, providing multiple exposures per second, and thus enables moving pictures to be taken. The crew made four runs alternately from north to south. After the fourth run the cameras stopped working and the crew returned home.

Amidst utmost secrecy, Beecroft's aircraft was fitted with another experimental cine camera. On 16 April, the crew were joined by Wing Commander Bennett, a Canadian photographic specialist. The cine camera had been built in Canada, however, precise details remain unknown. The crew took off at 2350 hours for Bremen but, as encountered frequently, the city was once again affected by ground haze and prevented positive target identification. However, a dummy aerodrome to the south-west of the target area presented an ideal opportunity to deploy the new camera equipment. As they turned for home, the starboard engine was hit by flak over the Dutch coastline and caught fire. Although the fire was extinguished, the propeller malfunctioned and fell into the sea.

Beecroft explained:

> The experience of night flying with an engine on fire is quite a hairy happening, especially for the rear gunner, Sergeant Roy Chandler, who could have made toast from his turret. Luckily, we dived and that coupled with the extinguishers put out the blaze but now our single Pegasus engine could not maintain height. We threw out every moveable object during the 116 mile drag across the North Sea but to no avail. About nine miles off Lowestoft, we ditched and clambered into the dinghy. Some four hours later we were found by our Commanding Officer Squadron Leader Ogilvie and he was able to direct the trawler HMT River Spey to our rescue.

All but two of the crew managed to board the rubber dinghy, and the two unfortunates spent the whole time in the sea hanging on to the lines. The dinghy was slightly damaged during the release from the Wellington. It must have been a great relief when they were circled by the Spitfire and subsequently rescued by the trawler *River Spey*.

The crew's rear gunner, Sergeant Chandler, later wrote down his memories of the incident in a letter to Beecroft. The accounts of Chandler and Beecroft were later published in *Wellington: The Geodetic Giant* by Martin Bowman:

> At first all went well. The Wellington crossed the enemy coast at 10,000 feet and arrived in the vicinity of the target area where there was a considerable ground haze. Elliott found a clear patch about twelve miles south west of Bremen and

a parachute flare was launched. Almost immediately it was extinguished by anti-aircraft fire. Undaunted, the Wellington crew made a run-up on a dummy aerodrome and photographs were taken. About five miles from the enemy coast the port engine burst into flames. Although the crew managed to extinguish the flames all was not well, as Sergeant R. F. 'Chan' Chandler, the rear gunner, explains: 'Eventually the airscrew fell away. I drew Flight Lieutenant Elliott's attention to this fact and after throwing everything we could out of the Wimp [Wellington]' and finding that we could not maintain the height required, we ditched! We ditched approximately nine miles from the enemy coast. It was 5 am and the water was cold. The first thing we saw was an He 111 flying east at about 5,000 feet. We hoped it would "go away". Sergeant Evans, the cameraman, and myself, spent the whole time in the sea, hanging on to dinghy lines, as there was just no room in the dinghy. The side had been badly holed on release from the Wimp' and despite chewing gum and the multi-pressure of flat hands on top of the tear, the dinghy was going down very quickly. It was a most welcome PRU blue Spitfire, piloted by Squadron Leader Ogilvie, that found and circled us. On the horizon came smoke and very soon, HM Transport River Spey came alongside our rapidly deflating dinghy and took us aboard. They were painting an emblem on the funnel as they had just had a successful engagement with an E-boat. We were given a warm change of clothing and large quantities of hot drink and rum. At Lowestoft Evans and I were rushed off to the local hospital. Eventually we arrived at Oakington to be given a royal reception in the Sergeants' Mess.'

His Majesty's Trawler *River Spey* had been called up for naval duties in 1940. The trawler was armed and fitted out as a minesweeper. She served in the North Sea on anti-submarine duties with the Royal Naval Patrol Service. Charles Rose, Royal Navy Reserve, was the skipper from May 1940 to October 1941.

Beecroft's pilot, Flight Lieutenant Elliott, later became an exceptional squadron commander in Air Vice-Marshal Don Bennett's hand-picked Pathfinder Force. Men were selected from within Bomber Command squadrons by Group Captain Hamish Mahaddie for the Pathfinders, who pinpointed and illuminated targets for the main force. The Pathfinders were distinguished from other airmen by a coveted gold Pathfinder winged badge worn below their wings.

No. 3 Photo Reconnaissance Unit was then transferred from Oakington to Boscombe Down. Flight Lieutenant Elliott and his second pilot, Eric Jackson, were selected and posted to Benson for conversion to fly Spitfires. Beecroft retained a photograph of a fly past of Spitfires, writing on the reverse, 'Farewell to Oakington 21 July 1941'. Beecroft was himself posted to 15 Squadron at Wyton, Cambridgeshire, leaving behind tales of a dangerous ditching among other unique experiences during that historically important experimental night photography period of 1941.

In the summer of that year there must have been satisfaction that within just eight months No. 3 Photographic Reconnaissance Unit had proven the worth of night reconnaissance imagery and established many of the principles of bomb damage interpretation. Scientific and technical solutions to improve bombing accuracy such as new bombsights, navigation aids and ground-mapping radar were evolving through some of that work. Winston Churchill said:

> The air photographs showed how little damage was being done. It also appeared that the crews knew this and were discouraged by the poor results of so much hazard. Unless we could improve on this there did not seem much use in continuing night bombing.

The day after Beecroft's introductory flight with 15 Squadron on 25 July 1941 with his new pilot, Flying Officer Thompson, his name appeared in operational orders. His new surroundings were still very fresh, as was the sight of the significantly larger four-engine Short Stirling heavy bombers positioned around the aerodrome. No longer was he a Jack of all trades combining navigation and bomb aiming. The Stirling had a large crew of seven men that included a dedicated bomb aimer and a flight engineer in charge of fuel management and airworthy maintenance. Beecroft was the individual accountable for getting the crew to the target and home again by navigation. He had only had thirty minutes in the air in a Stirling before the expectations built for his first operation in that mighty aircraft. Seven crews received news that they were to fly into the heart of Germany, the target Berlin.

Beecroft's crew took off from Wyton in Stirling N6029. Flight Lieutenants Thomas Henry Bryan Tayler and Frank Thompson were in the cockpit. The remaining crew were Sergeant John Day, Sergeant Brian Denis Beecroft, Sergeant Frank Smith, Sergeant Lawrence Titterton and from New Zealand Sergeant Haydn Neil Guymer. The operation drew out as well as possible for the crew in that the target was reached successfully and all the equipment appeared to have functioned properly. The return journey, however, became seriously problematic, although there are different versions of what actually happened. One report suggests that they were attacked by a Ju 88 off the coast of Rotterdam, which caused significant damage to the fuel tanks and eventually caused them to run out of fuel. However, Flight Lieutenant Tayler wrote after the war that the error was simply with the aircraft's compass and he states that they flew off course and subsequently ran out of fuel. For clarity, later research in the AIR81 archives casualty file 7889 states Stirling N6029 was attacked by a Ju 88, which caused significant damage to the bomber's fuel tanks.

The Australian pilot, Flight Lieutenant Thompson, successfully ditched the stricken bomber in the North Sea at 0540 hours. The flight engineer, Sergeant Day, had monitored the falling fuel readings closely and it was estimated that the fuel finally ran out when they were about 30 miles into the North Sea. Without engine power the heavy bomber silently and gently lost height before it struck the sea surface. The escape hatches were already opened with ditching stations taken before the inevitable happened. Having survived unscathed without any injuries, the crew immediately transferred to the inflated rubber dinghy. The time of year was a welcome factor, with warm temperatures and shorter hours of darkness. Stirling N6029 was a huge mass of metal supported by the enormously large wings and it floated on the water not far from them. The aircraft stubbornly refused to sink for what was estimated to have been three hours.

At Wyton, the radio message of 'operation complete' had been received from the bomber's crew. A later message indicating they were short of fuel had also been received. A line of bearing was calculated and once it was apparent the Stirling had not made it back to any airfield, numerous aircraft were sent to search the nominated sea areas. Those searches all drew a blank, despite the reasonable weather conditions. However, had any rescue aircraft flown over the correct area the Stirling would have been easily seen on the surface. Sometime later the crew spotted both German aircraft and distant shipping, neither of which responded to any of the rescue flares they sent up. Sergeant Beecroft knew they were some distance off the Dutch coastline and the initial sightings had provided hope of an early rescue. However, they simply fell at the mercy of the sea and without much nourishment for seven men. The first full day in the dinghy drew to a close with failing light, the weather worsening due to rain and the sea becoming rough with the prevailing winds.

Daybreak arrived and the rain had not lessened and the waves were sufficient to induce sickness, conditions that did not diminish throughout the entire day as the crew embarked on the second night afloat. Rough seas and heavy rain created grim and difficult conditions through the dark hours and into the third day. On the evening of 29 July, a sighting of shipping with escorting aircraft sparked a clamber to use the rescue flares again, however everything had been subjected to hours upon end of driving rain and they were useless. The coldness intensified and the morale reduced as energy sapped from each man. They had received a daily ration of two Horlicks tablets, a biscuit and piece of chewing gum each.

As dawn broke on 30 July, there was a sign of land far in the distance. During the day the men tried to keep the horizon in sight but the tides influenced the movements of the dinghy much more than any attempt at paddling in a specific direction. Over the next eight hours whatever energy they had was expended on paddling and this resulted in them reaching a shoreline. There were German troops observing the dinghy, which made ground on the island of Schouwen, one of the larger Dutch islands along the coast in that area.

The troops, having established the bedraggled survivors as RAF men, took them into custody. Initially they were taken to a Luftwaffe base hospital at Willemstad. They were given food, medication and a change of clothes before being transferred to an Amsterdam prison for interrogation. On 2 August 1941 the survivors were transported to the Luftwaffe interrogation camp at Frankfurt. From there they were distributed to various prisoner of war camps, Beecroft being sent to Kirchhain IIIE. There he came across Sergeant Price, who had endured an almost identical time adrift for days in a dinghy. Price's extraordinary experiences are outlined in the next chapter. It is possible these two men worked on the famous tunnel that later facilitated the escape of fifty-two fellow prisoners. Sergeants Price and Beecroft remained in close association as prisoners of war. Both were moved into Stalag Luft III before the mass tunnel escape and no doubt walked the exercise yards as good friends until they were repatriated in 1945.

The survival of the crew was entirely down to the design and construction of the rubber dinghy that protected them on those dangerous seas. However, for Sergeant Beecroft this was his second experience of being saved in a dinghy, by far more intense than the first, and quite extraordinarily he now had an entitlement to wear an additional blue embroidered wave beneath his Goldfish membership badge.

*Chapter 12*

# Sergeant Frederick Price – Goldfish Club, Adrift for Six Days, Prisoner of War

Frederick William Price was born 25 October 1915. He enlisted in the RAF on 23 August 1940 and volunteered for aircrew training. Selected as an air gunner in Bomber Command, he served in 149 Squadron. This particular squadron saw many Australian volunteers posted into it directly from the Empire Air Training Scheme. The scheme supplied tens of thousands of aircrews to fight in the air war over Europe during the Second World War. The majority of Australian aircrew, along with their Commonwealth colleagues, were posted as individual crew members who would eventually crew up, often with a multinational aircrew comprised of men from all over the Commonwealth.

Pilot Officer Patrick Leslie Dixon was one such Australian who commanded a Wellington crew in 149 Squadron. Frederick Price became his rear gunner, and this crew were exceptionally lucky to survive a traumatic experience in the North Sea in 1941. The other crew members involved were Sergeant M. E. Adams, second pilot; Sergeant J. N. Grace, New Zealander navigator observer; Sergeant A. Lawson, wireless operator; and Sergeant F. J. Woods, air gunner.

The second pilot, Sergeant Michael Adams, had been a public schoolboy and undergraduate at Oxford University. In the spring of 1939, he was touring Europe but the political turmoil induced him to return home, arriving at Newhaven on the English south coast on 2 September 1939. Germany had invaded and bombed Poland the day before and the RAF committed ten Fairey Battle squadrons, part of the Advanced Air Strike Force, to operate in France. Adams returned to Oxford, where a recruitment board for all three military services was actively encouraging enlistments. An interview saw him accepted for training as a pilot, not an unusual outcome as the recruitment from the RAF perspective was positively aimed at selection from the prestigious universities. What followed was a lengthy and protracted process of limited progression. He subsequently sailed to Egypt, the country of his birth and where his father worked at the National Bank of Egypt. In June 1940, he presented himself to the RAF Headquarters in Cairo and was treated suspiciously, which was not unusual in the circumstances. However, with Italy entering the war, the Mediterranean was no longer a safe passage back to England. By persuasion or other means, he was sent to Kenya for pilot training with two other individuals. On 15 July 1940 he departed for Khartoum, the capital of Sudan, and onward to Uganda and then Nairobi. Into August 1940, there was still no sight of any constructive training. The Battle of Britain was raging above London and the Home Counties while Adams languished at Nairobi airfield. Along with twenty or so others, Adams was transported to Eastleigh airfield across the other side of the city and training finally commenced. Most of the students were colonial servants or farmers. The instructors were reservists commanded by a South African, with just four Tiger Moths and an Avro Tutor acquired from private owners in East Africa and no prospect of replacements.

The basic flying instruction provided was insufficient for Adams to progress past elementary standards. In October 1940 the long passage by train and shipping commenced to England. Twenty-five pupil pilots eventually arrived at Cranfield aerodrome near Bedford. Before attaining his wings, the reality of the dangers of flying present themselves when Adams witnessed the death of a student in a crash. Dispatched to Mildenhall in Suffolk, he joined 149 Squadron and was allocated as second pilot to the crew of Wellington W5399 'Q' Queenie captained by Australian Pilot Officer Patrick Dixon. Every crew in Bomber Command had a mixture of young men from many walks of life. No doubt Sergeant Adams would have been looked upon as a wealthy university graduate and rather distant from the many working-class men that surrounded him at that time in his life. The practice of carrying a second pilot was commonplace early in the war. The prevalent opinion at that time was that pilots needed more experience before taking on the responsibility of commanding a crew.

Wellington W5399, known variously as 'The Wizzard [sic] of Oz' and 'The Ozard of Whiz', carried the squadron code 'OJ' and the aircraft identity letter 'Q' on the fuselage. Below the cockpit the aircraft carried the distinct nose art of a comical cow with a full udder. This particular Wellington had been converted to give it the capability of carrying the newly deployed 4,000lb blast bomb. It was also an aircraft of choice for Squadron Leader James, a renowned personality on the squadron.

In 1941, Brest was a repeat target for Bomber Command crews. On 15 May 1941, the Secretary of State for Air requested to know the total number of bombing raids that had been made on the French port, and the German battle cruisers in those docks. The Under-Secretary of State for Air reported that the docks at Brest had been attacked on forty-seven occasions, twenty-four of which included the German battle cruisers among their objectives.

It was on 7 May 1941 when Sergeant Price climbed into the rear gunner's turret of Wellington X3176, flying his first operational raid upon the docks at Brest. From his rear turret, Price witnessed the Wellington's stick of bombs fall away towards the dry dock target but conditions prevented any opportunity of seeing the results. As with any first operation, it would have created anxiety and excitement in Price in equal measures but the target had been a good introduction to operational flying.

A briefing held on 3 July 1941 confirmed a new target of Essen. The Krupp factory in the industrial town was a prime target for Bomber Command, as it had a significant ability to produce artillery, ammunition and other armaments from its steel plants. Just before midnight, Price and his crew attempted to take their bomb load into the air. They were carrying one of the new large 4,000lb bombs. Pilot Officer Dixon gained sufficient air speed but as he did so, the port wing dipped and the aircraft fell heavily back on to the runway and after the undercarriage collapsed it eventually tore across the airfield and into a barley field.

The second pilot, Sergeant Adams, had joined Pilot Officer Dixon's crew so his ability could be assessed. Following the loss of a Wellington the previous night, the replacement aircraft required flight testing and Adams was requested to undertake a circuit and landing at Mildenhall with the rest of the crew on board. However, he mistakenly failed to put the flaps down and this caused the 13-ton Wellington to be too high for any landing and also to be coming in too fast. Adams almost forced the Wellington on to the runway but with too much speed. Adams' enforced and heavy use of the rudder bar in order to avoid parked aircraft swung the Wellington's direction of travel and as it did so the undercarriage gave way and the aircraft slid sideways, coming to rest at right angles to the runway. This event resulted in the crew being given leave as any rear gunner in a landing that featured such errors of judgement like that would have experienced profound shock. Price would have rightly been concerned about the second pilot's ability after experiencing a landing with such consequences.

On 14 July, Pilot Officer Dixon once again took his crew up on a pre-raid test flight, during which Adams made a couple of landings without incident. Bremen was the target that night. Eleven crews sat through the briefing, with take-off scheduled for 2300 hours. The briefing advised that 103 bombers were to attack the railway yards in Bremen. The operational records advise that Price flew in Wellington T2737.

Adams describes the events:

We reached Bremen around 2am and recognised it by some waterways shining in the moonlight. Things seemed pretty quiet and we made a trial run over the town, untroubled at first by anything except a few wandering searchlights. Then the flak started to come up, I was standing in the Astro hatch halfway along the fuselage and bursts looked like cheerful fireworks. After this a long period of darkness, we lost the target and guns were inactive. Around 2.30am Jim Grace, the New Zealand Navigator, said he could see the target and Dixon turned for a bombing run. Then things did start to happen. One searchlight flicked onto us and held us, and a dozen more joined it, then the guns opened up all around us different coloured bursts of fire. I couldn't see how we could get through it unscathed, the aircraft started to lurch about in the sky as though it was being pummelled by unseen fists.

There was quite a bit of chat over the intercom, the gunners commentating unfavourably on the nearness of the flak bursts. When at last we came over the target the bombs wouldn't come off, I suppose the connections to the arming panel were shot away. The flak was still intense, it was a matter of getting out of it as soon as possible. Dixon jettisoned the bombs over a searchlight battery but then the bomb doors would not close, reducing our speed seriously, the hydraulics had been shot to bits and the fuselage smelt of petrol. I took over from the pilot when he assessed the situation. The instruments were damaged, the airspeed indicator was reading absurdly high. There was a big crack in the glass just in front of my face, the smell of petrol was strong and oil was slopping about on the floor. I flew over the Zuider Zee just before we left the Dutch coast when two searchlights picked us up, one had another Wellington in its beam about 1,500 feet above us to starboard. I did a few S turns to try and shake them off but without success, then we were over the sea and the main tanks were exhausted and switched to the nacelle tanks. Both engines picked up and we carried on at 6,500 feet. I had the nose down slightly to increase speed.

Dixon took over, announcing that we could not make England and must prepare to come down in the sea. I was sent back to check the dinghy release and flotation gear. Sandy the Wireless Operator and Fred Air Gunner joined me to remove the Astro hatch off, which was jammed. Jim Grace showed me where the dinghy release was and returned to Dixon. The petrol was finished and the engines were now quiet. I hopped up in the Astro hatch to see how close we were to the water. We were only a few hundred feet up so I stood by the flotation gear and told Fred to be ready to hop out first followed by Sandy. I was still plugged into the intercom and Dixon asked if I had everything ready. Just before we hit the water I pulled the three handles of the flotation gear, then caught hold of the dinghy release handle.

We hit the water with a wallop, I was thrown to the floor and a surge of water came rushing down from the cockpit and whirled me around in the fuselage. For a moment I thought it was all over but standing up I was able to get my head and shoulders out of the water. I saw Fred clambering out and Sandy behind him as I fought the water to the Astro hatch, where I gave the dinghy release another pull to make sure as I pulled myself up through the hatch into the air. The others were all out so we clambered into the dinghy and pushed off.

After about ten minutes, she sank. We were in the middle of the North Sea, six of us in a rubber dinghy about seven feet across and shaped like an ancient coracle.

It was just after 0500 hours on 15 July 1941. The sea was a bit choppy and the dinghy drifted according to the tide and winds. All hopes were on the wireless operator's urgent messages for an early rescue, but none came. Two crew at a time rested in the well of the dinghy while the others sat around the inflated rim. Being adrift in the North Sea would have been an exceptionally lonely experience. They were in favourable summer conditions but day followed night with regularity and the winds swept up waves that soaked everyone. The leak stoppers, part of the dinghy equipment, worked well despite their bulky and improbable design in dealing with one leak in the rubber skin of the dinghy. The dinghy proved robust in design and was the means that enabled the crew to survive. The constant movement of the crew had no ill effect on the durability of the rubber. Pilot Officer Dixon took charge of the survival rations, issuing the most meagre of quantities of biscuit or concentrated chocolate, raisins and Horlicks tablets. Drinking water was supplemented by collecting rain water to refill the three-pint bottles that were very much the lifeline of survival, as was the single ration of rum that Dixon was exceptionally careful to distribute when conditions were at their worst.

After three to four days without any sightings of shipping or aircraft, the helplessness and desperation would have inevitably set in as water and nourishment diminished, no doubt with endless calculations of how long the survival rations could be eked out, combined with the hope of being rescued. At midday on 21 July, a faint sound of aircraft was heard and four twin-engine aircraft were spotted. A Messerschmitt Bf 110 fighter flew over and investigated the dinghy. Three other aircraft also took a closer look before disappearing. Speculation as to the consequences of the sighting provoked all manner of possibilities in the minds of the crew. Before dusk, further aero engines announced a return of aircraft in the form of a Heinkel He 115 seaplane. The conditions were too rough for a landing, so the seaplane dropped another dinghy pack, which started to sink but not before the crew took some of the rescue equipment. As darkness fell, the waves grew in intensity with high winds. This was the sixth night in the dinghy. It must have been difficult to endure as those conditions always had the potential to flip the dinghy and cause those inside to fall in with little chance of survival. Luckily the weather subsided as the sky grew lighter and the Messerschmitts returned, escorting the seaplane. The seaplane landed not far away and taxied towards the rubber dinghy. As it reached the dinghy a trapdoor opened and one by one the Wellington crew were assisted inside.

All the survivors had lost the use of their legs, with almost all unable to support themselves. After a short flight they were taken to a hospital for feeding, followed by a prison somewhere in central Amsterdam. In isolation from each other, the crew rested and recovered as best as possible. They were then taken on a train to Frankfurt for interrogation as prisoners of war. Fifty-two prisoners were taken collectively from the interrogation camp to Stalag IIIE Kirchhain and this included crew members Adams, Lawson, Price and Woods. Dixon went to Stalag Luft III and for some reason Grace was sent to Stalag VIIIB.

While at Kirchhain, Price applied to join the Goldfish Club by writing to P. B. Cow and he was accepted. Few members had endured such a long period of survival in a rubber dinghy as he had. Many men made applications directly from prisoner of war camps.

In April 1942, a move to Stalag Luft III was announced. There was discontentment among the PoWs on hearing that news because Adams and others had been digging a tunnel with some ferocity. It was likely to be finished towards the end of June. The first party to leave Kirchhain on 28 April consisted of 100 men. The following week another transit of prisoners was scheduled. The escape tunnel was approaching 90ft long. It was not possible to make the progress required to reach out past the perimeter fence for the first departure but all effort was put in place to have it ready before the second tranche of men departed the camp. Adams was removed from the camp in the first wave. Unbeknown to him, the tunnel – which reached 163ft long – was completed within two days of their departure. The tunnel was a remarkable achievement and on 11 May 1942, fifty-two prisoners escaped, a number only to be beaten by the Great Escape from Stalag Luft III in 1944.

Promoted to warrant officer in captivity, Price spent time in four prisoner of war camps before his liberation on 8 April 1945.

*Chapter 13*

# Flight Sergeant Victor Jarvis DFM – Air-Sea Rescue

Victor Jarvis was born on 19 September 1904. He enlisted in the RAF in 1921 and during the Second World War he witnessed the development of measures to recover ditched airmen from the sea. He then became the first member of the air-sea rescue services to be awarded the Distinguished Flying Medal. Later, he served in a unique position, flying over the United Kingdom in enemy aircraft that had been captured and were being test flown to determine their capabilities.

Enlisting on 6 September 1921, Jarvis served at Leuchars and Gosport for some four years. He was permitted to volunteer as an aircraftsman for air gunner duties and gained intermittent time in the air. In 1927, he was selected for official training in air gunnery while attached to 25 Squadron. This inter-war period was challenging for any aircraftsman aspiring to fly as the post of air gunner was not given any recognition. In September 1929, Leading Aircraftsman Jarvis was posted to the Middle East and he served with several squadrons at Ismailia, north of the Great Bitter Lake in Egypt, before returning to the United Kingdom in November 1932. The Auxiliary Air Force Reserve of Officers was formed in September 1932, and only those who had served in the Auxiliary Air Force were eligible for a four-year commission. Having served in excess of ten years in the Auxiliary Air Force, Jarvis was able to discharge himself from service the following year.

Jarvis was recalled to the RAF in May 1938 and was sent to Gosport while awaiting a posting. After war was declared he was sent to an Army Co-operation Command squadron. He was posted as an air gunner flying in Westland Lysanders, an aircraft that had only entered service in May 1938. The first unit to receive the aircraft was 16 Squadron, based at Old Sarum, the birthplace of Army Co-operation training. When the British Expeditionary Force went to France, six Lysander-equipped squadrons formed part of the contingent. Leading Aircraftsman Jarvis was in 2 Squadron. In October 1939, he was deployed to France as part of 51 Army Co-op Wing, alongside 26 and 59 Squadrons. Victor's squadron had detachment flights at Labuissière, in Belgium, and Senon, north-eastern France.

In early May 1940, 2 Squadron was thrust headlong into the war. The Army Co-op Wing Lysanders were flying contact patrols looking for the enemy and were regularly subjected to ground fire as they flew low over the advancing forces. They were affiliated to Army divisions working directly under Army commanders. On 14 May, the squadron moved to advanced landing grounds in Belgium, 'A' Flight to Béthune–Labuissière and 'B' Flight to Abbeville, followed by 'C' Flight to Wevelgem. The squadron was ordered to consolidate at Béthune–Labuissière due to the German Army's rapid advances. On 19 May, the squadron would be tasked to reconnaissance the vital bridges where the British Third Corps were retreating across the Scheldt River. In the chaos, it was not known who was controlling the bridges. The strength of the enemy in the air was overwhelming and eventually orders arrived to withdraw from France. The ground crews made for Cherbourg, while any airworthy Lysander was flown back to Lympne airfield in Kent, where it would continue to operate with the Army in tactical reconnaissance.

An estimated fifty out of a total of 174 Lysanders that were operational in France made it back to the British Isles. Unfortunately the official squadron records of their activity in France were lost and exactly what part Leading Aircraftsman Jarvis undertook remains unknown. The September 1939 to May 1940 operational record books detail very little and only October 1939 has a form 541 detailing the work undertaken during that period, with an additional partial entry made for May 1940.

Saturday, 25 May was probably the most significant day in the battle of France as the British forces were ordered to withdraw. In the afternoon, the Secretary of State for War, Anthony Eden, sent Brigadier Claude Nicholson, the commanding officer in Calais, a message that read:

> Defence of Calais to the utmost is of highest importance to our country as symbolising our continued cooperation with France. The eyes of the Empire are upon the defence of Calais, and H.M. Government are confident you and your gallant regiments will perform an exploit worthy of the British name.
>
> Every hour you continue to exist is of greatest help to the British Expeditionary Force. Government has therefore decided you must continue to fight. Have greatest admiration for your splendid stand.

Records of activity in England provide details of operational flights taken by Leading Aircraftsman Jarvis in support of the British garrison besieged in Calais in May 1940. Early in the morning of 26 May, the German bombardment resumed with additional artillery having been brought up from Boulogne. The British and French troops were encircled by German forces. A plan for Lysanders from Hawkinge to drop supplies directly into the encirclement had been devised and would commence at first light. No. 2 Squadron were to engage with the drop over the citadel encirclement while 26 and 613 squadrons were dropping supplies to the troops on the beaches.

Unfortunately, the citadel drop required exceptionally low altitude as the drop zone was by then approximately only 400 yards by 200 yards. Flight Lieutenant Drysdale and Leading Aircraftsman Clark were to lead the operation, which engaged seven further crews and included Leading Aircraftsman Jarvis accompanying his regular pilot, Pilot Officer Dudeney.

The squadron record book confirms that on 27 May 1940, eight aircraft took off at 0945 hours to drop water, ammunition and supplies on the beleaguered garrison. The supplies dropped on the citadel were released at a height of 50ft and only one container fell outside the target area. However, unknown to Whitehall or the participating aircrews, the citadel had actually fallen before the War Office request was made to the Air Ministry. Calais was in enemy hands on the evening before the Lysanders set out on their dangerous mission. Nonetheless, it had been a bold action by the RAF to supply the provisions using the vulnerable Lysander.

Leading Aircraftsman Jarvis was promoted to sergeant as 2 Squadron received orders for a new kind of warfare, gas spraying. Four squadrons were to be trained for low-level gas spraying over the potential invasion beaches of the east coast of England. The threat of German forces invading was seen as real and spraying gas was seen as a possible defensive action. Pilot Officer Dudeney and Sergeant Jarvis were among the crews of A Flight, 2 Squadron, that were posted on 24 October 1940 to be part of the initial gas-spraying crews. Along with 'B' Flight from 26 Squadron, they reformed into 268 Squadron at Westley to the west of Bury St Edmunds, Suffolk.

The main activities for Pilot Officer Dudeney and Sergeant Jarvis were dawn and dusk anti-invasion patrols along the coast, and in late 1940 to early 1941 they were involved in anti-aircraft co-operation work with gunners at Gatwick. Jarvis was listed regularly as air gunner for Dudeney until his pilot was posted to join Bomber Command in February 1941. Jarvis remained with the squadron until

Advertisement publishing the Irvin parachute, 1939.

News of the Goldfish Club spread as the war progressed. In January 1943 the BBC broadcaster Wynford Vaughan-Thomas interviewed two recent members of the club at the P. B. Cow factory. In a dinghy surrounded by life rafts with an illustrated air-sea rescue backdrop, Sergeants Albert Ricketts and Ron Thompson sat next to Charles Robertson describing their daylight raid on the Phillips Radio Works in the Netherlands on 6 December 1942. Returning to base, their Lockheed Ventura ditched into the sea about 7 miles off Felixstowe. The dinghy inflated correctly and within an hour they were rescued and taken to Felixstowe. *C. A. Robertson*

The broadcaster Wynford Vaughan-Thomas holds the microphone as Charles Robertson talks to Sergeants Albert Ricketts and Ron Thompson. The recording was broadcast to the public in March 1943. The two sergeants from 21 Squadron also reported to the Air Ministry to give an account of how the Ventura had performed in the ditching. *C. A. Robertson*

The Goldfish Club artwork design upon the reverse side of the waterproof, sealed membership card. The yellow doughnut life raft is clearly defined, as is the single-man dinghy and a parachute. This artwork was undoubtably created by Charles Robertson.

An air-sea rescue launch with three crew helping board a ditched airman wearing his Mae West life jacket from the sea. The 64ft launch provided little security for the crew other than the grab ropes and rails that are being used by two of the rescuing seamen. The third seaman is negotiating the rope net used for climbing onto the launch from the sea.

*Left*: The cloth woven membership badge of the Goldfish Club showing a white-winged goldfish flying above two symbolic blue waves of the sea.

*Below*: An early wartime example of the Irvin Caterpillar Club membership card, awarded to Corporal Foster.

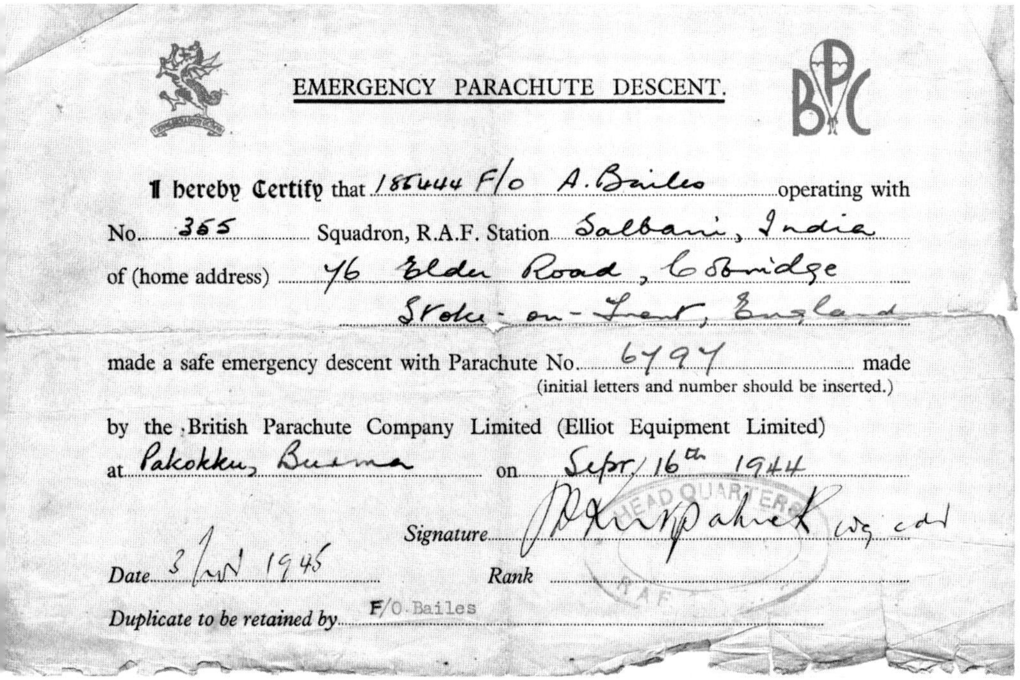

EMERGENCY PARACHUTE DESCENT.

**I hereby Certify** that 186444 F/O A. Bailes ................operating with
No. 355 Squadron, R.A.F. Station Salbani, India
of (home address) 46 Elder Road, Cobridge
Stoke-on-Trent, England
made a safe emergency descent with Parachute No. 6797 made
(initial letters and number should be inserted.)
by the British Parachute Company Limited (Elliot Equipment Limited)
at Pakokku, Burma on Sept 16th 1944
Signature ...................................... W/Cdr
Date 3/JAN 1945 Rank .........................
Duplicate to be retained by F/O Bailes

Warrant Officer Bailes' British Parachute Company emergency parachute escape certificate for parachute serial number 6797. *Via Matt Poole*

An early period Irvin Caterpillar pin attached to the recipient's Distinguished Flying Cross medal ribbon.

Six aircrew from a ditched aircraft using the dinghy paddle and hand oars to manoeuvre the rubber dinghy towards a Sunderland flying boat. Three of the rescued airmen are wearing yellow skull caps, which were thought to have improved the possibility of aerial recognition by rescue aircraft.

Six aircrew from a Whitley that ditched in the waters off Iceland were rescued from their dinghy and rowed ashore by two civilian rescuers, who are seen manning the oars with the rubber dinghy in tow. The medical staff at the Royal Air Force station in Reykjavik treated the crew.

The 16ft-long type Q dinghy was equipped with an inflation cylinder positioned on the upper rib and a high twin-sectional telescopic mast for a mainsail and foresail. The crew are climbing from the dinghy into the Lindholme boat, which was powered by a two-stroke engine and contained waterproof clothing, food and medical supplies. One of the parachutes that supported the boat when it was dropped to the survivors can be seen semi-submerged at the forward section.

Wellington bomber crew wearing their lightweight yellow Mae West life jackets with ties, grab handles and an additional pocket to the right side. The crew hang their helmets and masks over their shoulders, while one member carries the crew mascot. The aircraft fuselage displays the identity 'Flak Happy Harry'.

Flight Lieutenant Brayshaw wearing his Mae West illustrated with an elephant good luck mascot. In October 1943 his life was saved by this life jacket after his Typhoon ditched and sank immediately. In another incident in February 1944, he endured another ditching off the French coast. His body was never located and his life is commemorated on the Runnymede Memorial.

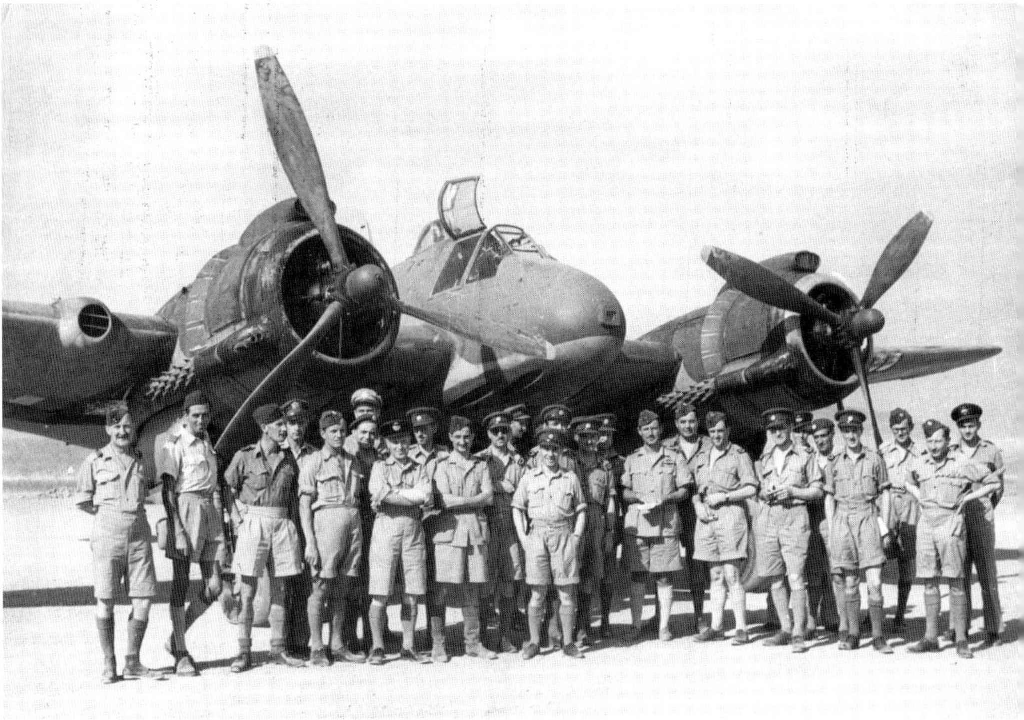

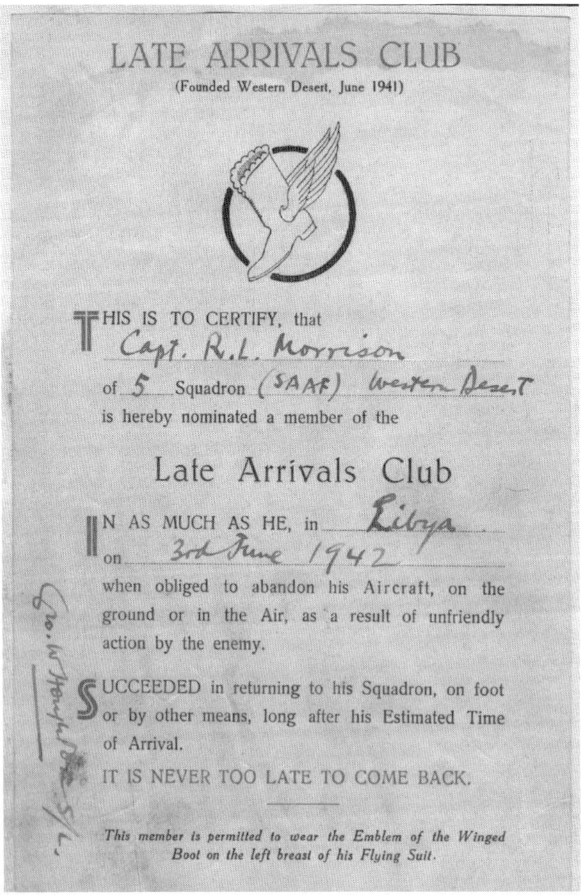

LATE ARRIVALS CLUB

(Founded Western Desert, June 1941)

THIS IS TO CERTIFY, that Capt. R.L. Morrison

of 5 Squadron (SAAF) Western Desert

is hereby nominated a member of the

Late Arrivals Club

IN AS MUCH AS HE, in Libya

on 3rd June 1942

when obliged to abandon his Aircraft, on the ground or in the Air, as a result of unfriendly action by the enemy.

SUCCEEDED in returning to his Squadron, on foot or by other means, long after his Estimated Time of Arrival.

IT IS NEVER TOO LATE TO COME BACK.

*This member is permitted to wear the Emblem of the Winged Boot on the left breast of his Flying Suit.*

*Above*: Air correspondents visited North Africa in October 1943. Squadron Leader Houghton, a pre-war journalist, had created the Late Arrivals Club. This captured the imagination of war correspondents, who reported that it was never too late to come back. Squadron Leader Houghton is seen far left in front of a Desert Air Force Beaufighter with the newspaper reporters. During his time in North Africa, Houghton awarded the membership badges and signed certificates personally.

*Left*: The South African Air Force Late Arrivals Club certificate of Captain Morrison, signed and awarded to him by Squadron Leader Houghton in June 1942.

*Above*: The Western Desert had remote landing grounds where aircraft were made ready for operations over enemy-held territory. On 22 November 1941, Sergeant Robert Turton bailed out of his burning aircraft, having flown from a similar landing ground. During three days of walking, sand snails were his only source of food and moisture. He reached safety, becoming a Late Arrivals Club member.

*Below*: Major Morrison's Kittyhawk fighter-bomber of 5 Squadron, South African Air Force, seen on an Italian airfield in the summer of 1944. Having previously become a member of the Late Arrivals Club, Morrison was killed in September 1944 attacking a gun emplacement.

The Irvin Caterpillar Club membership card awarded to Sergeant Percival Lindsay Miller. This emergency escape occurred on 11 August 1942, and the membership card is an unusual type and infrequently seen. The signature is of Leslie Irvin.

The Irvin Caterpillar Club membership card awarded to Flight Sergeant James Forsyth Burness. This emergency escape occurred on 5 February 1943. The membership card is the more usual wartime design with the personal signature of Leslie Irvin.

 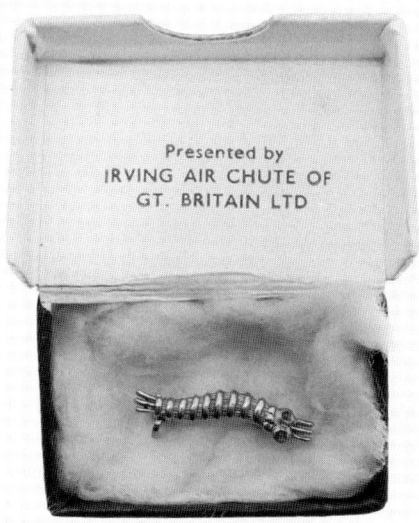

*Above left*: The medals and Caterpillar Club membership pin awarded to Sergeant John Lord, who parachuted into captivity on 15 September 1941. His Caterpillar pin was awarded while a prisoner of war. He lost his life from injuries sustained when his prison column was attacked, mistaken as enemy troops while being marched into central Germany. The 1939 1945 Star, Air Crew Europe Star and British War Medal were sent to his family with the nation's gratitude.

*Above right*: In 1930, Mappin and Webb jewellers created a silver commemorative piece for Amy Johnson's solo flight from England to Australia. This may well have influenced Leslie Irvin into commissioning the jewellers to manufacture the early engraved Caterpillar pins for his club. The pin was presented in a small box that identified both the Caterpillar Club on the inner lid and the jewellers on the outer box lid.

*Below*: The hand engraving of a later wartime economy Caterpillar pin.

*Above*: Two ditched crew wearing the additional yellow scull hats in their inflated dinghy. A pair of hand paddles designed to enable some form of propulsion or control over the dinghy are in use. By 1941 all multi-seat aircraft had been supplied with dinghies to accommodate different numbers of crew members.

*Left*: A Beaufort crew seen below their aircraft. The crew are wearing their life jackets over the Irvin leather flying jacket. Above them the rear-facing defensive gun is well illustrated. This gun was fitted in an area originally designed as a forward escape hatch for the crew and only featured on the early Beauforts.

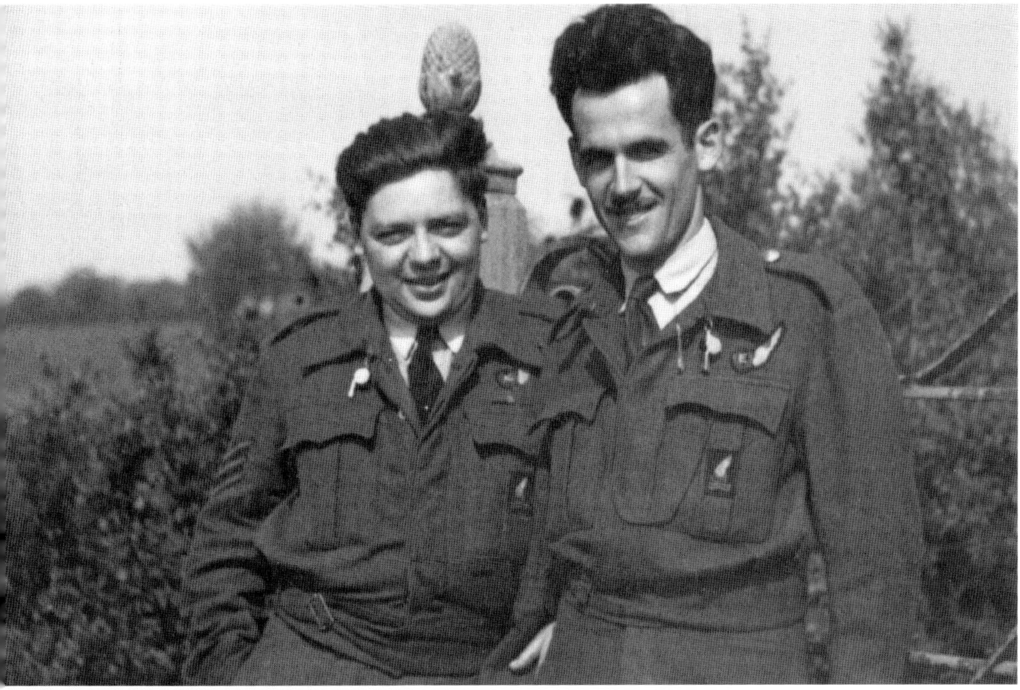

A rare example of both survivors wearing their Goldfish Club membership badges sewn upon their tunics. Sergeants J. Wilson and D. Hughes ditched in their 214 Squadron Stirling heavy bomber on 23 November 1943. Both men later added membership of the Caterpillar Club during subsequent operations. *Via Steve Palmer*

Membership Card

This is to Certify that
P/O. R.W. Osborn
has qualified as a member of the Goldfish Club by escaping death by the use of his Emergency Dinghy on
16th September, 1943.

Signed
CHARLES A. ROBERTSON
Hon. Secretary

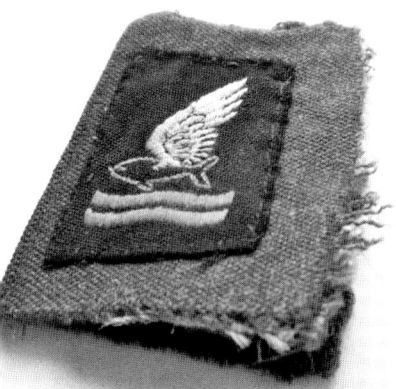

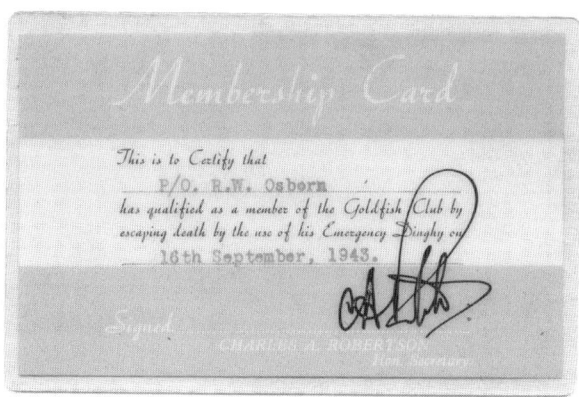

*Above left*: Pilot Officer Osborn's woven Goldfish badge, which to be compliant to dress regulations was sewn under the left lapel of his uniform tunic. The lapel was later cut from the tunic, which has thankfully preserved it among his wartime memorabilia.

*Above right*: Pilot Officer Osborn's Goldfish Club membership card signed by Charles Robertson certifying his survival on 16 September 1943.

| Date | Hour | Aircraft Type and No. | Pilot | Duty | Remarks (including results of bombing, gunnery, exercises, etc.) | Flying Times Day | Night |
|---|---|---|---|---|---|---|---|
| | | | | | Time carried forward :— | 208.05 | 45.00 |
| 8.9.43 | 12.20 | BEAU VI No 8444 | F/L FERGUSON | NAVIGATOR | N.F.T. | 00.30 | |
| | 19.30 | " | " | " | TO FWD BASE - COLTISHALL | 00.40 | |
| | 21.35 | " | " | " | "OPS" - TARGET CHANNEL PORTS - TRIP ABANDONED - WEAPON BENT | 01.45 | 01.45 |
| 14.9.43 | 10.55 | 8803 | " | " | N.F.T. - WEAPON BENT | 01.20 | |
| " | 14.35 | " | " | " | N.F.T. - All O.K. | 01.00 | |
| 15.9.43 | 12.00 | 8803 | " | " | N.F.T. ; | 00.35 | |
| | 18.00 | 8803 | " | " | TO FWD. BASE - FORD | 00.40 | |
| | 22.15 | " | " | " | "OPS" - TARGET MONTLUCON. PORT ENGINE CUT ON RETURN JOURNEY CRASHED INTO SEA 5 m. OFF FECAMP. SPENT 4½ HRS IN DINGHY. PICKED UP BY A.S.R WALRUS | | 02.55 |
| 17.9.43 | 01.00 | WALRUS | SGT. FLETCHER S/M. BAR | PASSENGER | TO FORD | 01.00 | |
| 22.9.43 | 11.35 | BEAU VI 8744 | F/L KELSEY | PASSENGER | N.F.T - FELT FINE ! | 00.40 | |
| | | | | | TOTAL TIME ... | 214.30 | 49.4 |

*Above*: Flying Officer Osborn's log book entry for his ditching on 15 September 1943. The renowned Walrus rescue pilot Sergeant Fletcher has been recorded by Osborn as his rescuer on 17 September.

*Left*: A 282 Squadron air-sea rescue Warwick carrying an underslung Lindholme boat. A bombsight was operated to drop the rescue boat as near to the ditched air crew as possible. It was dropped from an altitude of about 700ft suspended by parachutes.

An air-sea rescue Lindholme boat with the sail and rigging being checked by ground crew before stowing and securing in the under-fuselage position of the Warwick. The assembly at the rear of the boat designed to assist with aerial stability can be seen, and the red cloth covering over the fore and aft shelters are easily defined with white numeral identification numerals.

Spitfire pilot wearing the complete parachute assembly. Although it looks cumbersome, once in the cockpit the pilot sits upon the parachute pack. The D Ring ripcord was partially enclosed within a cloth pouch to protect it from unintended deployment. This 602 Squadron aircraft has the name 'Bogus' painted beneath the cockpit.

Returning from Dieppe early on 19 August 1942, Sergeant Czachla of 306 Polish Squadron was low on fuel. On the approach to Northolt airfield as his engine cut, Malvern Avenue lay in front of him as he lost height. The pilot tried to land on the road in an effort to avoid the houses, illustrating the measures taken by many pilots to save their aircraft.

# LATE ARRIVALS CLUB
(Founded Western Desert, June 1941)

THIS IS TO CERTIFY, that SERGT. H.T. ROLPH of 148 Squadron MIDDLE EAST is hereby nominated a member of the

## Late Arrivals Club

IN AS MUCH AS HE, in CYRENAICA on 5TH APRIL 1942 when obliged to abandon his Aircraft, on the ground or in the Air, as a result of unfriendly action by the enemy.

SUCCEEDED in returning to his Squadron, on foot or by other means, long after his Estimated Time of Arrival.

IT IS NEVER TOO LATE TO COME BACK.

*This member is permitted to wear the Emblem of the Winged Boot on the left breast of his Flying Suit.*

*Left*: The Late Arrival certificate awarded to Sergeant Rolph and signed by Squadron Leader Houghton in April 1942.

*Below left*: The Late Arrivals Club badge awarded to Sergeant Rolph. Aircrew coming to grief over North Africa and the Middle East carried booklets of tear-out chits to assist the local population. Chits were printed in Assyrian, Azerbaijan, Arabic, Kurdish and Turkish.

*Below right*: The 1939–1945 Star Pacific Star and war medal awarded to Sergeant Lockwood, who has attached his Caterpillar pin to the medal ribbon.

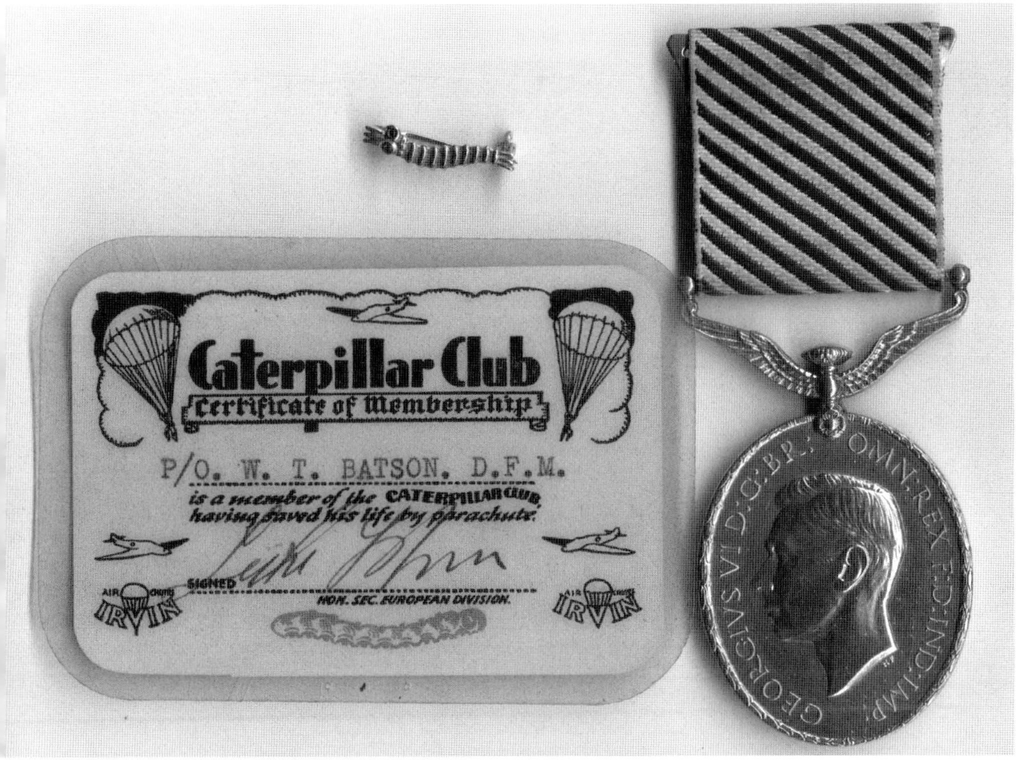


*Above*: Pilot Officer Batson's Distinguished Flying Medal with Caterpillar Club membership card and membership pin.

*Right*: The acceptance letter from the Caterpillar Club sent to the prisoner of war camp that enclosed Pilot Officer Batson's membership card.

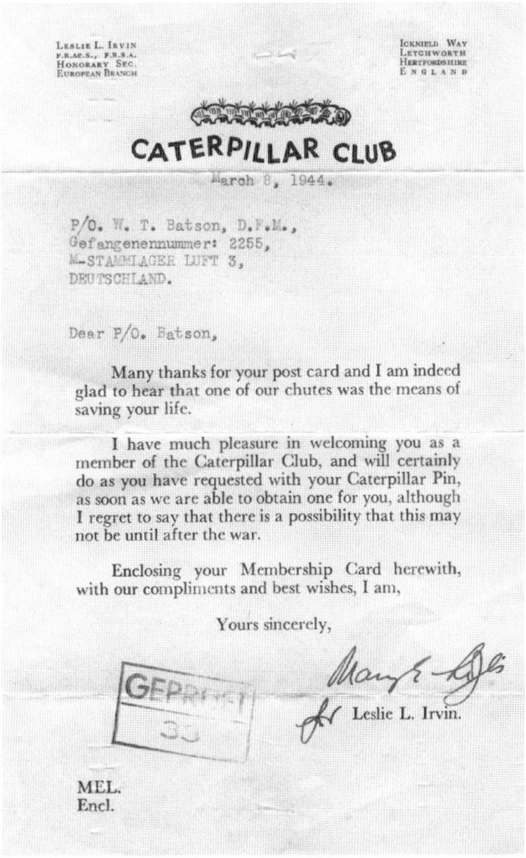

Leslie L. Irvin
F.R.Ae.S., F.R.S.A.
Honorary Sec.
European Branch

Icknield Way
Letchworth
Hertfordshire
England

CATERPILLAR CLUB

March 8, 1944.

P/O. W. T. Batson, D.F.M.,
Gefangenennummer: 2255,
M-STAMMLAGER LUFT 3,
DEUTSCHLAND.

Dear P/O. Batson,

Many thanks for your post card and I am indeed glad to hear that one of our chutes was the means of saving your life.

I have much pleasure in welcoming you as a member of the Caterpillar Club, and will certainly do as you have requested with your Caterpillar Pin, as soon as we are able to obtain one for you, although I regret to say that there is a possibility that this may not be until after the war.

Enclosing your Membership Card herewith, with our compliments and best wishes, I am,

Yours sincerely,

for Leslie L. Irvin.

GEPRÜFT
33

MEL.
Encl.

*Above*: The flying log book entry made by Sergeant Beecroft on his ditching and the post-war, vehicle-mounted Goldfish Club badge.

*Left*: In January 1941, twelve Lysander aircraft were borrowed from Army Co-operation Command for air-sea rescue duties. This Lysander is dropping a dinghy pack from the undercarriage pannier. This aircraft was lost in unexplained circumstances on 24 August 1942 flying rescue sorties with 276 Squadron.

A heavy bomber crew in a dinghy. The survivors have raised the rubber weather aprons fitted on the inflated dinghy chambers. The additional survival equipment known as Lindholme gear is floating in sequence along the trailing rope line. The rear aileron of the rescue aircraft can be seen in the top left section of the image.

Corporal Hills seen wearing his Guinea Pig Club badge on his tunic breast pocket. In the background, wearing glasses and bow tie looking onwards, is Archibald McIndoe. Hills, a ground crew mechanic, had been officially accepted into the prestigious aviator's club and later served as McIndoe's chauffer.

The Defence and War Medal with Guinea Pig Club badge awarded to Corporal Hills. In all probability a unique example of medals to an entitled club member.

Warrant Officer Taylor's letter of membership of the Goldfish Club and the question answered by Charles Robertson on the wearing of the woven badge.

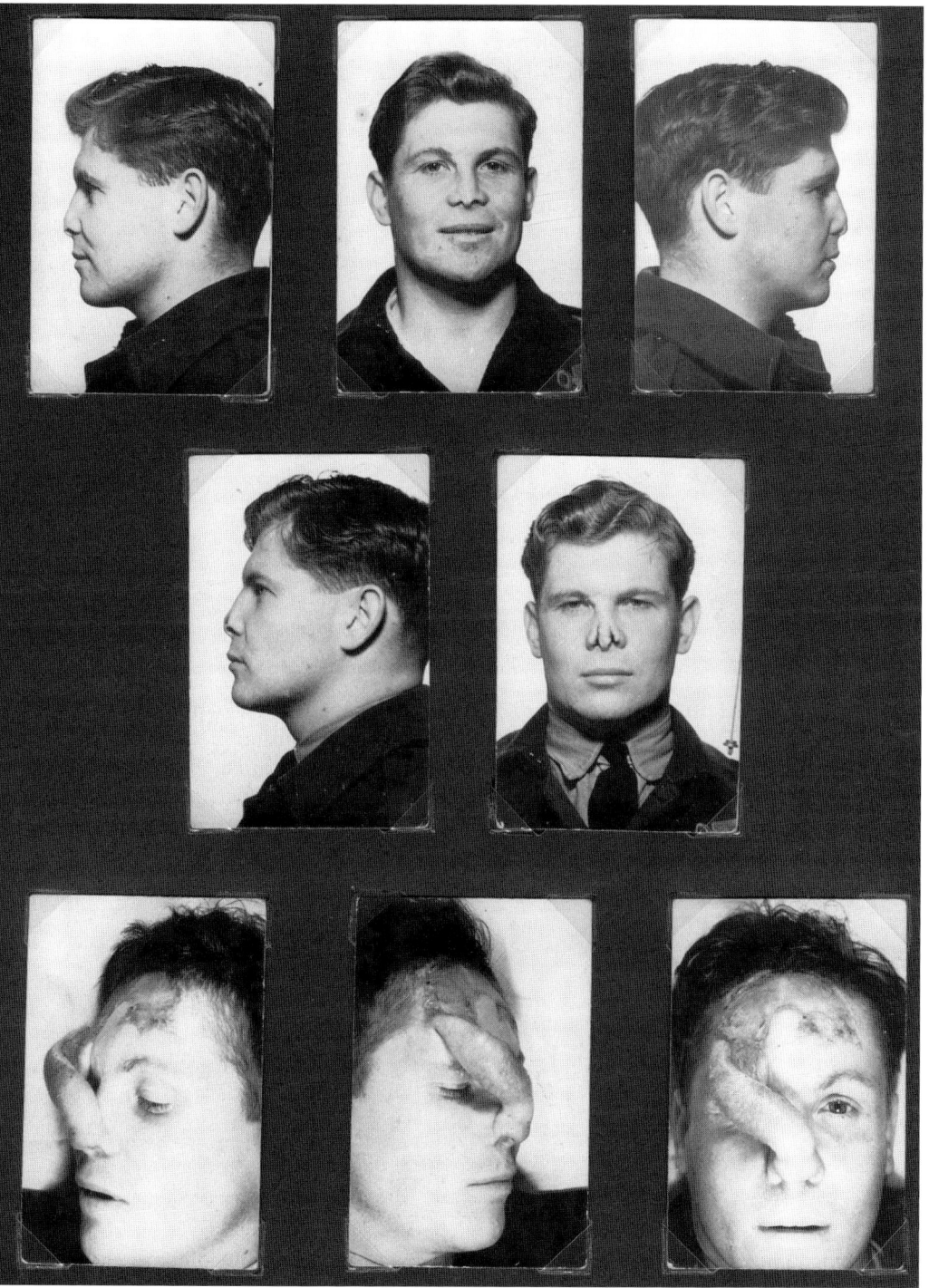

The sequence of facial images plotting the operations undertaken by Archbald McIndoe upon Warrant Officer Taylor. The pedicle skin harvest of tissue allowed the operation to be completely successful.

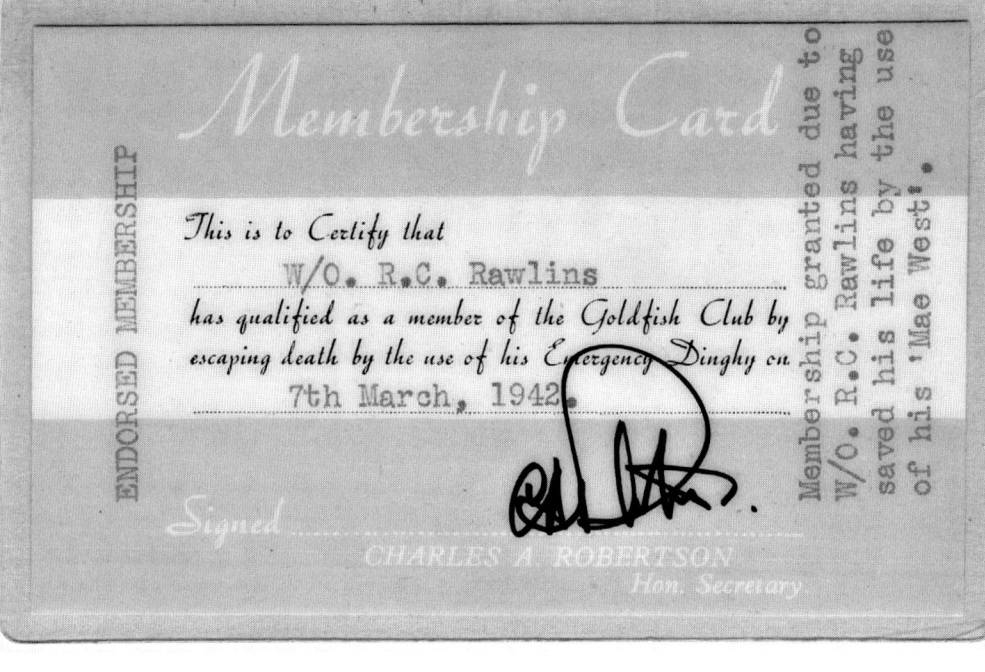

*Above*: The Goldfish Club Endorsed Membership card issued to Warrant Officer Rawlins for the events on 7 March 1942. Examples of such cards are rarely seen.

*Left*: The Goldfish Club letter to Warrant Officer Rawlins commenting upon the malfunction of the dinghy and the inflation system of his Mae West jacket on 7 March 1942.

The manufacturing of what appear to be inflated type H dinghies. The women in the foreground are attaching sea anchor chambers to the base of the dinghy, which were designed to create greater stability for the occupants. This dinghy had a seating capacity for five persons, and a rope ladder greatly improved access for the survivors.

The unique GQ parachute club members gold lapel badge engraved number 449 awarded to Pilot Officer Altham in 1945. The GQ badge was awarded in limited numbers. Each applicant was required to evidence that the chute used was GQ manufactured and not an Irvin type made under licence by GQ Parachutes Ltd.

The GQ parachute club certificate of membership awarded to Pilot Officer Altham. Each certificate was personally signed by Raymond Quilter and identified both the recipient and the badge number awarded.

Pilots sat on their parachute when in the cockpit, and the harness, frequently referred to as 'the Sutton', strapped the pilot into his seat. The Sutton harness was fitted with a quick-release buckle, which meant that in the event of an emergency the pilot would be released from the seat while still retaining the actual parachute and its own harness.

early April. As context for these postings, late March to early April 1941 witnessed a growing number of pilots and air gunners posted to meet demands from Bomber Command. However, for the newly promoted Flight Sergeant Jarvis, a very different posting occurred.

In April, Jarvis was posted back to RAF Hawkinge. During the Battle of Britain, it became apparent that an improved system was necessary to increase the chances of survival for pilots whose aircraft were forced to ditch into the sea. In an attempted solution, Fighter Command borrowed Lysanders from the Army Co-operation Command and placed them under the operational control of Fighter Command. These aircraft were given a fighter escort and sent out after each air battle to search the coastal waters and beyond. The main rescue equipment was a rubber dinghy, which was carried in the pannier rack of the landing wheels. Despite close co-operation with the Royal Navy, only limited success was achieved. However, with high losses occurring in October 1940, the Chief of Air Staff proposed a significant expansion of the sea rescue capabilities.

Accordingly, the Directorate of Air Sea Rescue Services was formed at a meeting held at the Air Ministry on 14 January 1941, under the chairmanship of the Deputy Chief of Air Staff and representatives of the Royal Navy and Royal Air Force operational commands. It was agreed that sea rescue of aircrew personnel had become of such importance that it required the full-time attention of an air commodore. However, despite the important function of the new directorate, no aircraft or aircrews could be spared specifically for rescue purposes. Therefore, the operation of the rescue service was to remain the responsibility of the operational commands. It was decided that the directorate was to be responsible directly to the Deputy Chief of Air Staff, but the director and his staff were to be attached to Coastal Command for close co-ordination with sea and air authorities concerned with search activities. The British Isles were divided into four geographic areas coinciding with the regions of responsibility of the Coastal Command groups. Close-in search, to a distance of 20 miles from shore, became the responsibility of the Directorate of Air Sea Rescue. The directorate started to function with only twelve Lysander aircraft made available on temporary loan.

Heavy losses of personnel in the sea, with an average of 200 per month during 1941, became the deciding factor for change. Accordingly, in May 1941 the Lysanders were transferred to Fighter Command and a further six were made available. Flight Sergeant Jarvis was posted to join the air-sea rescue flight at Hawkinge that April. He was a very experienced observer air gunner on Lysanders and in September the number of the type allocated to air-sea rescue was further increased to thirty-six, divided into four squadrons. The expressed need for amphibious aircraft was also finally accorded recognition, and in July 1941 three Walruses were provided for sea-landing rescues, with an additional six following in the next month. These additional aircraft were assigned to the four squadrons, which became composite units designated as air-sea rescue squadrons. They were 275, 276, 277 and 278 Squadrons.

In late 1941, two Hudson squadrons, 279 and 280, became engaged in air-sea rescue, however they did not become fully operational until March 1942. Throughout all the rapid developments of the air-sea rescue services, Jarvis had engaged with its evolution while actively taking part in rescue sorties. For that work, he was recommended for the very first Distinguished Flying Medal to ever be awarded for air-sea rescue duties. The award was published in *The London Gazette* on 21 November 1941.

The recommendation states:

> This Non-Commissioned Officer has taken part in thirty-nine searches and patrols in the Dover Straits as Wireless Operator Air Gunner on Air-Sea Rescue work since May 1941, including six successful rescues. He is of outstanding

character and personality, shows judgement and resource, and has assisted considerably in the evolution of a technique for Air-Sea Rescue work. He is forty years of age and has an approximate total of 1300 hours flying to his credit since joining the Royal Air Force in 1921. Prior to being posted for Air-Sea Rescue work he was employed on Army Co-operation aircraft including operational flying in France.

Jarvis was responsible for saving the lives of several pilots. On 31 July 1941, Spitfire Pilot Robert James Boyd of 609 Squadron parachuted into the Channel off Calais. Jarvis and his pilot, Pilot Officer Hunt, located him in Lysander V9473. Tragically, Boyd was killed in action over Normandy on 6 September 1943, once again shot down. This time, his parachute failed to function properly.

Not all rescues were successful. A Canadian pilot, Leonard Basil Fordham, who had flown Spitfires during the Battle of Britain, was shot down over the Channel in July 1941. Jarvis, with his pilot Sergeant Waddington, engaged in an extensive search to locate him. His subsequent rescue was successful but concluded with an entry in the records advising that although Fordham had been found in the water, he had died after completion of the rescue operation. He was buried in Brookwood Military Cemetery, Surrey.

Throughout the autumn of 1941 and into 1942, British air-sea rescue was able to save more than a third of those who ditched or bailed out into water. In the fourth quarter of 1941, 160 out of 473 ditched aircrew were saved. In the same period in 1942, there were 205 out of 568. By mid-1942, more than 150 sea rescue boats, high-speed launches and seaplane tenders were available for rescue operations.

By August 1942, the provision of air-sea rescue had been improved significantly. Control rooms were managing distress signals, positions were plotted and the information phoned to the control staff of the nearest area headquarters, which in turn notified the controller of the group in whose area the aircraft had ditched. The controllers contacted the nearest Coastal Command station, and a reconnaissance plane was dispatched immediately. In addition, combined headquarters notified the nearest naval station, which would put rescue boats to sea and these were in turn directed by the reconnaissance plane crew. The aircraft circled the sighting constantly to ensure that their position would not be lost. Weather permitting, relays of aircraft would relieve each other, and if the delay was prolonged, they would drop supplies to the survivors.

Only one Distinguished Flying Medal was ever awarded to the Hawkinge Rescue Flight, that being the award to Jarvis. The officer's equivalent, the Distinguished Flying Cross, was awarded on several occasions. One example was a recommendation for the Distinguished Flying Cross and later bar to the Canadian pilot, Flight Lieutenant John Alexander Spence of 277 Squadron, who served alongside Jarvis. Both men had joined the Hawkinge Flight within weeks of each other. Spence's award was effective on 23 March 1943. The Public Record Office Air 2/4951 has the recommendation:

> Since joining the Air Sea Rescue Service on 3 June 1941, this officer has carried out seventy-three rescue sorties over the Straits of Dover and Channel, flying Lysanders and Defiants, and has been instrumental in rescuing seven survivors from crashed planes. On 11 December 1942 when flying a Defiant off Dungeness, he was attacked by a Focke-Wulf 190. In spite of the fact that his aircraft was damaged, he was successful in evading the attack and landing safely at base. On another occasion he persevered with a search one mile north of Calais in spite of fire from the German ground defences until he was recalled. On 28 February 1943 Flight Lieutenant Spence made his first operational sortie in a Walrus, having completed his training on this type of aircraft

only two days before. This sortie took him to within five miles of Le Treport, where he landed and picked up a Canadian Flight Sergeant Pilot who had been shot down three hours before. He then took off and returned safely to base. The visibility was deteriorating fast, and this rescue is typical of the skill, courage and resourcefulness that this officer has so frequently exhibited. During the last seven months Flight Lieutenant Spence has commanded the detached flight of No.277 Squadron at Hawkinge with distinction and has set a fine example to his pilots and air gunners.

Flight Lieutenant John Alexander Spence – Bar to Distinguished Flying Cross, 277 Squadron. Award effective 9 July 1943:

In June 1943, this officer undertook a flight to search for a pilot who was adrift in his dinghy in the English Channel. He succeeded in locating the dinghy some two and a half miles from the French coast. The sea was exceedingly rough, but he brought his aircraft down safely on to the water, then taxied to the airman, who after a strenuous effort, was hauled aboard. Owing to the heavy seas it was not possible for the aircraft to take off again so, disregarding enemy minefields in the vicinity and the possibility of attack from the air, Flight Lieutenant Spence resourcefully taxied his aircraft across the Channel to a home base. His gallant achievement was worthy of high praise.

Jarvis eventually left the air-sea rescue service on 13 November 1942 when he was posted to 1426 Enemy Aircraft Flight. This unit had been formed on 21 November 1941 to test and evaluate captured enemy aircraft. Flying Officers Forbes and Kinder, Pilot Officer Lewenden and Flight Sergeant Goug, all test pilots from

41 Group, were the first posted into the unit. They worked with the Air Fighting Development Unit, which was established to test enemy aircraft abilities and develop tactics to combat them. To gain intelligence on the capabilities and characteristics of these aircraft was of significant importance. As a result, the flight gained the nickname 'The Rafwaffe', although it did also evaluate an aircraft of the Regia Aeronautica Italiana.

One of the first detailed evaluations was of a Heinkel He 111 that had been shot down and subsequently crash-landed over North Berwick in early 1940. Around this time the flight also came into the possession of a Messerschmitt Bf 109E-3 that had been captured by the French in late 1939 and a Junkers Ju 88A-5 that had landed due to navigational error at Chivenor. All captured or recovered aircraft were repainted with RAF markings and given appropriate serial numbers, effectively becoming Allied operational aircraft.

The flight received specialist airmen for the many duties required to maintain these enemy aircraft. No. 1426 Enemy Aircraft Flight was officially a detachment of 12 Group, Fighter Command. As the war progressed, further aircraft came into the possession of the flight, including a total of seven Messerschmitt Bf 109s, four Fw 190s, and five Junkers Ju 88s. The flight also had the aforementioned Heinkel He 111, a Messerschmitt Bf 110, a Messerschmitt Me 410, a Henschel Hs 129 and an Italian Fiat CR.42 Falco.

Jarvis had been posted into the Enemy Aircraft Flight at its conception and his stay was to be a lengthy one. He would later be promoted to warrant officer and subsequently asked about and was recommended for a commission to officer rank. His trade was still that of air gunner. Based at RAF Collyweston, the unit was unique. The Enemy Aircraft Flight flew several tours to airfields, where their presence was always enthusiastically appreciated. During 1942 alone they visited seventy-four aerodromes. On 10 November 1943, the flight suffered the loss of their Heinkel He 111 in a tragic accident at

Polebrook aerodrome in Northamptonshire. The Heinkel spun into the ground while avoiding the flight's Ju 88, which was landing from the other direction. The accident took the lives of seven men and injured four others. The casualties were primarily aircraftsmen, all ground trade personnel such as instrument mechanics, electricians, engine engineers or airframe engineers who were being carried as passengers for the flight experience.

In early May 1944, the flight became resident at Thorney Island aerodrome on the south coast for a five-week duration. The Allied fleet was building in readiness for the invasion of France and Europe. In order to assist the Navy with enemy aircraft recognition, well-planned flights were flown conducting recognition exercises across the many English ports, which were holding thousands of Allied vessels.

In early September 1944, the enemy aircraft flight was requested to fly to an airfield near Toulouse in France. The French resistance had secured an undamaged Heinkel He 177 aircraft that was airworthy. Wing Commander Roland Falk, the chief test pilot at Farnborough, flew a Hudson to France carrying a crew selected to fly the He 177 back to England. The flight was protected by two Beaufighters and as light faded, they safely reached Blagnac airfield in Toulouse. However, immediately after the Hudson landed, the landing lights were switched off, leaving the Beaufighters stranded flying in darkness. With no communication possible, they turned to make for another airfield that they had previously overflown. After little success, the two Beaufighter pilots took differing emergency actions. Squadron Leader Hood force-landed but found himself injured and unknowingly within Vichy France territory, while Flight Lieutenant Martin had made for the coast but had to bale out when his fuel ran dry. He parachuted into Allied-held territory and duly became a member of the Caterpillar Club. Hood, meanwhile, was taken to a field hospital and with sympathetic assistance his uniform was removed and he was placed among some German wounded soldiers. It was a chaotic situation whereby an amusing situation developed when a German officer appeared and distributed decorations to the wounded patients. Hood then mutely received an Iron Cross, second class.

The Heinkel He 177 was repainted with the Allies' black and white invasion stripes and bold RAF roundels. The French Maquis added the words 'Prise de Guerre' to the aircraft's fuselage before it flew from France to Farnborough. It subsequently appeared in a more refined livery and was allocated the serial TS439.

At the end of January 1945, the flight reformed at Royal Air Force Tangmere as the Enemy Aircraft Flight of the Central Fighter Establishment. A small number of Luftwaffe aircraft survived the war, with examples now on display at the Royal Air Force Museum at Hendon.

Flying Officer Victor Jarvis was responsible for saving ditched airmen and for influencing the effectiveness of the early days of rescuing them from the sea. He then flew in the Luftwaffe aircraft that had engaged in actually shooting down those airmen into the sea. It was an extraordinary set of circumstances for an air gunner to have experienced.

The post-war years in Jarvis's life provide additional evidence that his sense of service was high as he volunteered as a special constable in the police. He was awarded the special constabulary long-service medal after completing nine years' voluntary service. There will have been many occasions when he would have been asked about the Distinguished Flying Medal ribbon that he wore upon his police tunic and what he did in the war. He was an integral part in the rescue of many men who lived to become members of the Goldfish Club.

*Chapter 14*

# Sergeant James Burness – Caterpillar Club, Dinghy Dropping

James Forsyth Burness enlisted into the RAF at the outbreak of war. He volunteered to serve as aircrew and subsequently passed selection for training as an wireless operator/air gunner. This entailed extensive wireless operating training and to a lesser extent in air gunnery. In late May and early June 1942, Sergeant Burness was posted for operational duty with 279 Squadron. The squadron had been formed on 16 November 1941 at Bircham Newton in Norfolk as an air-sea rescue unit. It became fully operational in March 1942, later becoming the first air-sea rescue squadron to carry airborne lifeboats and deploy detachment flights flying the Lockheed Hudson. The Hudson was a military version of the American Super Electra airliner and was ordered for the RAF in June 1938. The Hudson entered service with Coastal Command in 1939 and was used extensively over United Kingdom waters on anti-submarine and general reconnaissance duties.

No. 279 Squadron created a most positive impact between May and June 1942, when six ditched crews, a total of thirty-five airmen, were saved after the sighting and directing of rescue craft by the Hudson crews. They were stationed in south-west England for operations over the Bay of Biscay and the Western Approaches between April 1942 and December 1943. The squadron records evidence operational flying, searches undertaken, and rescue sorties throughout an eighteen-month period between June 1942 and November 1943. The term 'deep search squadron' was used within the rescue service for 279 Squadron. Sergeant James Burness was actively engaged in attempting to rescue aircrew survivors who had ditched into the sea, many of whom would become members of the Goldfish Club. Burness, while acting as rescuer, would himself join one of the exclusive clubs by parachuting from his aircraft and becoming a member of the Caterpillar Club during a rescue flight.

The 279 Squadron operational record book entries record a total of forty-nine operational sorties undertaken by Burness between June 1942 and November 1943. Typically, entries recorded the sighting of a dinghy with one or more occupants, guiding rescue launches to the survivors as well as the sighting of empty dinghies. Various survival packs had been developed for dropping from rescue aircraft, including the dinghy pack, which consisted of a well-equipped dinghy into which survivors could transfer, containing four containers stocked with food, warm clothing and distress signals. Distress signals had been subject to much scrutiny as the standard marine distress signals stowed in dinghy packs had been prone to fail in operation. In 1942, waterproof red star Verey cartridges were included and subsequently an improved lightweight 1in Very pistol was provided to fire the star distress cartridges. The problem of water provision was solved by deploying tinned containers. Later an airborne lifeboat was developed that originated from a conception by Group Captain E. F. Waring, who was operational at RAF Lindholme in Yorkshire. He had invented and perfected a series of five containers, the largest of which was the converted tail unit of a bomb fin that held the rubber dinghy. The four smaller units contained water, food and protective clothing. The five containers were linked together by floating ropes, which allowed ditched aircrew to grasp them easily. The advantage of this apparatus was the ability to drop a larger dinghy of robust construction, and essential supplies that all connected and floated.

Group Captain Waring devised a means of carrying the motor-driven lifeboat and dropping it by parachute with the support of a boat-building expert. His desire was to drop boats powered by a combination of sail, oar and a motor capable of accommodating up to seven ditched survivors. Most cleverly, to overcome the problem of the boat drifting out of reach of the survivors, it would be fitted with a rocket-fired weighted drogue attached to the bows to act as a sea anchor. The GQ Parachute Company devised the parachute release gear, which was equally as important. To prevent the boat capsizing, buoyancy chambers triggered by the deployment of the parachutes operated automatically. The Lindholme boat was capable of being carried and dropped by aircraft, initially slung under the Hudson fuselage and later carried by a much larger aircraft, the Vickers Warwick. No. 279 Squadron's Hudson aircraft became operational with the lifeboat in January 1943. They were provided with signalling aids, food, drinking water, waterproof suits and first aid kits for a crew of up to seven men. A compass and sea charts were provided along with materials and tools to effect repairs stowed in the boat's lockers. There were instructions to enable survivors to operate the boat with petrol, oil, sails, masts and navigation.

The Lindholme boat was slung in a way that had little effect on the Hudson's flying controls. Visually it created an impressive sight. No. 279 Squadron personnel spent endless hours in the air searching for ditched aircraft in addition to distressed or missing motor torpedo boat crews. Several inflatable dinghies from sea ditchings were spotted, some with survivors and others with deceased occupants. Wreckage of shipping and aircraft was frequently located with no sign of survivors. Empty dinghies were inevitably sunk by gunfire to avoid other sightings of them that could instigate additional searches.

One of Sergeant Burness's first rescue flights saved the life of Sergeant Gordon Richmond, who had qualified as an air gunner in October 1940. His story of service illustrates well how fate took its part in survival. He joined Bomber Command's 35 Squadron in May 1942, taking part in his first operation to Cologne on 30 May

1942. This would be the first of the famous thousand-bomber raids. The second of these raids was to Essen on 1 June 1942. Sergeant Richmond returned to Essen again on 8 June 1942. These massive raids were instrumental in Bomber Command's development of targeting and destroying the war factories of Germany. There was no doubt that the infrastructure of expected losses and ensuring the readiness of air-sea rescue services in supporting crews returning from Germany had been well planned. Sergeant Richmond was to become one of those predicted casualties. Coming back from their bombing raid on 8 June 1942, his aircraft was hit by anti-aircraft fire. The port inner and outer engine failed and the crew were forced to ditch off Great Yarmouth at 0330 hrs. After some seven hours at sea, they were overflown by a Hudson and Burness, who was in the aircraft, was responsible for spotting the ditched crew. The system of reporting and shadowing the survivors' position was flawless and line of sight of the survivors was maintained throughout before the ditched crew was subsequently rescued by an air-sea rescue launch at 1030 hours. Burness captured the scene of rescue using his hand-held camera.

Sergeant Richmond and his crew were granted well-deserved survivor's leave after the ditching. It was to be a very short interlude and he then notched up three more operations before his third and final thousand-bomber raid on Bremen on 25 June 1942. Richmond was enrolled into the Goldfish Club and received his membership card. With little respite, he completed a full tour of operations in Bomber Command, with his final operation on 1 March 1943.

Sergeant Burness had himself experienced the dangers of wartime flying. On 5 February 1943, while over the North Sea on yet another rescue flight, his Hudson encountered severe weather. The automatic pilot, which used a set of gyroscopes from a magnetic compass to maintain course, became unserviceable. Forced to return to Scotland, the weather conditions had shrouded the ground, inhibiting the sight of flares. Two unsuccessful attempts were made to land and then the pilot consulted the crew and gave orders to prepare to bale out. The Hudson climbed to 3,000ft but without warning the aircraft went into a spin and fell about 500ft. The aircraft then spun in the opposite direction, causing the air gunner Sergeant Pertus to shout incoherently as he rushed towards the emergency exit door. Burness tried to restrain him but was unable to prevent him from jumping. Meanwhile, the Hudson regained control and once stable, the pilot gave orders for the remaining crew to parachute out at 2130 hours. The crew followed orders, each man suffering minor injuries either in the flight or upon the parachute landing. Pertus's body was later recovered from the sea and taken to Tayport on the mouth of the River Tay. His body now lies in Leuchars cemetery on the east coast of Scotland.

Burness wrote to the parachute manufacturer Irvin and reported that life had been saved by the emergency use of his parachute and requesting membership of the Caterpillar Club, which was accepted willingly. He joined the club on his thirty-eighth operational sortie with 279 Squadron. His membership card and Caterpillar pin were to remain with him for the rest of his life. This had been a rare case of two men, both of whom joined exclusive clubs that celebrated their lives being saved; one upon the water, the other by a silken canopy.

James Burness was commissioned in the RAF as a probationary pilot officer in late 1943. He was promoted to flying officer April 1944 and flight lieutenant in November 1945. Many ranks were temporary during war service, and rank reductions thereafter became common place. Burness was accordingly appointed as an acting pilot officer, Training Branch, in September 1946, and eventually resigned his commission in the RAF on 23 April 1949.

*Chapter 15*

# Warrant Officer Robert Rawlins – Goldfish Club Endorsed Member

Prior to enlisting Robert Rawlins had been an insurance broker's clerk. He lived in Hammersmith, London, and had been educated at the City of London College, at that time situated near Moorgate Station. Eleven months after the outbreak of war he enlisted in the RAF at the close of July 1940. His journey into service life took him along a rather unexpected route. It commenced with training as a wireless operator, always a challenging course of instruction and endless assessments, all of which he mastered. In early 1941, he married his fiancée, Winifred, in Fulham and juggled the requirements of lodgings and anticipated operational postings.

Sergeant Rawlins was eventually posted to the Middle East theatre of operations, destined to fly in the Vickers Wellington. He was to serve in 109 Squadron, which had been formed from the Wireless Intelligence Development Unit at Boscombe Down in December 1940. The investigational work performed by the unit required the employment of specially trained wireless operators and Rawlins was selected for his skill and capabilities in those duties.

In the late summer of 1941, several aircraft were tasked with airborne high-frequency jamming missions in support of offensives by the Eighth Army in the Western Desert. The jammer, a Marconi transmitter code-named Jostle, was modified by the British company Ecko and was already established in use against Luftwaffe communications. No. 109 Squadron had been engaged in secret research into radar and radio navigation aids, developing both German and British equipment simultaneously. The squadron continued to perform that important development role until it was dispersed in January 1942. At that time, it was devolved into three flights: the Wireless Development Flight, the Wireless Reconnaissance Flight and the Wireless Investigation Flight.

No. 109 Squadron sat within 257 Wing operating from Kabrit, Landing Ground 224, and Shallufa. The squadron flew Wellingtons in North Africa from 20 November 1941 until late 1942. It appears that they were developing and experimenting with the jamming of German tank communications, monitoring radio and radar activity, jamming enemy radar and calibrating their own. The Wellington crews were popularly known as 'Winston's Wellingtons', primarily because Churchill himself had a strong interest in their use against the Afrika Korps. The electronic battle fought in the air by airborne jammers targeted enemy tactical communications, particularly in tanks during battlefield engagements or during movements. The specific testing of special equipment designed to detect enemy radar was under the supervision of Lieutenant Philip Thomas Windley Baker, Royal Navy Volunteer Reserve. In September 1938, he had been promoted to Scientific Officer in the Admiralty's Scientific Research and Experiment Department. Only a handful of specially equipped Wellingtons were involved in the secret work. Sergeant Robert Rawlins was to work alongside him, involved in those covert operations bound by the Official Secrets Act as amended in 1939.

As early as 1940, Lieutenant Baker had led an attempt to identify possible German use of the centimetre systems waveband for radar at sea. His small team had fitted a number of convoy escort vessels with a crystal detector and an amplifier type of receiver. Clearly an expert, he was an authority on Allied electronic counter-deployments, which explains why he was attached to 109 Squadron. He flew in Royal Navy uniform and maintained a Navy tradition of deploying a hammock within the Wellington fuselage, an unusual set of circumstances that

Rawlins witnessed. Lieutenant Baker was in a multinational crew comprising Australian, Canadian, British and Royal Navy personnel, all deployed on secret duties. The Wellington was fitted with a gun-mounted Yogi aerial in the front gunner's turret. Effectively it looked to the casual observer like a standard aircraft, however the aerial was capable of detecting and pinpointing the location of German Würzburg radar, and the equipment needed a special operator. This was not a duty for Rawlins as he normally manned the standard wireless operator's position during operational flights.

In February 1941, the Italians abandoned Benghazi, a strategically important port, and retreated westward down the coast road to El Agheila. British forces occupied Benghazi and El Agheila but with overwhelming forces against them they were forced to evacuate Benghazi the next month and began a retreat into Egypt, losing great numbers of tanks to the Afrika Korps.

The detachment flight of 109 Squadron at Kabrit was at first referred to as 'the Signals Squadron'. The squadron's operational record books are not well detailed or complete, and the detachment flight itself is not readily identified. However, they do record some events. Wellington Z8907 was on a special operation on 20 November 1941 when it was shot down by Italian fighters near Halfaya Pass near Sidi Omar. Lieutenant Colonel R. P. G. Denman of the Royal Corps of Signals lost his life alongside that crew. This First World War veteran was commissioned into the Royal Signals on the outbreak of the Second World War as a specialist in radio countermeasures. The captain of the Wellington was a Canadian, Flight Sergeant Herbert Wolf. His wireless operator was Sergeant Donald Cross, probably associated with Sergeant Rawlins through their specialist briefings. The wreck of the Wellington was later found burnt out in the desert. The finding of the wreckage led to the casualties being recovered but it was only much later that the body of Lieutenant Colonel Denman was identified. The crew in its entirety now lie in the Halfaya Sollum

War Cemetery. Denman's widow, Charlotte, subsequently joined the Special Operations Executive and for the remainder of the war ran the clerical aspects of the Signals Directorate, for which she was appointed an MBE for her service to the SOE in 1946.

Lieutenant Baker strongly suspected that the armaments and searchlights protecting the Benghazi and Derna areas were radar controlled. Benghazi was a high-priority target for the RAF and it appeared with great frequency on the numerous desert air force operation lists. Some investigation flights with Baker on board flew enticingly over the areas many times to collect and collate readings in an attempt to calculate the range and height of the suspected detection equipment. Lieutenant Baker was significantly important to the scientific work being undertaken and it was acknowledged that measures should be in place not to expose him to greater dangers than absolutely necessary.

Baker's experimental efforts resulted in the confirmation that eight Würzburg and thirteen Freya radar stations existed in the central and eastern Mediterranean areas. The dangers were very evident to any operational crew. On 22 November 1941, five Wellingtons of 109 Squadron were flying over the battle area when Wellington Z8944 was damaged by Italian fighters. The pilot, Flight Lieutenant Wills, managed to escape successfully but his wireless operator had been wounded. These exposed aircraft, often flying in a relatively confined area of sky, were highly vulnerable. That same day Wellington X9988 was flown by Sergeant Nicholson. His crew, which included an Australian and Canadian, was shot down by Italian fighters. The crew's wireless operator was Sergeant Malcolm Forrest, one of the most experienced working alongside Sergeant Rawlins. With the exception of one casualty, the crew now lie collectively in the Knightsbridge War Cemetery close to the Benghazi to Tobruk highway. Flying Officer David Jefferies, the Australian, perished but has no grave. The desert was capable of thwarting the recovery of victims most effectively. His life is commemorated on the Alamein Memorial.

On 25 November 1941, the squadron flew five operations to jam enemy communications. However, damage by various means and unforgiving desert conditions resulted in just one Wellington remaining fully serviceable. The arrival of additional tanks for the German forces in early 1942 allowed General Rommel to mount a strong offensive drive across the desert. The physical war on the ground and intelligence-gathering efforts in the air continued with as much vigour as possible. Sergeant Rawlins was by now well versed in the special duties he was undertaking. The desert environment was challenging for all of these men, while the secret scientific work continued alongside them.

The second and third week in January 1942 saw two Wellingtons flying with T1360T transmitters to test them against recovered German tank receivers and establish their height and range effectiveness. Rawlins also flew sorties to search for enemy chain radar stations, testing S27 receivers along the Crete peninsula. The squadron strength was six aircraft but servicing and reliability issues rarely saw more than four available at any one time. No. 109 Squadron had been detached to Egypt in name, however little changed for the special signal squadron other than it became 162 Squadron in late February 1942.

On the night of 6 March 1942, disaster struck on a radio intelligence operation to Rhodes. Sergeant Rawlins was an old hand in the crew, and also accompanying Lieutenant Baker on 6 March 1942 was an Australian, Sergeant Robert Tregenza. He was a trainee special operator, and would have greeted the sight of Baker's Navy-style hammock strung up inside the Wellington's fuselage with bemusement as it was highly irregular. The crew of eight consisted of the pilot Sergeant Knowles, Lieutenant Baker wearing an engineering branch naval uniform and Sergeants Murrel, Tregenza, Westbrook,

Levy, Drever and Rawlins. In the early evening, they climbed into Wellington Z8905 at Shallufa. Also on board was Leading aircraftsman Connor, who alighted when the barren desert landing ground 09 was reached. Leaving 09, they departed to Rhodes. The squadron record book confirms that the area of operation was the Dodecanese islands on the south-eastern side of Greece.

During the flight, Baker and his apprentice Sergeant Tregenza were advised by the pilot that the aircraft was becoming unairworthy and that they had little time left in the air. At that time, they were not far from enemy-held territory. The pilot made all possible effort to reach the deepest water possible, desiring the Wellington to be sunk to prevent any salvage attempts. The crew jettisoned all scientific equipment before the inevitable ditching. The eventual impact upon the water was greater than anticipated. Sergeant Tregenza suffered a dislocated shoulder and Sergeant Rawlins' thumb was almost fully detached as he tried to actuate the dinghy release toggle. The dinghy did not inflate by the immersion switch system and the crew were all reliant on the help of their life vests for support in the water. Rawlins' bad luck then continued because his inflation bottle refused to work. Gas was usually released into the life jacket's bladders by pulling down a lever on the lower right side of the vest. As the lever actuated, the brass threaded stud snapped off, releasing $CO_2$ into the bladder. Sergeant Rawlins inflated the air bags as best possible by blowing into the inflator tube that was normally used to top up the bladders. Wearing flying gear and an under-inflated life vest with a torn-away thumb while trying to swim to a distant shoreline must have been a daunting prospect.

After an estimated ninety minutes of endurance swimming, the men eventually saw the beachline ahead. It was lined with Italian troops. The bedraggled crew all made it to the beach and once searched they were taken to a guardhouse. The Italians were drawn to the Naval officer among the airmen. Lieutenant Baker had torn off his engineering branch badge, anticipating interest in his uniform. His story that he was simply being carried back to Egypt as a passenger was accepted. In reality he was probably one of the most important and valuable prisoners of war to have been captured. The survivors were taken to a hospital for treatment and then were taken together to a military barracks.

A Navy cypher on 12 March 1942, later repeated to the RAF as message 1522B at 1714 that day, stated that a German broadcast station had reported that a Wellington had been shot down on the night of 7–8 March and seven survivors picked up. The enemy statement was assessed as being made simply due to a crew having been captured, as opposed to having been shot down. The circumstances strongly indicated the broadcast related to the Wellington that Baker was flying in. There were actually eight people on board that aircraft, therefore a very good chance existed that Lieutenant Baker was a prisoner of war. Naturally, anxiety grew around the circumstances of his capture because of his importance.

Rawlins documented his time as a prisoner and noted his released from hospital as 14 March 1942. He was at Rhodes Island barracks until 26 April 1942; prisoner of war camp PG 75, Bari, Italy, until 12 August; prisoner of war camp PG 70, Italy, until 8 September 1943; and then Mühlberg, Germany, until April 1945. The latter was known as Stalag IVb and was a large camp on the eastern bank of the River Elbe, situated near the town of Mühlberg. The camp brought much horror for the Russian prisoners of war, among whom abuse and starvation rations caused a great loss of life to that segregated populus. The Russian forces liberated the camp on 23 April 1945 and Rawlins, now officially a warrant officer, was swiftly interviewed by MI9 intelligence and returned home to Hammersmith.

On 2 August 1945, Rawlins wrote to P. B. Cow's Beehive Works in Honeypot Lane, Stanmore, Middlesex. His letter was addressed to Mr Robertson, Secretary of the Goldfish Club. After reporting the malfunction of the rubber life raft and that his life jacket required his own intervention to blow up the bladders, he received a sympathetic reply. It also advised that he had been entered on the membership list of the club and he was registered as an 'Endorsed Member' in that his life was saved by the use of his Mae West. It is not known if any other survivor from the ditching of Wellington Z8905 applied for or became a member of the club.

Endorsed membership was effectively an anomaly because the club had only been formed in 1942 to grant recognition to those airmen who had been through the ordeal of using an emergency dinghy, and thereby saving their lives. In 1943 the club disclosed that membership was not restricted to dinghy users. Men who had their lives saved by a Mae West were accepted, with a membership card endorsed in an appropriate manner and with red typed endorsements upon the laminated membership card certifying the recipient and date of incident.

Lieutenant Baker was never suspected by the enemy of anything other than having been a passenger on a Wellington bomber that ditched into the sea. Three months after becoming a prisoner of war, Admiralty Fleet Orders announced in a supplement to *The London Gazette* on 30 June 1942 that Temporary Lieutenant Philip Thomas Windley Baker, Royal Navy Volunteer Reserve, was awarded the Distinguished Service Cross for outstanding courage, skill and enterprise.

Following the 1943 North African campaign, the British were holding a significant proportion of Axis prisoners of war. An international agreement was made for an exchange of prisoners and Baker was repatriated in one of the first swaps about a year after his capture. Nearly 5,000 men were released from the German prison camp infrastructure and sailed to England. Baker was on one of the five voyages that took place. He carried many secrets and his survival is testimony to the entire crew, who were likewise engaged in secret duties but disclosed nothing.

Because of the sensitivity of the work involved, a strong sense of identity and common purpose existed among men such as Warrant Officer Rawlins. The veil of secrecy that had prevailed for decades only began to lift in the 1960s. However, it was not until some thirty years had passed before the official report of events involving scientific measures applied to detect enemy radar was released by the authorities.

This account is interesting in that it represents a crew who survived the experience of a malfunction to the deployment of a rubber dinghy. In differing circumstances that malfunction would have probably sealed their fate. Their survival was only possible because of their proximity to land and the support given to them by their Mae Wests. That said, Sergeant Rawlins provides a rare first-hand account about the mechanical failure to inflate his Mae West life jacket properly. Survival so often engaged with luck or good fortune and Rawlins certainly drew on both to survive and join the rather exclusive few who carried an endorsed membership card of the Goldfish Club.

*Chapter 16*

# Flight Sergeant Alexander Sutherland DFC – Goldfish Club

Alexander Sutherland, throughout his life known as Alistair, was born in Aberdeen. The early 1920s saw him experience the busy and developing district of Ferryhill, where his family lived. The railway line and River Dee were close to his home, no doubt creating an interesting environment for a young boy to experience. He did well in his schooling and became an under training chartered accountant. Scotland could be regarded as the birthplace of British accounting as Queen Victoria granted a royal charter to the Institute of Accountants in Edinburgh, which effectively created the profession of chartered accountancy in 1854. Sutherland began working as a trainee accountant in an office in the northern district of Ferryhill run by J. Milne. His early working years witnessed the developing turmoil in Europe and the eventual outbreak of war with Germany.

In early 1941, Sutherland volunteered to join the RAF with an ambition to fly. His initial training as Leading Aircraftsman 174225 Sutherland saw him join the selection pool of young men for pilot training. An unexpected posting to Craig Field, Alabama, in the United States meant a long Atlantic crossing before he could experience service life as a pilot under training. It was an experience far removed from the raging war in Europe. The skies were safe and the weather invariably good for flying. Upon qualifying he was recommended to fly single-engine fighter aircraft, no doubt the ambition of the vast majority of young men who gained their wings.

A long-overdue period of leave saw Sutherland return to Ferryhill in April 1942. He wore the uniform of a sergeant pilot with the King's Crown pilot's wings sewn above his left breast pocket of his tunic. Sutherland was among the first British pilots to qualify at Craig Field. He had also been gifted the American pilot's wing.

During February 1943, the Mediterranean Air Command, known as the Desert Air Force, was formed under the command of Air Chief Marshal Sir Arthur Tedder and Sutherland was posted to 244 Wing. The unit had been formed in February 1942 as a mobile offensive fighter wing, which controlled three fighter squadrons at flexible locations. It served over the Western Desert with the Eighth Army and on into the Tunisian campaign. Sutherland initially served in the 244 Wing Training Flight to gain experience of the unique requirements needed to fly in the area of operation and on 24 March 1943, he and fellow Sergeant Thomson were both posted to 145 Squadron, Desert Air Force. Barely twenty years old, Sergeant Sutherland was about to embark on operational flying in a Spitfire to protect the Allied landings in Sicily.

Sergeant Sutherland's Spitfire carried the desert camouflage scheme of sand and grey with the squadron identification letters painted blue with white outline edges to help identification. To take Sicily, the Allies had to embark on an aerial assault well aware that they were facing strong forces of Italian and German front-line troops. Enemy armoured strength consisted of nearly 200 German tanks and numerous Italian armoured fitting vehicles. These forces were distributed with troops holding the coastline while field divisions were left in reserve inland to deal with any threatened attack. In the air, the Axis had more than 300 German fighters, with fewer fighter-bombers and ground-attack aircraft, plus nearly 200 Italian fighters based in Sicily and the toe of Italy. Within easy reach on Sardinia were further German and Italian fighters. Sicily formed a natural bridge between the tip of Tunisia and the Italian mainland.

The western point, Cape Boso Lilibeo, sits 90 miles north-east of Cap Bon in Tunisia. The south-eastern area, Cape Passero, points south to Malta only 55 miles away, and the north-eastern area, Cape Peloro, is separated from the Calabrian peninsula at the toe of Italy only by the Strait of Messina, which narrows to a width of barely 2 miles. These were geographically challenging environments for the Allied commanders to consider.

Sergeant Sutherland climbed into a Spitfire to fly numerous operational sorties comprising of convoy protection, escort to light bombers and many scrambles to intercept enemy activity. He flew numerous Spitfires according to availability and as allocated to him on orders.

At the completion of the Sicilian operations in September 1943, Sutherland was promoted to flight sergeant. His operational flying continued in a similar vein, supporting the Allied landings on mainland Italy and engaging in targeted sorties to secure beachheads and the advances into occupied territories. Sutherland was by now a well-established pilot on the squadron. He was addressed by his peers simply as Jock, his Scottish decent being very apparent, and associated with fellow pilots from across the Commonwealth.

In the new year of 1944, 145 Squadron were briefed upon the operation to break the deadlocked advance through mainland Italy by using an amphibious force to land further up the coast at Anzio, 30 miles south of Rome. The aim was to draw German forces away from Monte Cassino, allowing a breakthrough and subsequent advance towards Rome and then relieving the Anzio beachhead on the advance. The operation, named 'Shingle', was launched on 22 January 1944. Sutherland would once again fly protection cover for the Allied forces. It was a bold plan but tragically many British and Commonwealth men lost their lives during it. More than 3,000 Anzio fallen are commemorated at the Anzio War Cemetery and also at the Beach Head War Cemetery. The 145 Squadron records for 26 January 1944 state that all efforts were again devoted to the Shingle theatre. The composer of the record book entry noted: 'The only incident being on the last patrol. Flight Sergeant Sutherland developed a glycol leak and had to bale out over Gaeta Bay from three thousand feet. After ten minutes in the water, he was picked up by the destroyer Kempenfelt which could not do enough for him.'

Glycol was used in the engines because of its low freezing temperature and its lubricating properties. Any minor leak would produce a gradual loss of coolant and induce a gradual increase in operating temperatures. A major leak could result in the engine seizing within seconds and normally produced white smoke pouring from the engine exhaust stacks, providing clear evidence of the pilot's dilemma for those who saw it. Clearly Sutherland was forced to abandon his Spitfire, an incident that would probably have been seen by vessels below supporting the bridgehead. Gaeta Bay was a huge expanse of water south of Anzio. Sutherland's survival was by no means assured and landing into water was always regarded as dangerous as he needed to detach the parachute immediately. From January 1942 Spitfire pilots had been issued with the K Type dinghy, a one-man life raft. The model or type was dependent upon the parachute manufacture. Sutherland's life raft was attached to his harness assembly, which was clipped to the seat of the parachute harness. Sutherland parachuted into a sea that was not much warmer than the English Channel. It was by good fortune that the destroyer HMS *Kempenfelt* was in the area where he came down.

*Kempenfelt* was part of the 19th DD Flotilla, tasked in the shelling of enemy-held positions at Anzio before the landing of the Allied troops and upon selected tactical targets thereafter. The ship's crew rescued Sutherland and treated his facial injuries before arrangements were put in place to transfer him to the mainland. No. 145 Squadron records state that by 31 January 1944 Sutherland was assessed as fit to return to full flying duties. He immediately resumed flying in February, flying speed and armament tests and, on 3 February, he was back over the same area protecting shipping. No doubt thoughts of his ditching in the waters below crossed his mind during that sortie and during the following fifteen that he flew that month.

In March 1944 the famous Squadron Leader Neville Duke took command of 145 Squadron. Intelligence reported that the Luftwaffe had appeared with fighter aircraft carrying new identity markings, intimating a more tenacious enemy offensive over Anzio. No. 601 Squadron was the first to engage with the new Luftwaffe unit on 7 March, when five Spitfires tangled with Bf 109s over Anzio at 0900 hours. Flight Lieutenant Henderson failed to return from the engagement. Four days later, at 0731 on 11 March, Sutherland chased a Fw 190 fighter in Spitfire JF952 and they engaged in combat for several minutes. The Fw 190 tried to escape at low level but Sutherland chased it and fired into the wing root from about 300 yards. The Fw 190 gained height and the pilot fell away from the cockpit to deploy his parachute. After so many operational sorties, Sutherland was at last able to claim a destroyed enemy fighter, and he later composed a combat report so he would be officially credited.

In the afternoon of 24 March, Sutherland submitted another combat report, detailing that he and others were patrolling Cassino when Luftwaffe aircraft were seen issuing vapour trails above them. Upon climbing, the flight of four Spitfires sighted six plus Fw 190s, whereupon the majority dived away, chased by the flight leader. Sutherland singled out one Fw 190 and fired from around 250 yards as he chased it. Strikes were seen and immediately glycol poured from the engine but the Spitfire's ammunition was spent other than one gun that had jammed. Informing Flight Sergeant Thomson, who had joined 145 Squadron alongside him, and Lieutenant Wells, the South African, both were able to finish off the damaged Fw 190 and later each pilot claimed a third of a confirmed combat claim. The Luftwaffe pilot was seen to bale out before his aircraft burst into flames and crashed.

Sutherland flew twenty-two operational sorties during March. The intensity of flying became onerous but the elation of any Spitfire pilot's ambition of becoming victorious in aerial battle was reward for the hours of flying. The following month saw Anzio patrols feature once again as well as covering bombers attacking road and rail bridges throughout the central Italian areas of battle. Fifteen sorties were flown in April. The battle-worn Sutherland was nearing the end of a very long tour of operations.

During May, he received a commission and was promoted to pilot officer. He left 145 Squadron tour expired and returned to Scotland, where he was greeted with the news that the local newspaper had published an extensive account of his escape by parachute in February.

The article was titled 'Flight Sergeant Sutherland City Pilots Escape Thrill Over Anzio Beachhead'.

> 'I am meantime off flying duties suffering from a cold.' Thus wrote Flight Sergeant Alistair Sutherland, an Aberdonian to his mother.
>
> Shortly afterwards it was revealed by the Air Ministry in a letter sent to his parents that the young man had been slightly injured in operations in the Mediterranean area. But even that communication left much to be told. Behind the Flight Sergeant's injury lies the story of an amazing escape over the Anzio beachhead.
>
> He was patrolling in a fighter plane 20,000 feet up when his engine cut out. Nothing could be done to repair the fault and Sutherland brought his machine down to 17,000 feet. He spotted some ships below him and decided the circumstances for a parachute descent were favourable. So, he pushed the

stick right forward, his plan being that when the fighter nose-dived, he would be thrown clear. It almost worked out as he planned but as he was projected from the cockpit his head was hit by the tail plane. Everything blacked out on him and he hurtled down 7,000 feet unconscious.

He came to at 10,000 feet and began to fumble for his parachute ripcord, finding at the same time that his right glove was soaked in blood. It looked as if he would never get the chute open. He was feeling sick and shaken when he was pulled up with a jerk by the parachute opening. When he had reached 3,000 feet he again lapsed into unconsciousness, although he just noted that he was near a ship. He did not revive until he struck the water. His dinghy then opened and a short time later he was picked up by a destroyer.

One of the first to welcome him on board was the surgeon Lieutenant James Catto of Kirkcaldy, who had been a school friend of Sutherland. They had not previously met since their school days. Sutherland suffered from a gash across his face, and this was promptly treated. He had to remain on board the destroyer until she completed her patrol, which included the bombarding of enemy positions near the Anzio beachhead.

The newspaper report contains more detail of events than the squadron records. Regardless, the events over the Anzio invasion beaches were celebrated by his family in Scotland and an official application was made to P.B. Cow to join the Goldfish Club. This was simply because the life raft that deployed on his entry into the sea was effectively the flotation device that saved his life and this was manufactured by P.B. Cow.

It becomes debatable why the more obvious life-saving device, his parachute, was not seen as the primary life-saving device and an application to join the Caterpillar Club held merit in the circumstances. However, it is possible his issued parachute was not an Irvin, and he assumed wrongly that this would have denied him the opportunity to apply.

Seven months passed before Flying Officer Sutherland commenced a second tour of operations in January 1945. Among many younger and inexperienced pilots, he was seen as an old hand and had lots to offer by way of advice and experience. However, he himself was to experience new challenges, flying the Spitfire as a bomber with 43 Squadron during the continued offensive into Italy. Extensive partisan activity had developed behind the German lines in the north. The fascist puppet state was still supported to some extent despite Italian dictator Benito Mussolini having been overthrown. The Germans, along with Italian fascists, carried out many reprisals against civilians suspected of supporting the partisans and Allies. The war in Italy was becoming more diverse and problematic.

No. 43 Squadron were operating from Rimini on the east coast of northern Italy with part of 324 Wing Desert Air Force, supporting the ground forces. The Spitfires were kept bombed up and ready for deployment at all times. Targets of identified strongholds, bridges, and those that were transport related, were the fodder of their daily sorties. In February 1945, Sutherland was frequently leading armed reconnaissance flights of six Spitfires seeking transportation targets of opportunity. Shooting up trains became favoured by the pilots as it also provided the ability to destroy the railway tracks in addition to the rolling stock. A further promotion to flight lieutenant additionally saw him posted to command a flight in 111 Squadron stationed further north on the east coast of Italy at Ravenna. The Spitfires also attacked similar selective bombing targets in southern France. The squadron leader commanding 111 Squadron recommended Sutherland for the Distinguished Flying Cross in early May 1945. The group captain endorsed the recommendation, adding:

Flight Lieutenant Sutherland has shown the highest qualities of leadership and personal courage throughout his career as a fighter bomber pilot. He is a determined and aggressive fighter bomber pilot whose results with both bombs and cannon place him far above the average. By his example he has inspired his flight whose results speak for itself. Strongly recommended for the award of the Distinguished Flying Cross.

As the award was being processed, Sutherland departed Italy to attend a fighter leaders' course at Tangmere, Chichester, in Sussex. He married Florence Caroline Bittinec from Aberdeen on 23 June 1945, at Chichester. The Second World War had been won but Sutherland, now wearing the medal ribbon of his Distinguished Flying Cross, was posted to return to 111 Squadron in July 1945.

The squadron were part of the policing forces over Austria and Yugoslavia stationed at Klagenfurt. Clearly he had made a request to continue in service. In early 1946, he was flying the remarkably fast Spitfire F.21 with 122 Squadron at Dalcross, Inverness. No. 122 Squadron was part of 13 Group, Fighter Command. His daughter was born on 1 February 1946.

On 8 March 1946 four Spitfires from Dalcross were carrying out formation flying, with Sutherland piloting LA251. This aircraft had been built by Phillips & Powis's South Marston factory in March 1945. Just before 1000 hours that morning the formation was at 4,000ft, 2 miles off Lossiemouth. Sutherland was flying in number three position when his engine cut completely. Losing height, his initial reaction was to try to reach land. However, the Spitfire dived sharply into the sea from around 700ft. There had been no attempt to abandon the aircraft. The Air Historical loss card notes that the pilot was not wearing a life preserver or equipped with a dinghy. It was a few years after 1946 that life jackets became integrated into the flying suit but it seems odd that no life preserver of any type was being worn.

Sutherland's daughter was no more than five weeks old when his Spitfire plunged into the sea. His body was never recovered and he became the last recorded casualty of 122 Squadron, which was renumbered 41 Squadron the following month.

*Chapter 17*

# Sub-Lieutenant Reginald Singleton, Fleet Air Arm – Goldfish Club

The Fleet Air Arm operated predominantly over the water with airmen of the Royal Navy flying aircraft that often looked antiquated. The FAA had 406 pilots and 232 frontline aircraft available for operations in September 1939. It grew in both size and capability throughout the war and saw sea versions of the Hurricane and Spitfire evolve into highly capable naval aircraft complemented by Fulmars, Barracudas and Fireflies. The Royal Navy, its aircraft and aircraft carriers, played an essential part in the Second World War, providing air cover to the convoys that kept the Atlantic lines open, which was of the utmost importance to keeping the UK in the war. The FAA also supported the land campaigns in North Africa and Europe, was fundamental in changing the balance of power in the Mediterranean and subsequently helped secure victory in the Pacific. By the end of the war in Europe, the FAA had grown to 3,243 pilots and 1,336 aircraft.

One naval aircraft defied obsolescence and stood out from among all other aircraft. The biplane Swordfish served magnificently in the Battle of the Atlantic and throughout the war. It became a symbol of courage directly linked to the Fleet Air Arm. With its low speed, good manoeuvrability and design it fundamentally represented the Royal Navy in the air.

Reginald Arthur Singleton was an FAA pilot who flew the Swordfish operationally in a rather unusual duty for which the low speed and manoeuvrability was a distinct asset. He was a member of the Volunteer Reserve, which had been established in 1903 and was made up of volunteers who served both onshore and at sea. These men had received a level of training for service in the Royal Navy in time of war or emergency. The only distinguishing mark on the Navy uniform was an embroidered patch on the right sleeve.

This account explores the alternative training that FAA aircrew underwent and looks at the path taken by one particular pilot. Sub-Lieutenant Singleton had been an instructing pilot, training observers and pilots at Crail and Arbroath. The latter was one of the busiest FAA airfields of the time, opening in June 1940 as HMS *Condor*. The site had four main runways, while another much smaller runway was used for practice aircraft carrier landings. It was effectively a dummy deck painted on the tarmac. At Crail, FAA pilots and aircrew were taught the demanding skills of flying low over the water and dropping dummy and live torpedoes.

Singleton was posted to 836 Squadron, where all the observers bar one man were fresh from training. Crewing arrangements were haphazard with little planning, however the pairings, once made, became more or less permanent. Working as a team in the air and on the ground, these men worked relentlessly. There was formation flying and depth charge and torpedo dropping on targets near offshore targets. Additional targets for practice work with special equipment and radar were part of several exercises, which also saw the squadron change crews a good deal to replicate operational conditions.

On 9 August 1942, 836 Squadron was posted to Machrihanish, an air station on the Mull of Kintyre, Scotland, which was a training ground for all weather night flying. It was here that Singleton was complimented on attaining high standards during deck landings. Blind approach training using equipment to aid landing in inclement weather was something he also excelled at, and this skill would be evidenced exceptionally well later on in his operational flying.

In late September 1942, 836 Squadron was based at Landrail, a peacetime airfield that had been expanded for wartime use. The airfield itself was in a valley that cut between the mountains of the Mull of Kintyre from east to west. A week later they went to Crail on the Firth of Forth. There were other RAF and Naval Air Stations near at hand: Leuchars, Donibristle, Arbroath and Dunino. Navigation exercises were undertaken from Arbroath, using areas assigned to the observers' school that reduced the use of airspace over the vulnerable Firth of Forth. Drogue target shooting was something to enjoy in good weather at Machrihanish. Singleton recorded exceptional scores on the drogues and also on the simulated torpedo attack teacher used for carrying out after-dark exercises. His training was nearing completion having covered dive bombing, navigation in poor weather, dummy anti-submarine exercises and torpedo attacks by day and night and radar exercises locating submarines and to aid navigation. There were new aircraft, Blackburn-built Swordfish, nicknamed 'Blackfish', for 836 Squadron. They left Landrail on 26 November 1942 for air gunnery training at St Merryn in Cornwall and thereafter moved to Thorney Island on the south coast to begin night operations in the Channel and along the French coast.

Thorney Island was a large peninsular island at the boundary with Hampshire and Sussex. The southern extremity had a small church, St Nicholas, where Battle of Britain pilots from the RAF and Luftwaffe had been buried, the south coast having borne the brunt of Luftwaffe attention. There are fifty-two Commonwealth burials in the churchyard. Among the aircrew graves is an unidentified Allied airman. His body was washed on to the Sussex coast on 5 July 1940, having been in the sea for about three months. He was dressed in aircrew uniform but there were insufficient remnants to assist with any identification. At his funeral the coffin was draped with a Union Flag, and an RAF party fired a last salute over the grave. A verdict of 'found dead' was recorded at an inquest at Thorney. The young man's body now lies unidentified alongside the other brave men, with twenty-one German casualties buried in close proximity.

At Thorney Island, Naval Intelligence lectures on security and evasion brought home the realities of operational flying. The men were not to commence operations carrying any personal effects other than identity discs. If captured, they were instructed to give only their name, rank and number, and they should try to evade capture if at all possible. It was a sombre experience, as they went on to be introduced to the paraphernalia of escaping. Tiny compasses were fitted into pipes, buttons or collar studs. Escape maps were printed on the backs of silk cloth, capable of being hidden in clothing. German marks and French franc notes were in escape pouches issued before flight and returned to stores upon landing.

Christmas leave in 1942 heralded the end of working up training and the beginning of operations. The vast permanent peacetime station of Thorney Island was now under the RAF's Coastal Command structure. Anti-aircraft guns defended the airfield, and balloon barrages provided some protection for nearby Portsmouth and Southampton. Such balloons were connected to the ground and rose to several thousand feet. Tragically, these also incurred losses to Allied aircrews. An FAA Walrus struck a balloon cable near Southampton, with the subsequent crash causing the loss of all four crew. At Thorney, enormous camouflaged hangars stood at separate locations and the Georgian-style three-storey living quarters were likewise impressive. Men from the Commonwealth were seen wearing their respective uniforms, while the FAA uniforms were most distinctive. The sailors of the air who landed their Swordfish using a mere fraction of the long runway available to them looked rather out of place, as did their aircraft, which was not only largely fabric covered but still provided simple open cockpits for its three aircrew. There was a disconnect between the services in this respect, but the extraordinary Swordfish confounded sceptics

# Sub-Lieutenant Reginald Singleton, Fleet Air Arm – Goldfish Club 151

as the war progressed. At Thorney Island, it enhanced the Hudson and Hampden aircraft that carried out nightly radar shipping sweeps to Le Havre and Cherbourg. The 836 Squadron Swordfish stood ready to attack any convoy or shipping discovered during the radar sweeping sorties. No. 836 Squadron would be strengthened within weeks with the impending arrival of another FAA unit.

Another specific weapon the Swordfish carried to attack enemy shipping was the sea mine. The code word for aerial mine laying was 'gardening'. This entailed flying across the Channel at a maximum of 150ft to avoid radar, deter enemy fighters and drop aerial mines accurately into enemy-held waters. A single 1,500lb mine could be carried under the Swordfish. Navigational accuracy was needed otherwise the whole exercise was pointless as it was important to know exactly where the mines were positioned. Navigation had to be attained by dead reckoning, calculating winds and track by taking back bearings on flame floats that were dropped on the sea.

From May 1940, Swordfish squadrons were loaned to Coastal Command and conducted mine-laying operations and convoy patrols in the Channel and North Sea against German, Dutch, Belgian and French ports. The Nazi Blitzkrieg against the Low Countries and France forced the RAF and FAA to call on every resource they had to stave off complete disaster. Coastal Command was operating out of Thorney Island, North Coates, Detling and Manston. They had four squadrons of Swordfish available for mine laying, bombing of naval and ground targets, spotting, and reconnaissance, often flying individually throughout the night. With the threat of invasion from Europe, the four squadrons were called upon to bomb the enemy stock of invasion barges in ports and to lay mines in the harbours to thwart the supply chain. These early operations led to a significant loss of both men and aircraft.

These mining operations called for incredible concentration from the pilots, who had to fly on instruments for three hours at a time at very low heights. Taking off at ten-minute intervals, they had no other aircraft to fix on. The big imponderable was the barometric pressure, which could and did vary on either side of the Channel. Thus, an altimeter set properly with the correct barometric pressure on take-off could be reading high or low if the pressure over Le Havre was different. The Swordfish often flew considerably lower than the altimeter indicated. Reginald Singleton quickly settled down into a daily routine but the Squadron spent more time than it would have liked standing by, ready for deployment should the Hudson flight locate any suspected targets. The duty rosters relieved their tedium with much-welcomed three to four day blocks of leave, especially after 825 Squadron joined them. Having returned from the Arctic, 825 Squadron became shore based with an attachment to 16 Group, Coastal Command, at Thorney Island.

Singleton soon became used to the briefings and the visits to the operations room at Thorney Island. The vast aerodrome required a bicycle to travel between stations and the serving of operational crew eggs and bacon at evening meals was always appreciated. Emsworth provided the closest civilian public house once the extraordinary long access road from the aerodrome on to the south coast road had been negotiated, which was no mean feat in darkness.

The mole at Cherbourg soon became a familiar landmark to Reginald as his knowledge of the French coastline grew. On 3 March at Le Havre, fellow pilot John Lisle's luck ran out when the barometric pressure across the Channel caused his altimeter to mislead him and, losing height to drop his mine correctly, he flew into the sea. Lisle and his air gunner Pat Solway survived in their dinghy, but Paddy Allen, the observer, did not make it. Lisle let off flares when the following Swordfish arrived in the gardening area, hopeful that this would enable the squadron to realise that there had been survivors after they failed to return to Thorney Island. Lisle and Solway were captured and sent to prisoner of war camps, the

## Sub-Lieutenant Reginald Singleton, Fleet Air Arm – Goldfish Club

former until the end of the war. Solway was taken ill in captivity and was invalided home, likely to be through the prisoner exchange programme overseen by the Red Cross.

On 7 March 1943, Singleton returned from a mine-dropping operation to Cherbourg at the same time as a German air raid was under way. Searchlight and anti-aircraft gunfire warned him that Southampton was under attack from a heavy air raid. He was flying in cloud and, unsure of landfall, he decided to steer east away from the raid for safety. The non-arrival of his Swordfish at Thorney Island created a dilemma for the station staff, and they kept the landing beacon on despite the air raid. At approximately 900ft above the sea Singleton became blinded by searchlights, which at his slow speed beamed intensely upon him. Having lost height and with Singleton totally blinded, his aircraft crashed into the sea. He managed to get onto the inflated survival dinghy, which fortunately ended up close to his position. Having inflated his Mae West life preserver, he tried his best to take stock of what had happened. It was apparent that he was the only survivor. He was adrift in the dinghy for five hours and despite his best efforts he never saw his crew during that time. The Channel tides washed him through a minefield and on to the Isle of Wight near Sandown. He was sighted by an Army patrol or possibly Home Guard unit, who rescued him, carrying him up the cliffs to safety. The news of his rescue was sent to Thorney Island. Sadly, his observer Billy Muir and air gunner Eric George had both drowned in the ditching, their bodies given up by the sea in the following days. Singleton was eventually conveyed back to his squadron. The body of his observer was cremated at Southampton by family request and the body of his air gunner was buried in the Haslar Royal Navy Cemetery, Gosport. Fate had saved the life of the pilot but the life vest and dinghy had ensured Singleton's survival, which was recognised by his membership into the Goldfish Club. The Royal Navy, or Fleet Air Arm in particular, appear to have openly welcomed the club badge being worn by its entitled men.

The detachment of 825 Squadron Swordfish returned to sea duty in March 1943, posted to serve on the carrier HMS *Furious* on further convoy escort duties. No. 836 Squadron also received orders to leave Thorney Island and flew to Machrihanish once again, where they exchanged their black Swordfish for new aircraft with different camouflage. Singleton began anti-submarine training all over again. On 27 March, the squadron moved to Ballykelly in Northern Ireland and scattered to stations such as Castle Archdale to gain experience of Atlantic patrols.

Singleton was eventually posted to serve as a pilot on the MV *Empire MacAlpine*, an aircraft carrier recently launched and completed in 1943. The *MacAlpine* was the forerunner of nineteen such Merchant Aircraft Carriers that came into service between 1943 and 1945. It was a merchant ship in that it carried cargo but also functioned as an aircraft carrier with its own aircraft and flight deck. On 7 May 1943, Lieutenant Ransford Slater of 836 Squadron made the first deck landing on *Empire MacAlpine*. The ship's flight deck was just over 400ft long and 60ft wide. An aircraft hangar for four aircraft had a lift to take the aircraft to and from the flight deck. Singleton's exploits serving on this ship are referred to in this extract from *MAC ships: Merchantmen with Clout* by David H. Grover.

> MAC ships had relatively few encounters with German submarines but, nevertheless, their planes and pilots had many harrowing adventures. Simply getting back aboard the carrier could become a nightmare for a Swordfish pilot. An incident in September 1943, within Halifax-bound Convoy ONS 18 dramatically illustrates this difficulty. This convoy marked the baptism of fire for the MAC ships and planes. With U-boats reportedly trailing the convoy, the *Empire*

*MacAlpine* was asked to launch an aircraft during a brief lifting of the heavy fog that prevailed. A Swordfish, piloted by Sub-Lieutenant R.A. Singleton, was launched, only to have the fog immediately close in again around the convoy. The plane carried out its assigned patrol but saw nothing. Returning to the socked-in convoy [a term used to describe heavy fog], the pilot used the images on his own radar to obtain a bearing on the convoy and also homed in on the output of the carrier's radar. The crew of the ship then streamed a fog buoy at a prescribed distance astern so that the pilot would have some means of judging the distance if he came in low. When the carrier crew heard the plane making its approach, they turned on signal lights to aid the pilot. However, in spite of all these procedures, Singleton was unable to see the ship even when it was directly beneath him. As the plane's fuel dropped to a disturbing level, Singleton recognized that he had to bring the plane down soon. He flew out ahead of the convoy, then circled to begin an approach to the *Empire MacAlpine*. With visibility of about 100 yards, less than the length of the short flight deck of the carrier, the pilot brought his plane down as slowly as he dared. His radar-assisted letdown left him in a relatively good position for landing but, when visual contact was eventually established, the batsman waved off the attempt with his lighted paddles, and sent the plane back around for another approach. Finally, with visibility reduced to about fifty yards, Singleton brought the plane in for a perfect landing. The entire evolution was a credit to the skill and nerve of the pilot and to the simple but reliable electronics of the ship and plane.

On 4 April 1944, *The London Gazette* confirmed that two Fleet Air Arm officers, Lieutenant Reginald Arthur Singleton and Lieutenant

Commander James Harold Palmer, who had achieved an amazing landing onto the deck of their escort carrier, had been awarded the Most Excellent Order of the British Empire for courage and skill in air operations. The award of the Member of the Most Excellent Order of the British Empire is the third highest-ranking order within the British Empire award structure.

In late September 1945, a month after the end of the Second World War, men who had joined for the duration of hostilities awaited demobilisation. As men returned home from foreign stations or disembarked from redundant aircraft carriers, it was inevitable that they found themselves once again among friends and comrades from earlier phases of the war. Three men, Reginald Singleton MBE, Philip Blakey and John Taylor did exactly that. They resolved to continue their fellowship through some form of informal club. They agreed that it be called the Ransford Club, in memory of their Commanding Officer, Ransford Slater. His notable career had ended tragically in a flying accident in 1944. They invited his widow to be the club's president. Jim Palmer agreed to be secretary and the first reunion and meeting took place at the Royal Navy Volunteer Reserve club in Pall Mall in June 1946. Thirty-five years later the Ransford Club was still in being but eventually the loss of the old comrades saw its demise.

*Chapter 18*

# The Late Arrivals Club

George William Houghton was born in Perth, Scotland, in September 1905. He was a pre-war journalist who was commissioned as a pilot officer in the Administrative and Special Duties Branch of the Royal Air Force Volunteer Reserve in April 1940. His journalist skills were sought to further the reporting of the RAF in the Middle East. In addition to his writing ability, he was also a competent artist, a skill he employed while in the Western Desert. The Desert Air Force was a unique environment to operate in as aircrew and he became aware of the extraordinary circumstances of men walking back across the desert and rejoining their units. These stories were reported upon as public interest, but more than that he saw the opportunity to celebrate the achievement by awarding a certificate and creating a club for the entitled men. He alone was responsible for promoting this concept.

The Desert Air Force agreed to the forming of the Late Arrivals Club in June 1941. Membership was exclusively for those personnel who, following the need to abandon their aircraft as a result of enemy action or mechanical failure, returned successfully to Allied lines having eluded the enemy and survived the harsh and inhospitable desert conditions. The Late Arrivals Club was unofficial, however a certificate was issued with the badge that stated: 'The member is permitted to wear the Emblem of the Winged Boot on the left breast of his flying suit.' The badge, made in the shape of a 'winged' desert flying boot, was originally sand cast in silver and made by local jewellers and silversmiths in Egypt. The boot signified the walk back from behind enemy lines. The certificate also stated that: 'This airman when obliged to abandon his aircraft on the ground or in the air as the result of unfriendly action by the enemy, succeeded in returning to his Squadron on foot or by other means long after his estimated time of arrival. It's never too late to come back.' At its conception it became an accepted requirement for those applying for membership to have taken longer than forty-eight hours evading the enemy to walk to the safety of their own lines.

Wing Commander Houghton designed and commissioned the printing of the club certificates and the RAF permitted the issue of the badge in the Western Desert. The innovation captured the imagination of war correspondents, who reported the experiences of several recipients who had become members.

Promotion came to the popular Pilot Officer Houghton and his work was recognised by a mention in despatches as a squadron leader on 1 January 1943 and again as a wing commander in September 1943. It is not known if his creating and reporting of the Late Arrivals Club featured in any respect within the awards. His Western Desert diaries with artwork were published as *They Flew through Sand* in Cairo in 1942.

The late Bryan Morgan, who assisted the author with many aspects of accounts of survival and membership of the Royal Air Forces Escaping Society, confirmed that membership of the Late Arrivals Club was exclusive to the Middle East. However, due to the war correspondent's publicity, there were other groups of airmen in other theatre of operations who felt that the adoption of the badge was appropriate. The airmen who left North Africa and flew in the Italy theatre saw little distinction and this might explain some anomalies that appear to exist in relation to assumed entitlement to this rather exclusive club.

Wing Commander Houghton was posted as Officer in Charge of the Public Relations Section of the Allied Expeditionary Air Force in North-West Europe from 1944 to 1945, a role that included him witnessing the Normandy landings. He continued his association with the Air Officer Commanding the Middle East, Lord Tedder, under General Eisenhower's command. The Late Arrivals Club was left in the desert, where the tradition continued but the issuance of signed certificates ceased when Houghton saw service in France and Germany.

One of the first members of the club was a young pilot from 80 Squadron, Flying Officer Peter Wykeham-Barnes. On 4 August 1940, during the squadron's first serious aerial battle over Bir Taieb el Esem, Libya, Wykeham-Barnes engaged Italian aircraft in his Gloster Gladiator. Flying Officer Wykeham-Barnes shot down two enemy aircraft but was himself shot down and walked back towards the Egyptian border, where he was picked up by a British Army patrol. Although this action took place in 1940, prior to the club being formed, Wykeham-Barnes was welcomed as a founder member in early 1941. He was awarded the Distinguished Flying Cross in November 1940, and a bar to that medal in 1941. A Distinguished Service Order followed for operations in the Italian theatre in 1943, and later he took command of the Mosquito Wing in 2 Group. He led the legendary Mosquito raid on the Gestapo headquarters at Aarhus in Denmark, receiving a bar to his Distinguished Service Order. He continued to serve within the RAF post-war and reached the rank of air vice-marshal, probably the highest-ranking member of the service to have ever worn the winged boot.

When the American Air Forces Escape and Evasion Society was formed in 1964, it was decided to use the winged boot within the letterhead of the society logo. This no doubt accelerated the presumption that the Late Arrivals Club was associated with the US society, whereas no such connection existed. It should be considered as a tribute to the RAF, and in particular Wing Commander Houghton, who devised, organised and promoted the efforts of the

Desert Air Force personnel who with great sacrifice and courage, walked back to their units from the desert.

No evidence exists supporting any engagement with the Late Arrivals Club in the latter stages of the Second World War. Wing Commander Houghton's original publication in 1942 had delivered the story of his desert club to a significant readership and continues to do so today. There were two types of metal-winged boot badges that accompanied any membership and they always had a membership certificate. Any signed by the then-ranked Squadron Leader Houghton are indisputably members of that club, which has a most restrictive membership.

*Chapter 19*

# Sergeant Henry Rolph – Late Arrivals Club

Henry Thomas Rolph, born in 1920, was the only son to his parents, Thomas and May from Westcliff-on-Sea in Essex. His only sibling, sister Olive, remained a spinster all her life and she remembered her brother's valiant service in the RAF until her own death in December 2000. Olive cherished the photographs and official documents that to this day provide a personal insight into the family's pride for Henry along with the anguish and sadness that all too often occurred throughout families in the Second World War.

Henry Rolph was among many volunteers at the initial training establishment at Blackpool in 1940, surrounded by young men who were barely out of their teenage years. He was Airman 1176863 and was embarking on becoming an air gunner wireless operator. Sitting for a group photograph and wearing a white flash in his side cap indicated he was an airman under training for aircrew duties. This photograph sat in a frame at the family home from 1941 and thereafter for many years.

Rolph attained the standards required of any wireless operator and his anticipated promotion to sergeant was to arrive sooner than later. His flying hours were minimal at this time but his forthcoming experience at the operational training unit in Wellingtons would see him selected for service to Egypt with 148 Squadron. Equipped with Wellingtons, the squadron flew bombing operations against Axis forces in the Western Desert. Sergeant Rolph passed out of training at the end of 1941 and in early 1942 was crewed up on a new

Wellington bound for North Africa. A transit to Gibraltar took place before he arrived in Egypt in March 1942.

The new arrivals were not assigned a flight in the squadron until later that month. They were flying almost daily sorties to Benghazi, operations that became known as mail runs because of their frequency. The bombing of enemy shipping that was providing vital supplies to Rommel and the Afrika Korps was a priority. No. 148 Squadron had endured terrible losses flying in the desert conditions. The dangers of faulty engines, which was not uncommon, could swiftly create situations of total isolation after a forced landing into the inhospitable environment.

Rolph flew with Sergeant Nethercote in Wellington Z8359 on a subsequent attack on Benghazi on 4 April 1942. The operation was mounted from Kabrit at Bitter Lakes to the advanced landing ground 106. These were airstrips that had been constructed in the desert for Wellington deployments. Six bombers were to fly to Benghazi. The objective was to drop sea mines into the harbour, which also required in the case of Rolph's crew, bombing Benghazi as a distraction from the mining. A faulty rear turret on one aircraft resulted in just five Wellingtons taking off and these proceeded across the vast desert to the target.

As the flight progressed, at 0145 hours on 5 April 1942, Sergeant Nethercote commenced gaining height at a position some 5 miles from Benghazi. The required bombing height had not been reached when the starboard engine unexpectedly cut out completely. The only remaining engine was unable to cope in those circumstances and so the bomb load was jettisoned. The aircraft made a turn eastwards heading for Bitter Lake but it was progressively losing height. The crew responded to orders to jettison any removable articles in an attempt to lighten the aircraft but height continued to be gradually lost. It was estimated that the Wellington had covered about 130 miles after turning from the approach to Benghazi before

Sergeant Nethercote ordered his crew to brace for a belly landing. The two emergency exits, both in the upper fuselage near the cockpit, were prepared as these were likely to be the main escape points once the Wellington slewed into the sand. The crash site was about 7 miles east of the tip of Baltet ez zalagh in Cyrenaica. Rolph sent a wireless message about their emergency, which was received. It was acknowledged with the transmission: 'Abandon aircraft, walk due East, British lines near good luck.'

Having saved all food and water bottles, the crew set fire to the Wellington bomber at 0445. They set off east using a compass that was part of their emergency escape box. Resting at 0730, they saw movement on the southern horizon and finally identified an armoured car of unknown nationality. Red and yellow flare lights were being fired. These were not recognised as the colours of the day, and the crew stayed in hiding provided by the low shrub. The crew then decided to travel only by night. At 1000, from their resting place they saw two armoured cars and a motorcycle to the west. One car went towards the aircraft, which was still smouldering and then approached the hiding place of the crew, its guns trained upon them. The crew came out of hiding and discovered that they had been tracked by a Free French patrol. The survivors were subsequently taken to an advanced patrol of the 12th Lancers, via Bir Hakeim, El Adem, Tobruk, Capuzzo, Marsa Matruh and then to their advanced landing ground. The crew finally reached their base on the fourth morning after their forced landing.

In April 1942, Rolph joined the Late Arrivals Club. His certificate of membership is unusual in that Squadron Leader G. W. Houghton personally signed it and the certificate was supported by a pair of winged boot badges. It was accepted and unquestioned that recipients could wear the winged boot silver cast badges in the Desert Air Force theatre of flying. The crew took the entitled survivor's leave of seven days with a due date to return on 22 April 1942.

Sergeant Rolph subsequently returned to England as tour expired. After resting and fulfilling a training post, he returned to operations in the rank of warrant officer with 514 Squadron based at Waterbeach in Cambridgeshire. This was a heavy bomber unit within Bomber Command and Rolph then began attacking central targets in occupied Europe. He flew several operations with his New Zealand pilot, Flight Sergeant Hudson, in the Avro Lancaster.

An operation of note was to Frankfurt on 22 March 1944. Twenty-two 514 Squadron aircraft were detailed to bomb the target. One Lancaster returned early and two were later recorded as missing. One Lancaster landed at Mildenhall badly damaged with two gunners killed and two of the crew having abandoned the aircraft by parachute. The two gunners, Sergeants L. Warren and L. Blackford, within Lancaster LL703, had lost their lives during the night fighter attacks. On the same operation, Lancaster LL728 was being flown by Flight Sergeant Hudson with Warrant Officer Rolph in the wireless operator's position having dropped the bomb load satisfactory. The Lancaster turned ready for the return journey. The combat report states that at 2217 hours when 10 miles south of Luxembourg the mid-upper gunner reported an unidentified twin-engine aircraft on the starboard beam slightly up at a range of approximately 400–500 yards apparently closing in to attack. The mid-upper gunner immediately opened fire with a short burst of about one second and gave the order to corkscrew to starboard. The enemy aircraft was lost to view as soon as the corkscrew was commenced and was not seen again. No searchlights, flak or fighter flares were evident at the time. The visibility was fair with bright starlight. The mid-upper gunner, Sergeant Campbell, had fired fifty rounds. The rear gunner, Sergeant Granbois, no rounds. This operation to Frankfurt saw 514 Squadron gunners submit five combat reports having engaged night fighters. Two Lancaster crews had been shot down by night fighters.

On 22 April, Düsseldorf was revealed as the target selected for Bomber Command. No. 514 Squadron mustered twenty-two Lancaster crews to bolster the hundreds of other bombers that were going to fly to the German of the aircraft and crew strengths are officially recorded in the following entries, which include the death of Warrant Officer Rolph:

Lancaster DS669 flown by Flight Sergeant J. Harrison, Flight Sergeant E. Wilde, Flight Sergeant P. Kirkpatrick, Sergeant F. Nash, Sergeant A. Buttling, Sergeant W. Wilson and Sergeant R. Norris were killed. This Lancaster was hit by flak or possibly collided with Lancaster DS828. Sergeant Nash's body was never found, his crew were buried and now lay in the Reichswald Forest War Cemetery.

Lancaster DS682 flown by Flying Officer J. Morgan-Owen crashed in the sea. An SOS message was received at 0256 hours. Sergeants P. Sadler and D. Tetley are buried in Sage War Cemetery; the rest of the crew are commemorated on the Runnymede Memorial as no bodies were ever recovered, they were Flight Sergeant A. Green, Flying Officer P. Jacobson, Sergeant E. Gledhill and Sergeant S. Hayward.

Lancaster DS828 flown by Flight Sergeant Hudson, was possibly hit by flak or collided with Lancaster DS669 and crashed in the target area. The crew members Flight Sergeant P. Constable, Sergeant G. Goddard, Flight Sergeant C. Campbell, Flight Sergeant W. Granbois and Sergeant G. Jones are buried at Reichswald Forest War Cemetery. Flight Sergeant Hudson and Warrant Officer H. Rolph are commemorated on the Runnymede Memorial as both bodies were never located.

In guidance published in 1943, the Air Ministry circulated to its staff a policy concerning burials and funerals of Royal Air Force personnel that had a marked effect on public morale. It did not address the issue of airmen missing over enduring time periods. The story of how the Air Ministry corresponded with Warrant Officer Rolph's mother regarding that fateful night unfolds in the original documentation retained by his family.

The first news of Rolph's failure to return from operations was the Post Office telegram personally delivered to his mother at 67 Brightwell Avenue, Westcliffe-on-sea, Essex, on 23 April.

The next day Squadron Leader Reid at Waterbeach wrote to Rolph's mother:

> Dear Mrs Rolph.
> Prior to receiving this letter, you will have received a telegram informing you that your son 1176863. Warrant Officer H.T. Rolph has been reported missing as a result of an operational flight which took place on the night of 22/23 April 1944.
>
> It is with very deep regret I am writing this letter to convey to you the feelings of the entire Squadron following the news that your son has been reported missing.
>
> At about 2315 hours on Saturday last an aircraft and crew of which your son was the wireless operator took off to carry out a bombing attack on Dusseldorf. This flight was vital and one of the many fighting and courageous efforts called for by the Royal Air Force. The flight should not have taken many hours but although other aircraft completed their mission your son's aircraft failed to return.

The most searching enquiries through all possible channels and organisations have so far revealed nothing, but of course it will take some time for possible information to come through from enemy sources, and I can only hope your son and crew are prisoners of war. Meanwhile further information may come available, if so, this will of course be passed to you immediately.

A committee of officers known as a Committee of Adjustment has gathered your sons' possessions together and will communicate with you in the near future.

May I again express my personal sympathy in your great anxiety.

Yours Sincerely
Squadron Leader Commanding
514 Squadron

The chaplain at Waterbeach wrote a personal handwritten letter to Mrs Rolph on 25 April. This was followed by an official letter to Mrs Rolph from Waterbeach, which arrived on 27 April. The letter advised that the effects of her son were being forwarded to the central depository at Colinbrook.

It was not until 23 October that Mrs Rolph opened an Air Ministry letter from the Director of Personal Services advising that no definite news of her son had come to hand. A report had been received from the International Red Cross Committee, Geneva, regarding the occupants of two aircraft that were missing on the night in question after the attack on Düsseldorf. Unfortunately, the report had mixed up the two crews. Eleven men were listed with six others whose identity the German authorities were unable to establish, and who had lost their lives on 23 April 1944 and were then buried in Field IIIC of the North Military Cemetery at Düsseldorf. The report stated that as there were fourteen members in the two crews, it was not possible on the above information to ascertain who were the six that were unidentified.

On 6 November, Mrs Rolph received a personal letter sent by the family of Flight Sergeant Jones, the flight engineer in Warrant Officer Rolph's crew. The sharing of grief between the families is palpable, and it was clearly a letter wishing to comfort, while the Jones family were themselves torn apart with anguish and pain.

Mrs Rolph replied to the letter and this is worthy of including in its entirety:

Dear Mr and Mrs Jones.

My daughter joins me in thanking you for your loving letter of sympathy. Henry is our one and only as he always termed himself and we still have great hope of his coming home. If not then we shall go to him and to a better place than this where our dear lads can realise their ordeals.

We can be firstly proud of them. Three months ago, a nephew of mine who was a flight engineer Raymond Rolph was killed when near his base after returning from a job, they were nearly home, but evidently the plane caught fire. He was a splendid lad too. He came to see me after Henry was missing and said don't worry Auntie he will come home. He was also on the same job as our lads that night on 22 April but got back safe.

There is still hope that your son bailed out and is in hiding and if it is in God's providence that he shall come home then I shall rejoice. May God bless you and yours is the earnest wish of yours sincerely.

Mary Rolph

Sergeant Raymond Albert Rolph 1645930 of 578 Squadron was presumed to have lost his life alongside his entire crew when returning from operations on 6 July 1944 in Halifax MZ519.

On 27 January 1945, the Air Ministry wrote again to Mrs Rolph:

> With reference to the letter from this department dated 23 October 1944, I am directed to inform you, with great regret, that as no further information has come to hand about your son, Warrant Officer H.T. Rolph, the Department now propose to presume his death for official purposes. Before this action is taken, however, it is requested that you will be good enough formally to confirm that you have received no evidence of his survival. As soon as the necessary formalities have been completed, you will be notified.

On 29 January 1945 Mrs Rolph replied:

> In answer to your letter of 27 Inst. I am very sorry to say that no information has reached me concerning my son Warrant Officer Henry Thomas Rolph except that received from the Air Ministry.
>
> Yours sincerely Mary Rolph.

The Air Ministry replied to Mrs Rolph on 26 February 1945:

> Madam.
> I am commanded by the Air Council to state that in view of the lapse of time and the absence of any further news regarding your son, Warrant Officer H.T. Rolph 1176863, since the date on which he was reported missing, they must regretfully conclude that he has lost his life, and his death has

now been presumed, for official purposes, to have occurred on the 23 April 1944. The Council desires me to express again their sympathy with you in the anxiety which you have suffered, and in your bereavement.

The Air Ministry Casualty Branch from Oxford Street W1 wrote to Mrs Rolph on 29 June 1945:

> Madam
> I am to explain that the most exhaustive investigations are being carried out for news of the fate of all missing Royal Air Force Personnel, by the Graves Registration and Enquiry Services of the war office in those cases where some burial particulars have been received, and by the Royal Air Force Missing Research and Enquiries Service, in other cases. I am therefore to assure you that, if it is at all possible to discover any information, you will be notified at once. In the meantime, the Department is very sensible of the anxiety which waiting for news must cause you, and regrets most deeply that such news, if obtained, can but add to the sadness of your great loss.

The numbers and geographical spread of RAF crews whose aircraft had been shot down over Europe presented significant difficulties. In July 1945, the Casualty Branch of the Air Ministry estimated that approximately 31,000 aircrew were still listed as missing. By the time the Missing, Research and Enquiry Service Units engaged to try to find and identify the bodies of these men, the processes of decomposition, combined with the violent manner of many of these deaths, made this a terribly difficult task. They used a range of techniques to try and identify casualties, in particular, tooth charts. However, as many of the exhumations related to violent death situations, there was often little left to identify.

Mrs Rolph died on 26 January 1947, leaving her daughter Olive to deal with all family matters including the requesting from the Air Ministry of an official certificate of death for her brother, which was subsequently issued on 23 May 1947.

In May 1948, Olive received an official letter addressed to her mother from the Air Ministry. In entirety it read:

Dear Mrs Rolph

I am very sorry to renew your grief in the sad loss of your son Warrant Officer H T Rolph but am writing to let you know that a report has now been received from the Royal Air Force Missing Research and Enquiry Service regarding the fate of his aircraft and crew.

As you already know, two crews were involved in the crash over Dusseldorf on the night of 22 23 April 1944, and of the fourteen airmen who lost their lives, the Germans reported that five identified, and six unidentified airmen were buried in the cemetery there.

As a result of their investigations the Missing Research Service have located these eleven graves, and upon exhumation were able to identify individually all the occupants. Unhappily, however, no grave could be found for your son and his comrade Flight Sergeant Hudson, nor for Sergeant Nash of the other crew.

As the aircraft are known to have exploded in the air, it can only most regretfully be concluded that these three gallant men perished with their aircraft, and that there was no recoverable trace of them when the wreckage fell upon the bombed city.

In such sad circumstances, it has been decided that the great sacrifice made by so many of our fallen, who have no known grave, shall be commemorated by inscribing their names upon a memorial to be erected in this country. Its exact form and location is still under consideration by His Majesty's Government, but as soon as a decision is reached you may rest assured that public announcements concerning it will be made.

I sincerely hope the thought that your son's name will rank in such gallant company may be of some slight comfort to you in the great loss you have sustained.

Yours sincerely
P.416274/44/S.14.Cas.C.7. Air Ministry 2 Seville Street, London, SW1

Olive May Rolph died on 19 December 2000. The letters and in particular the Late Arrivals certificate with the medals awarded to her brother were among her treasured possessions at the time of her death.

*Chapter 20*

# Flight Sergeant Thomas Docherty – Caterpillar Club and Late Arrivals Club

Flight Sergeant Thomas Dalrymple Docherty had a route into operational flying that was unusual and unexpected. He volunteered for aircrew service immediately war was declared in 1939 and quite quickly found himself under training as a wireless operator air gunner. He would train for six days a week on the theory of wireless and how to maintain and operate various types of wireless sets, including the Marconi R1155 receiver and T1154 transmitters of the time. He probably had a natural ability to excel at the qualities required in wireless transmission as he achieved twelve words per minute as the required standard without issue. Instruction was also received in mathematics, Morse Code, voice messages and electronic and radio principles. Problem solving and temporary repairs were essential skills required in the event of a wireless failure in the air, as was the use of the signalling lamp for visual communication in Morse. Once qualified as a wireless operator, all students were posted to a bombing and gunnery school. Upon successful completion of that course, they became fully qualified, promoted to sergeant and more often than not posted for operational training duties.

Sergeant Docherty had endured more than five months of training. The posting he received in February 1940 was to become an instructor at an operational training unit. No doubt an unexpected posting, he must have demonstrated qualities of ability that were assessed as well placed in instructing others in wireless operating for operational training. The operational training unit's function was to instruct new crews and to train them to work as a team, ultimately for operational deployment. The fledgling crews at that time would normally comprise of pilot, navigator, air bomber, wireless operator and an air gunner. Based at Bassingbourn, Cambridgeshire, Sergeant Docherty served on the training flight of 11 Operational Training Unit, which flew primarily on navigation and landing exercises and other training operations.

Despite not being on operational flying, life held many dangers for the instructing staff and crews undertaking training. There were many incidents that proved fatal. On 8 June 1941, Wellington R1728 mysteriously disappeared on a night cross country training sortie. All six crew members were reported missing. Thirteen days later a rubber dinghy was sighted in the sea and once located by a rescue boat it was later confirmed that Sergeant Richard Burt and Sergeant William Hare from that aircraft had survived the ditching but had died during the thirteen days afloat. The remaining four crew were never found. They are commemorated upon the Runnymede Memorial to those with no known grave.

In January 1942, Docherty received a posting and left the training unit to go to Harwell for duties with an aircraft ferry group. RAF Harwell was a training base used by 75 and 148 Squadrons, 15 Operational Training Unit as well as being the base for a Middle East ferry unit. In July 1940, the Atlantic Ferry Organisation had been formed to ferry aircraft across the Atlantic. On 20 July 1941, that unit transferred to the RAF with the formation of Ferry Command, later renamed Transport Command in 1943. The main responsibilities were the transport of aircraft across the Atlantic to the United Kingdom and from England to the Middle East and beyond. Passenger and freight service routes were developed initially between Canada and Britain, but later throughout Europe, the Middle East and India. Aircraft from Transport Command also towed gliders and dropped paratroopers during the Normandy and Arnhem landings.

Flight Sergeant Docherty was posted to serve in 44 Ferry Group, Ferry Command, undertaking wireless operator duties flying to Egypt. The route for his first delivery, of Wellington Z8500, would be Harwell to St Eval on the western tip of England. Then, St Eval for Gibraltar, a flight of around nine hours along the northern tip of Spain and along the coast of Portugal. A ferry flight bomber crew usually consisted of the captain, a navigator, two wireless operators, and two gunners. The next leg would be Gibraltar to Malta, where the crew would fly low over the Mediterranean waters to avoid detection. The Axis forces occupied Sicily and transmitted spoof navigational signals to be picked up and confuse Allied aircraft. Crews needed to be vigilant otherwise any Wellington could inadvertently head towards Sicily in error. Wireless bearing required thorough checking to avoid any possible errors. The flight to Malta was estimated to be completed in just over eight hours. Wellington Z8500 arrived at Malta on 17 January 1942. The Axis had started a new offensive against Malta and 263 air raid alerts were sounded on Malta that month. On 21 January in Libya, General Erwin Rommel launched his second offensive, and as the situation in North Africa was directly linked with that of Malta, there were many events taking place as the crew sheltered for many hours in the bombing raids upon the island.

The RAF plan had originally been that on landing in Malta the Wellington would be refuelled with another crew taking it over and continuing to Egypt. This proved to be impossible to undertake as aircraft were being targeted in the bombing and blast walls were not effective in protecting the parked aircraft. Aircrews had accumulated on the island with nowhere to go, and no aircraft to fly. In all probability this explains the next task for Flight Sergeant Docherty's crew. They managed to reach Aboukir, on the Mediterranean coast of Egypt, on 28 January and remained there until 5 February, when they flew away from the coast to Shallufa, east of Cairo. Flight Sergeant Docherty and his crew were effectively attached to a flight within 38 Squadron, which was flying Wellingtons and attacking Mediterranean shipping targets with torpedoes. Flight Sergeant Docherty's and his crew's familiarity with the Wellington was not in question, but they had no experience of low-level flying over water. This might explain the shuttle flights of Wellington aircraft they undertook flying between the advanced landing grounds at Shallufa and Gambut from 21 February to 25 February.

On 25 February, the crew of Pilot Officer Knowles, Sergeant Bevan, Sergeant Durie, Sergeant Hammett, Sergeant White and Flight Sergeant Docherty took off from Shallufa in Wellington Z9108 and landed at the advanced landing ground 09. They were to take part in an operational mission to attack the shipping port of Benghazi, and their specific duty was to drop a sea mine into the anchorage waters at Benghazi. No. 38 Squadron briefed five crews to drop the mines while other aircraft from other squadrons were briefed to create a diversion by bombing the town and port facilities. Despite a wealth of flying experience, these were completely unknown circumstances for Docherty. As they reached the target, the anti-aircraft gunfire struck the Wellington with devastating effect in the cockpit area. Pilot Officer Knowles lost the majority of his instruments and he was wounded by flak splinters. The best possible effort was made to escape the area without any instruments but eventually the conditions made the Wellington impossible to control. The pilot gave orders for the crew to bail out over the Libyan desert at 0245 hours. It was daunting having to jump from the aircraft and to parachute into the vast desert, probably becoming separated and alone with limited chance of survival. In the semi-darkness Docherty jumped and parachuted safely. With daylight commencing within the next two or three hours, it takes little imagination to understand his feelings of anxiety and fear of being alone, totally isolated in an expanse of hundreds of miles of barren sand.

No. 38 Squadron records simply state four of the five participating aircraft returned to Shallufa safely. Z9108 'R', flown by Pilot Officer Knowles and crew, did not return to advanced landing ground 09. A search was undertaken but nothing was sighted. A second search was flown to cover additional areas but again there were no sightings. Late on 26 February, an Army unit reported that two members of the missing crew were safe at El Adem and the remaining men were thought to be uninjured and sleeping in the aircraft. The information was unconfirmed. Two days later, on 28 February, 38 Squadron received a message that Docherty had parachuted out 60 miles south-east of El Adem, had been located by an Army convoy and would be returning as soon as possible. On 2 March, Sergeant Hammett, the second pilot, and Sergeant White, the front gunner, arrived back at Shallufa. They were debriefed on the circumstances and made aware that their wireless operator, Docherty, had been located and was safe. A precis of their report is as follows:

> The aircraft approached Benghazi from the south and on reaching the Juliana Mole was engaged by the ground defence. The height was about five hundred feet and the aircraft was losing height in order to drop the mines. Suddenly one of the shells hit the door of the front turret and a piece of shrapnel pierced the oil feed, causing oil to spray all over the cockpit. The mines were immediately dropped and Pilot Officer Knowles made a superb manoeuvre which brought the aircraft clear of the barrage. Pilot Officer Knowles climbed and set course before mentioning that he had been hit in the leg. The only instruments in working order were the Air Speed Indicator, the altimeter and the compass and the second pilot took over with this knowledge. The aircraft flew for two hours slightly north of track hoping to reach Mersa Matruh.

The Air Speed Indicator suddenly gave out and as the conditions were very bumpy it was a hopeless job trying to keep the aircraft on an even keel. Realising this Pilot Officer Knowles took over and gave the order to bale out, an answer was received from every member of the crew. Sergeant White the front gunner baled out first, followed by Sergeant Hammett who saw Flight Sergeant Docherty following him.

Sergeant Hammett met Sergeant White in the morning and together they searched for the aircraft, the search being unproductive. They decided to walk and were later picked up by an Army Convoy at 1140 hours. The convoy took them east to Thalatha, and the officer commanding assured Sergeant Hammett that he would communicate with the squadron and tell them the approximate position of baling out and how many of the crew were safe. Resting on this assurance the two Sergeants made no further effort to communicate until two days later. Their message was distorted and when received contained the same information as the unconfirmed Army report of the 26 February.

A letter dated 3 March was received at the advanced landing ground 09 from 121 Maintenance Unit. The letter reported the finding of the body of Pilot Officer Knowles, who had been found outside the aircraft, while the remains of two other bodies were within the aircraft. They had been found by a padre, who had been taken to the scene by an Arab. The padre buried the three bodies and reported the matter at Bardia, from where a search was made immediately. Due to weather conditions this search was unsuccessful. This letter did not reach Shallufa until 11 March.

Docherty eventually arrived at Shallufa, where he advised that it had been the Royal Army Service Corps that came across him in the desert. He was reunited with his fellow two surviving members of the crew and told of the demise of their pilot, rear gunner and navigator, who appeared to have been unable to parachute to safety. Good fortune had seen the safe arrival of Docherty, and his experience of surviving in the desert with no water for nearly three days and the protracted journey returning to his station was recognised by him being officially presented with the certificate of membership to the Late Arrivals Club.

Docherty also chose to contact the manufacturers of the parachute that saved his life in the emergency jump from the ill-fated Wellington. His letter was acknowledged, recording him as a member of the Caterpillar Club, and he duly received his pin and membership card. His story of the events of 25 February 1942 enabled him to become a member of two exclusive clubs for survivors, altogether a rare set of circumstances had taken place following the events that had commenced as a routine ferry flight to the Mediterranean.

*Chapter 21*

# Major Robert Morrison DFC – Late Arrivals Club

Robert Lionel Morrison was from Eastcourt, Natal Province, South Africa, and was born on 26 January 1921. His father had served in South Africa and the Great War, in the New Zealand Expeditionary Force, Late Natal Field Artillery and Imperial Light Horse. He had worn the medal ribbons for the Natal, Relief of Mafeking, Transvaal conflict and later, the Distinguished Conduct Medal in 1918, having been previously awarded a mention in dispatches in 1916.

Robert Morrison enrolled in the 7th Brigade at Durban as a cadet officer in February 1939, later flying for the South African Air Force with the rank of major. The Union of South Africa differed in both rank and uniform structure to the Royal Air Force. When the Union went to war in 1939, the South African Air Force was fairly devoid of both equipment and personnel, primarily a result of the restrictions imposed by the pre-war economic depression. The statistics are staggeringly small: there were only 160 permanent force officers, 35 cadets and 1,400 other ranks. The inventory of just ninety-three aircraft echoes the derisory situation, especially as a high proportion were not airworthy.

An expeditious growth took place whereby at the end of 1941, the South African Air Force had more than 31,000 personnel, including more than 900 pilots. Robert Morrison was one of those men. He had commenced flying service having had previous flying experience in August 1940. By 1943, the number of personnel had further increased dramatically, whereby the pilot strength was more than 2,000. The story of Morrison's operational flying is both remarkable and tragic. The South African 5 Squadron in which he flew had been formed in April 1939 at Cape Town as a fighter-bomber unit. It was disbanded at the end of the year, only to be reformed on 7 May 1941 at Swartkop in the Eastern Cape province. The squadron relocated to the Desert Air Force in Egypt in December 1941, equipped with Curtiss P-40 Tomahawks. The Tomahawk was a single-seat fighter and ground-attack aircraft that first flew in 1938. No. 5 Squadron had joined 233 Wing as the fighter cover for 3 Bomber Wing, South African Air Force. They flew the Tomahawk operationally alongside 4 and 2 Squadrons.

Captain Morrison's first close call to tragedy occurred on 2 March 1942. Scrambled into the air, the fuel pump on his aircraft stopped working. He noted modestly in his logbook that he had managed to land with difficulty. Sand was one of the most dangerous enemies of desert pilots. If ingested into an engine it could prove disastrous in a matter of hours. All aircraft were fitted with special air filters that caused drag in the air and effectively reduced performance. Sand jammed gun mechanisms and Perspex cockpit canopies were scored and scratched by sand to such an extent that it was impossible to polish out. Morrison took that same troublesome Tomahawk up for the interception of a reported Ju 88 on 12 March. He was in company with Lieutenant Thornhill-Cook. A sighting some 20 miles from their desert landing ground saw the Ju 88 dive steeply, jettisoning bombs and fuel. The enemy pilot took steep turns and a chase occurred with the rear gunner firing tracer rounds during a clamber for cloud cover. However, before the German reached the clouds, Morrison engaged twice with long stern attacks and again fairly close-quarter frontal passes, seeing pieces fly off the cockpit area and silencing the rearward-firing gun position. The two South

African pilots secured a shared damage report over the German aircraft.

South African Cecil Golding was also posted to North Africa and was thrown into battle at a time where the German and Italian aerial forces had superiority in numbers and Allied losses were disturbingly high. On 25 March 1942, Golding joined 5 Squadron at Sidi Barrani in Libya. It had the top-scoring South African ace, Major Jack Frost, as its commanding officer. Due to the shortage of pilots, Golding was placed into the squadron without any meaningful operational experience in a Tomahawk. Captain Morrison was given the task of looking after the young pilot, who stepped up to the challenge well. The Tomahawk was without doubt inferior to the German Messerschmitt Bf 109 and that fact was reflected in the losses that were occurring. The squadron records show that at the close of March 1942, 339 sorties had been flown that month with two enemy aircraft destroyed, one probable and four damaged. The squadron's sorties had consumed more than 22,000 gallons of fuel.

On 8 May 1942, while on a flying sortie with Captain Botha, they were both surprised by a pair of enemy fighters. Captain Morrison's Tomahawk sustained four large cannon shell strikes and eighteen smaller rounds, which penetrated the fuselage and severed the hydraulic system. Being close to the landing ground, he managed to effect a crash-landing without incurring injury. His aircraft sustained significant damage and was written off, resting in the sand some 400 yards from their landing ground. Captain Botha was not so fortunate. He sustained shrapnel wounds in his thigh but despite two flat tyres he managed a good crash-landing.

Morrison had established himself as a reliable and competent pilot within the squadron. His first confirmed enemy kill came on 27 May 1942. The apprentice Golding was alongside Morrison, having scrambled from El Adem. It was 0950 hours when all available Tomahawks intercepted ten bombers escorted by ten fighters near

Gazala. In the aerial melee, Morrison's aircraft received nine holes from an attacking fighter. The mixture of Italian and German aircraft among the Tomahawks was quite a spectacle for Golding, who managed to get some rounds into a Luftwaffe bomber. Morrison wrote in his logbook the claim for the Italian Fiat BR.20 as destroyed. This low-wing medium bomber had entered service in 1936 and was popular among the Italian aircrews, serving in significant numbers. Four Tomahawks from the squadron had sustained damage during the combat, while two failed to return. Remarkably both pilots were known to have survived, a fortunate set of events considering the expanse of desert lacked landmarks and featured undulating sand that was difficult to navigate.

A sobering statistic for 5 Squadron was the loss of sixteen pilots in June 1942, either killed, missing or in hospital. Morrison recorded sightings of enemy fighters on every flight in June 1942. During an early morning sortie on 3 June he saw some fifteen fighters and he wrote: '0700 hours, sweep of Knightsbridge, diced for twenty minutes very enjoyable got in a few squirts no results seen.' The battle of Knightsbridge was fought by the Eighth Army in the Western Desert between 2 and 11 June 1942. During it the tanks of Rommel's Afrika Korps were able to overpower and captured many Allied soldiers. Later that day, at 1215 hours, Morrison was in the air again, ordered to carry out another sweep. Two Tomahawks collided head on as they taxied before getting into the air. The Tomahawk strength therefore reduced to nine aircraft as they made it to Bir Hakeim, deep in the Sahara Desert, a desolate crumbling old fort that Rommel had left to be held by the encircled Italian troops.

Overhead, Morrison and his fellow pilots engaged with twelve Stuka aircraft that were dive bombing Bir Hakeim. The Stukas were protected by a flight of Bf 109 fighters, which were the most significant threat and they attacked the Tomahawks as they arrived. Morrison estimated fifteen fighters and in the aerial tussles he received six cannon shells into his aircraft. However, more troublesome was the chunk of shrapnel that had embedded itself into his right knee. The Tomahawk was a robust aircraft but cannon shells were terribly destructive. Morrison became debilitated and, losing blood, he crashed into the desert.

The events of 3 June 1942 are set out in more detail in the squadron records and post-war accounts from numerous sources. Unsurprisingly, some information is conflicting but the circumstances were traumatic and the German claims add to the confused detail. Second Lieutenant Cecil Golding and Captain Bob Morrison combined had shot down a Stuka but both were themselves shot down as they did so. At least five Tomahawk aircraft were shot down in close vicinity of Bir Hakeim, all reputedly claimed by the German ace Hans-Joachim Marseille. Golding managed to make a controlled emergency landing and found a Stuka pilot who had been shot down, reputed to have been Leutnant Hans Deibl. He was still in his aircraft but trapped. The Stuka was burning but, together with the badly injured Captain Morrison and Lieutenant Vivian Muir, who had also been shot down, he rescued the Stuka pilot.

Marseille claimed six Tomahawks shot down on 3 June, including the three pilots who had assisted in rescuing the Stuka pilot. He had been born on 13 December 1919 and was one of the most accomplished fighter pilots of the Second World War. Known as the 'Star of Africa' against the Desert Air Force over North Africa, he flew a Bf 109 during his entire combat career. No other pilot claimed as many Western Allied aircraft as Marseille. On 3 June 1942, he was credited with shooting down six aircraft in eleven minutes. Marseille lost his life later that year, on 30 September.

The wounded survivors, including Morrison, were located by a South African armoured car operating behind enemy lines and this enabled the wounded pilots to be transported through the German lines and back to a hospital in besieged Tobruk. Although this was not an easy transit, clearly the armoured car crew were aware of navigating the desert expanses with expertise. Morrison was then evacuated from Tobruk to a hospital in Cairo on 18 June, just two days before the town was taken by Rommel. Morrison had suffered a significant injury through the back of his leg at the knee. He later received membership into the Late Arrivals Club, his certificate being signed and issued by Squadron Leader Houghton to celebrate having succeeded in returning to his squadron.

On 5 June, the commanding officer of 5 Squadron, Major Jack Frost was shot down in the Knightsbridge area, fortunately landing in the lines of the 1st South African Division. Two days later, on 7 June, he was back in the air and claimed a probable Bf 109 over Knightsbridge. On each of the following days over Bir Hakeim, he damaged two further aircraft, both probably destroyed. Bir Hakeim eventually fell to the Axis on 10 June.

Tobruk was to feature in more significant aerial battles but tragically Major Frost was eventually shot down and lost his life on 16 June 1942, near Bir Hakeim. Lieutenant Derham was also shot down and became a prisoner of war. Repeated searches were made for Major Frost in the days after his failure to return, but neither he nor his wrecked aircraft were ever found. His successor, Captain Louis Botha, was killed on the very next day, and Major Dennis Lacey, who subsequently commanded the squadron, was himself shot down on 7 August. Within a short period of three weeks during June and into July 1942, the squadron had lost three commanding officers. Consequently, the highly regarded Major van der Spuy took command of the squadron.

Captain Morrison climbed back into the cockpit of a Tomahawk on 18 October 1942. He was still on the strength of his old squadron. Initially his injury caused some issues for him in respect of flying but he soon mastered what was needed to gain back his confidence. His logbook recorded an engagement with Bf 109s on 20 October where the Tomahawk of another pilot, Lieutenant Coleman, collided with an Italian fighter west of El Daba, northern Egypt. Both aircraft crashed in flames. The intensity of operations was relentless in October, carrying out bomber escort and fighter sweeps. Morrison recorded enemy aircraft engagements on almost all of his eighteen sorties that month. Things calmed down in November and December with shipping patrols and those of less significance.

Although the Kittyhawk was Morrison's regular aircraft, he did have the opportunity to fly a Spitfire in February 1943. The logbook states: 'Like riding a racehorse after a Donkey', so he was clearly impressed by the iconic British fighter. He returned to flying the Kittyhawk and recorded many sorties, noting opportunities to ground strafe targets of opportunity. It was while attacking a similar target on 8 March 1943 in a flight of Kittyhawks that ten Bf 109s pounced on them. Morrison dropped his bomb and turned to attack the enemy fighters. One passed into his gunsight and he struck it accurately, upon which it dived steeply and crashed into the ground. He recorded, 'destroyed' in his logbook as his operational tour of duty drew to a close. The wing commander endorsed his book, which registered one Breda 20 destroyed (there was no such type but he could have meant a Fiat Br. 20), one Me 109 destroyed, half a Ju 87 destroyed and one Ju 88 damaged. Morrison was posted to the Middle East Staff college until July 1943 and then on to an operational training unit, where he became an instructor flying the Kittyhawk until March 1944.

On the cusp of the German retreat at Rome, 5 Squadron welcomed back the promoted Major Morrison as he commenced his second tour of operational flying over Italy. The German forces would make successive stands on a series of defensive positions known as the Trasimene, Arezzo, Arno and Gothic Lines. It was here that Morrison would once again fly the Kittyhawk. A seriously impressive thirty-five sorties were flown in May 1944, with every entry in his logbook detailing the targets of bridges, railways, roads, embankments and any transportation sighting of opportunity. These were low-level air-to-ground attacks and had inherent dangers. Morrison recorded on 15 May: 'Force landed, old habit, near Cassino. Hit by flak, successfully belly landed.' Recovering from the forced landing, the remarkable intensity of attacking ground targets continued with eighteen sorties carried out in June, twenty-six in July and fourteen in August.

The strategic purpose of the Allied attack on the Gothic Line in Italy in August 1944 was to engage the enemy and prevent the transfer of German divisions to France or the Eastern Front. Morrison had led endless sorties to specific targets, some no more than a single emplacement gun or troop concentration in woodlands or villages. On 2 September 1944, he led six Kittyhawks to an identified road bridge target. Unexpectedly intense anti-aircraft gunfire came up from the protected target and one Kittyhawk flown by Lieutenant Dickson was badly damaged. He was able to take to his parachute but the anti-aircraft gun fire prevented any observation of his descent. It transpired that he had been wounded and treated as a prisoner of war but he died of his injuries sixteen days later.

On 13 September, Morrison led five Tomahawks on a cab rank sortie directed to attack an enemy-held defended ridge at a specific map reference. The cab rank was devised to allow very specific targets to be attacked direct from ground force intelligence. This target was in a well-camouflaged, elevated position, and Morrison flew a reconnaissance of the area to identify the target before going in to bomb. Diving towards the ridge at 1,000ft while selecting his target, his aircraft was damaged by anti-aircraft fire and it fell out of control, plummeting onto the ridge and disappearing into trees. Lieutenant Barret took command of the flight and led the remaining aircraft to attack the ridge, which was thought to have been successful. Barrett flew low to try and locate Morrison but nothing could be seen. The forward control cab rank was requested to make whatever steps they could to locate Morrison's crash location but this proved to be impossible.

Major MacMurray, the squadron commanding officer, wrote to Major Morrison's mother providing as much detail as was possible. This was based on facts provided by the pilots that had accompanied Morrison that day. Major MacMurray informed her that the target attacked was approximately 5 miles within enemy held territory.

It was not until 22 February 1945 that Morrison's next of kin were advised that the Kittyhawk serial FX772 had been located 22 miles north of Florence at map reference L82103. The pilot's body bore a major's crown on both shoulder red tabs, pilot's wings and a notebook in the pocket. The aircraft's identity plates and notebook had been forwarded to the squadron, who identified them as the property of Major Morrison. The aircraft bore the markings FX772/A-041197.

Morrison was initially buried in the Sal Lorenzo Military Cemetery. After the war, many graves were moved into the Florence cemetery and on 20 April 1945, Morrison's remains were respectfully interred there. He was just twenty-three years of age and had accomplished many deeds of valour before his life was taken. The certificate of membership of the Late Arrivals Club had been pasted into the front of his flying logbook. It was clearly something that was most meaningful to him.

Major Morrison's operational service was worthy of recognition and a recommendation for a Distinguished Flying Cross by his commanding officer was submitted, effective on 12 September 1944. This was the day prior to Morrison's death as the Distinguished Flying Cross could not be awarded posthumously. The recommendation read:

> Major Morrison has taken part in a large number of operational sorties. On his first tour of duty, during the strenuous period of retreat from Gazala to El Alamein, he

flew on numerous low-level missions and bomber escorts and destroyed at least one enemy aircraft. Later this officer led many attacks on the enemy's lines of communication and inflicted considerable damage on mechanical transport. Major Morrison consistently displayed great courage and devotion to duty and his fine fighting spirit never wavered, even in the face of intense anti-aircraft opposition.

The terminology of the recommendation clearly has relevance to his death inflicted by anti-aircraft fire. Morrison was one of just 407 men serving in the South African Air Force to be awarded the Distinguished Flying Cross. *The London Gazette* published the award on 12 February 1946.

The Governor General of South Africa invited Morrison's mother to Government House, Pretoria, on Friday, 26 November 1948, where she was to receive her son's Distinguished Flying Cross medal. The added sadness of this ceremony was that Morrison's father had died in the months prior to the ceremony. He had written to the war records office in Pretoria in March 1948 requesting a piece of ribbon for the medal that had been awarded to his son.

The most unusual if not unique circumstance of a mother being able to hold the identification plates and aircraft manufacturer's plate of the aircraft in which her son lost his life are testimony to the commanders of his South African squadron in which he had served. The efforts to unite the flying logbook and the wings that were worn on his tunic with the aircraft plates and importantly the Late Arrivals Club membership certificate illustrate the respect held for her son.

*Chapter 22*

# Guinea Pigs

As the Second World War progressed, RAF station medical officers issued every member of aircrew with a small personal first aid pack and these were often carried in the pocket of the Mae West life jacket. At the time of issue, no doubt it was just another item of issue among many for these service personnel. It was a well-devised first aid pack and any man requiring it often needed to get the contents in emergency situations. Therefore, the outer waterproof covering had been precut on a bias at each corner to assist in opening. The whole pack could be ripped open diagonally in a moment. The covering material of the pack was treated to be non-inflammable, protecting the contents in event of a flash fire.

Aircrew burn injuries needed to be treated at the earliest moment possible to reduce infection. The first principle in the first aid treatment of burns was to exclude the air from the exposed surface. Burns to hands were always likely and a pair of oiled-silk gloves containing an antiseptic powder were in the pack contents. In use, they fastened at the wrist by means of a strip of bandage material tipped with adhesive plaster. For burn injuries other than to the hands, a tube of anti-burn jelly and two ampoules of morphine were immediately available. A large wound dressing and a safety pin completed the contents. This sounds basic but in many cases this emergency pack was used by aircrews effectively, in particular among the RAF bomber crews.

Hospital general surgical wards were presented with difficult circumstances in treating burn cases. Among many patients in busy wards, cross-infection was almost impossible to avoid. Burn dressings required more attention and were usually time consuming. Often to avoid cross-infection they would be undertaken late on daily dressing changes; they were often distressingly painful. In July 1940, the RAF consultants in surgery and the civilian consultant in plastic surgery Archibald McIndoe formed a committee on burn treatment and recommended the segregation of these patients into special burns centres, self-contained or adjacent to the hospital. Four hospitals – Halton in Buckinghamshire, Ely in Cambridgeshire, Rauceby in Lincolnshire and Cosford in Staffordshire – became burn centres. These were not fully equipped and operational until mid to late 1941. The important special dietary provision of high-protein fluids for patients with facial and jaw injuries was perfected at this time. Each hospital had around twelve beds and two saline baths. There were significant photographs taken of patients' injuries as treatment progression. The images were ideal for medical staff consultation and many patients actually retained personal copies.

The emergency medical centres established at St Albans, Basingstoke and East Grinstead were the first operational facilities to receive casualties, the latter known for treating fighter pilot cases from the Battle of Britain in 1940. During that time terribly distressing burn injuries were sustained by pilots during attempts to escape the flames that engulfed cockpits from engine and fuel fires. Archibald Hector McIndoe, a New Zealand-born surgeon, was at that time embarking upon the development of burn treatment for victims. He revolutionised the field of plastic surgery, working from the Queen Victoria Hospital in East Grinstead, Sussex. McIndoe had two key members of his operating staff with him at East Grinstead, Sister Jill Mullins and John Hunter, who was his chief anaesthetist. However, it would be remiss not to acknowledge the nursing orderlies who always took the greatest interest in the patients, becoming excellent dressers of wounds and having inexhaustible patience with some ghastly injuries. Towards the end of 1940, the training of surgeons commenced at East Grinstead in the fundamentals of plastic and jaw injury combined with burn cases. Nursing sisters underwent short attachments at East Grinstead and often departed to the larger burn centres to apply what they had learned.

Initially the standard treatment for serious burns had been to cover the wounds with tannic coagulation hoping that this would dry out the burnt areas and allow the dead skin to be removed. This process was extremely painful for patients and often induced extensive scarring. McIndoe noted that the burnt pilots who had bailed out by parachute but landed into the sea recovered with differing and in many cases better healing results. McIndoe subsequently developed the practice of bathing patients in saline. This proved to be a much gentler treatment process, with the saline solution improving healing times. A prototype saline bath was installed at East Grinstead but because of the technical issues with the corrosive salt, all materials used had to be resilient to the corrosive actions and the Air Ministry Directorate of Works assisted to resolve these matters. Each bath needed to be effectively isolated or earthed as any metal parts were subjected to electrical conductivity caused by the saline. Each bath facility required stretchers or ward beds to access and facilitate patients being lifted without obstruction. After the patient was lifted out of the bath, the burned areas were cleansed, dusted with sulphonamide powder and covered with tulle gras dressings before skin grafting could be undertaken. This work required heavy lifting and selected male nursing orderlies were required for undertaking the tasks surrounding the maintenance and nursing services of the saline bath units.

These saline-bathed pilots were the inaugural Guinea Pigs for Archibald McIndoe and the men who later established the famous Guinea Pig Club in the Second World War. Within this book there is the account of Dennis Taylor, who required a pedicle graft. These were probably the most visually impacting aspects of the work at East Grinstead. This type of graft created a skin tube with its own blood supply to the tissue. The skin grew and extended between its two points of contact on the patient. Once sufficient skin growth had taken place, the new skin was grafted. Tube pedicles were often used by McIndoe to recreate an airman's nose, forehead or lips. Dennis Taylor underwent eight operations to reconstruct his injuries and he was enrolled as a member of the Guinea Pig Club, becoming a stalwart member for the rest of his life. Taylor retained the sequence of photographs that illustrated his pedicle graft, its growth and the application to rebuild his nose, and he kept them for the rest of his life. Patients with tube pedicles feature predominantly in published images of the work undertaken by McIndoe and his Guinea Pigs.

There was an escalation of burn injuries as the air war intensified and by 1945 the vast majority of the Guinea Pig Club members were men who had sustained burns flying within bomber aircrew. Although men from all nationalities joined the Guinea Pig Club, the Canadians were significantly represented with 176 members, the largest non-British contingent. In addition to the airmen, doctors and surgeons were made honorary members of the club. There were also recognised friends of the Guinea Pig Club who were presented with a special membership badge.

An Air Ministry Pamphlet, produced in 1944, was distributed to medical officers at squadron bases who were likely to deal with burn cases. The booklet covered the effects of avoiding burns and gave clear image evidence of the protection afforded by gloves, helmets, goggles and other flying clothing. It also dealt with burn shock and how burnt aircrew could appear to be well and initially fare better than less seriously burnt men. Burn shock victims were always likely to deteriorate rapidly if not treated swiftly and appropriately.

It must be made clear that the infrastructure of hospitals treating injured airmen across the country was significant, and the number of patients treated for burn injuries across that network is not known. The hospital at East Grinstead grew in reputation and it naturally became the centre of expertise and had revolutionary success in treating seriously burnt airmen. McIndoe was expertly skilled in harvesting sheets of tissue paper-thin skin grafts using an open razor with a 10in blade. Tissue harvesting was essential to his work in treating burns. Each harvest was individual and McIndoe demanded that this skill was attained by his staff.

McIndoe himself often accessed and selected patients from other hospitals where he felt they would attain the best option for recovery and where certain cases offered him the opportunity to engage in specific medical challenges. This explains well how becoming one of McIndoe's Guinea Pigs evolved into the rather exclusive club with a select membership of just 649 men.

McIndoe had recognised the importance of rehabilitation in the overall healing process. He encouraged the forming of their own club with social reintegration into normal life. McIndoe was instrumental in organising social events inside the hospital and encouraging his patients to get out into the community. The RAF originally required any patient to be rendered fit for service within six months or invalided. Clearly this was too short a time when applied to serious burn injuries. The period was prolonged and eventually in selected cases enabled patients to be retained in service and under treatment for two and a half years. This resolved the worrying issue of deprivation of rank and pay and improved morale. McIndoe's Guinea Pigs also benefited with the Air Ministry's engagement with the Ministry of Labour in locating appropriate employment once fully recovered. One of the major problems arising from the war and peculiar to East Grinstead hospital was the rehabilitation of the long-term plastic cases; long term because in order to complete their treatment many of the Guinea Pig Club members needed multiple operations that extended over many years.

After the Second World War specialised burn units were created throughout the country, including one at Stoke Mandeville Hospital. The number of war injuries had reduced, resulting in a burn unit for all three services being set up at Halton, a few miles from Stoke Mandeville. A close relationship between the hospitals developed that led to military surgeons being posted to Stoke Mandeville for training in the care of burns and an introduction to plastic surgery.

It is also worthy of mention that medical rehabilitation had been well recognised within the RAF. Marchwood Park in Southampton became the residency for recuperating patients from East Grinstead. In 1950, Headley Court was officially opened by the Duchess of Kent as a Medical Rehabilitation Unit for pilots and aircrew who had been injured during the war.

Archibald McIndoe was knighted in 1947 and in May 1950 the French Government made him a Commander of the Legion of Honour. The citation read:

> During the war of 1939–1945, he founded and organised to the profit of the Allied Forces, the East Grinstead Plastic Surgery Centre, and has thus enabled many disfigured French servicemen to return to their normal lives after long and difficult treatment which demanded the greatest care in every detail and which brought into play the highest qualities required of a surgeon. He displayed true genius in his operations and has obtained the most prodigious results. Since the founding of the plastic surgery centre, he has shown an untiring devotion and boundless energy. By making possible for many French servicemen a life which otherwise would have been indeed difficult, Sir Archibald McIndoe deserves the recognition of the French Army.

East Grinstead has honoured the work of Sir Archibald with the installation of a statue to him that stands in front of Sackville College. The statue, created by sculptor Martin Jennings, was unveiled by the Princess Royal in 2014.

The Guinea Pig Club supported the diverse membership of men through the war and into the post-war years, retirement and ultimately their final days for a total of eighty-two years. The club was unique, exclusive to those men who were operated upon at East Grinstead Hospital. The last two living members of the 649 men that became Guinea Pigs died in October 2023, both had reached the age of 101. The Royal Air Force Benevolent Fund had administered the club's welfare funds in the final years.

A memorial stone dedicated to the Guinea Pig Club stands in the Staffordshire arboretum. It is inscribed with the words 'Out of the flames came inspiration'.

*Chapter 23*

# Sergeant Dennis Taylor – Guinea Pig and Goldfish Club

Dennis Taylor had an unusual and interesting connection to two of the aviation survivor clubs that evolved during the Second World War. His story engages with events that took place on the first day of June 1942, events that would shape his life thereafter. He was born on 7 August 1920 in Penwortham, on the south bank of the River Ribble close to Preston, Lancashire. Dennis grew up with a brother, Jim, and stepbrother, Richard.

Several men from the Preston area, the majority of whom were not known to each other, would eventually become bonded together as a result of the Second World War. One young man in particular, Ronald Edwards who served in the Loyal Regiment, would spend years in the company of Dennis. Edwards' story would see him returning to Penwortham, where he died in 1946, aged twenty-seven, and is buried in Penwortham churchyard. Dennis's stepbrother, Richard Staveley, also joined the Loyal Regiment in Preston and served in the 18th Reconnaissance Corps. Initially known as the Loyal North Lancashire Regiment, it recruited primarily in Preston, Chorley, Bolton and Wigan. Dennis's brother, Jim, joined up to serve in the Royal Navy and Dennis followed, later volunteering to serve in the RAF. Prior to the war, Dennis had been employed as a sorting clerk with the Post Office. He enlisted to serve on 28 January 1941.

Dennis volunteered as aircrew and trained as a navigator at the Air Observer School, West Freugh, in the south-west of Scotland in late 1941. In training, he was a leading aircraftsman and once qualified he was promoted to sergeant. After the formal training process was completed, Sergeant Taylor was posted to become a member of 218 Squadron. No doubt a clerical error occurred because almost immediately after arriving he and the other men expecting to serve as a crew together were directed to 57 Squadron at Feltwell, Norfolk.

After arriving at Feltwell, the crew, which consisted of sergeants and a Canadian pilot, John Kormylo, were instructed to fly the Wellington on night operations over occupied Europe. After the normal assessments of ability and flight testing scrutinised by their flight leader, their first operation was to bomb Dieppe, on 29 May 1942. Six Wellingtons took part, and Cologne was to be the target the following day. It was no normal briefing because this operation to Germany was to be the first raid by over 1,000 aircraft. Bombers from across Bomber Command and the command's training groups participated. Twenty Wellingtons from Taylor's squadron took part, and it was considered to have been a well-executed operation with good bombing results.

The third operation saw the crew support Bomber Command's second 'Thousand Plan' raid, attacking Essen on the night of 1 June 1942. The aircraft for Dennis's crew was Wellington DV816. Bomber Command failed to accumulate the desired 1,000 bombers, but nevertheless the briefing for such monumental numbers of bombers converging over one place would have brought forth questions in the minds of crews like that of Sergeant Taylor, and even more so those receiving briefings who were still at training establishments with no operational experience at all.

At 2355 hours on 1 June 1942, Wellington DV816 left Feltwell bound for Germany. The crew then set about their business of surviving the flak and Luftwaffe night fighters. The 'Thousand Aircraft Operation' to Essen flew over Zeeland and the south Netherlands. Crews experienced great difficulty in finding the target as the ground was covered either by haze or a layer of low cloud. Bombing was very scattered and Wellington DV816, having dropped its bomb load, commenced its return to Feltwell. At 0243 hours, while flying low to avoid enemy fighters, the Wellington was suddenly hit by accurate anti-aircraft flak fired from a flak ship protecting the coastline near Flushing. That ship was undoubtedly a converted Dutch fishing vessel, part of the 32 Minensuchflottille, which were protecting the Dutch coastline in the Western Scheldt west of Flushing. The unpredictable presence of these anti-aircraft ships with their dangerous six heavy anti-aircraft guns and fourteen light anti-aircraft guns amounted to significant capabilities of firepower. It would appear that the Wellington's damage was sufficient to force the pilot to immediately ditch into the sea. In all probability, the Wellington crashed as little time existed for a controlled ditching. The crew suffered injuries from both the light flak and also from the violent ditching. The Wellington had struck the water at speed and the traumatic crumpling of metal and kinetic forces caused violent mayhem. The crew survived, but Sergeant Taylor had suffered serious facial injuries from the incident, including the partial severing of his nose by flak splinters. Eight bombers were shot down in the Zeeland and adjacent waters, as well as the sailing waters of the Wielingen, which was the North Sea approach to Walcheren Island.

The crew of Wellington DV816 had extricated themselves from the fuselage of the Wellington and were able to climb into the dinghy, which had automatically inflated. The opportunity for immediate first aid was taken, stemming the blood loss from Taylor's huge gash across his nose and this was relatively successful. The crew were adrift for nine hours in the water before the dinghy was sighted. They were picked up by the German Navy and taken ashore to receive medical treatment.

Taylor commenced his prisoner of war experience at Stalag VIIIB in July 1942. This camp was situated at Lamsdorf on

German territory between Breslau and Krakow. The camp held separate compounds for definitive groups, which included men from the British Army, Canadian Army and Indian service personnel. The Germans actively chose to separate the Royal Air force and Royal Australian Air Force personnel from other prisoner groups. Generally, aviators were considered by the Germans as requiring higher security, and therefore this well-established camp had always held considerable numbers of air force personnel. Frequently deployed as a holding camp, in 1942, it was consuming airmen primarily from Bomber Command on a regular basis, essentially casualties from the gathering growth of Allied air force activity over France and Germany.

By 1943, the famous camp for Allied airmen in Sagan – Stalag Luft III – had become so overcrowded that an estimated 1,000 men, mostly non-commissioned aircrew, were transferred to Lamsdorf. Part of Lamsdorf camp had been separated by building new barbed-wire fences, resulting in a camp within a camp being created. Lamsdorf was never to become a dedicated airmen's camp during its long existence.

Stalag VIIIB's notoriety is centred upon an order to bind the hands of the RAF prisoners in retaliation for a number of reasons, one being the Allied raid upon Dieppe in 1942. During the raid, the British and Allied combined Commando forces secured a number of German prisoners and temporarily tied their hands behind their backs. This decision was made as the small raiding party was limited in men and it reduced the requirement of having to guard the German soldiers. The German High Command chose to create a significant amount of propaganda over the tying up of prisoners. Because of this episode, the Germans took reprisals, focusing them upon the air force prisoners in Lamsdorf. From 8 October 1942, they endured daily hand binding from 0700 hours to 1900 hours for more than a year. Prison life for these men was terribly difficult and they were inhibited from engaging normal but mundane activities to pass the time. Respite at midday saw the restraints temporarily released for a meal and ablutions. The binding or handcuffing of the air force prisoners of war was a blatant contravention of the Geneva Convention. Prisoners that released themselves from the binding and were found to have done so by the guards faced immediate retribution. They would be marched to the guard house to stand facing a wall with verbal abuse inflicted upon them on a regular basis. Handcuffs replaced the temporary bindings on 20 November 1942 and it was only on 18 November 1943 that the practice ceased altogether.

Sergeant Taylor was aware of the Goldfish Club and wrote from the prisoner of war camp to the secretary of the club, Charles Robertson at the Beehive Works in Middlesex. He requested to become a member of the club and outlined the ditching circumstances in his initial letter. On 23 March 1944, Robertson replied, sending the letter to his mother, Mrs Taylor, 332 Leyland Road, Penwortham, Preston, Lancs.

Dear Mrs Taylor

News of the above club has penetrated to Royal Air Force prisoners of war camps in Germany, and as a result of this, I have heard from Sergeant Dennis Taylor, and understand he wishes to become a member.

As I have details of his ditching, you will be pleased to learn that he has been elected a life member, and accordingly I am enclosing herewith his Club badge and official membership card, with the intention that you should retain them until his return to England, which the Club Patrons sincerely hope will not be long delayed.

No membership fee of any kind is involved in this Club, as it is purely honorary, and intended to recognise the grand work put in by these air force Allied aircrews.

Yours sincerely.
C A Robertson Hon Secretary.

Stalag VIIIB held a significant number of prisoners but due to a mutual interest in a boxing club, two men recognised each other among the many faces. Sergeant Taylor knew Private Ronald Edwards, who was serving in the Loyal Regiment, both having lived in Penwortham. It appears that Edwards had been captured in 1940. Both men shared time engaged in the camp boxing club, using the equipment and sports vests provided by either the Young Men's Christian Association or the Red Cross, who endeavoured as best as possible to provide books and recreation material for prisoners of war. There were permitted movements for men between the prison enclosures, primarily for sporting activities including boxing and football. Sergeant Currie, an Australian, of 12 Squadron, had been shot down over Saint-Nazaire on the west coast of France on 25 March 1942. This rear gunner, who also flew in a Wellington, became a formative figure in the camp's RAF football team.

In January 1945, the German military authorities received high command orders to evacuate, among others, Stalag VIIIB and its associated work camps in Lamsdorf. The German orders were under the pretext that Article Seven of the Geneva Convention required prisoners of war to be moved out of danger away from a fighting zone. Prisoner of war camps in Poland and eastern Germany would be evacuated westwards as Russian forces advanced towards them. The German forces forcibly marched more than 20,000 prisoners of war west into central Germany, often making them walk as far as 20 miles per day. The majority of Stalag VIIIB inmates were marched through Czechoslovakia, to the north of Prague, ending their journey three months later in April 1945. It had been the coldest winter for many years and many men died from the enduring weather conditions and lack of nourishment.

Dennis Taylor was effectively promoted to the rank of warrant officer as his time as a prisoner accumulated. He survived the years behind barbed wire and the evacuation march with its privations, which must have affected everyone associated with it. He was below 8st in weight on completion of the forced march, which had been undertaken in forty-four days. Warrant Officer Taylor calculated that he had covered 645 miles on the forced march westwards into Germany.

Despite all the events that had taken place, almost as soon as he was freed and repatriated after the war he wrote to Charles Robertson. A reply arrived with him on 25 April 1945, it read:

Dear W/O Taylor.
I was very glad indeed to receive your letter and hear that you are once again back in England. I hope that you are now fit and well and have completely recovered from your experience.

Regarding the wearing of the Goldfish badge, I understand that it is allowed to be worn on flying suits and battle dress, but of course, not visible on the tunic. However, I believe that the whole matter is left to the discretion of the Commanding Officers.

The post war plans of the club have not yet been settled. Our chief difficulty in coming to a decision is the fact that our members are scattered all over the world.

Yours sincerely.
C A Robertson Hon Secretary Goldfish Club

There were other pressing matters for Warrant Officer Taylor to deal with. The facial injuries he sustained in the ditching had healed but the severe nose injury had left him disfigured. The repatriation medical that the majority of returning prisoners of war underwent saw fit to send him for admittance to a hospital in Cosford. Following a medical assessment and consultation with the staff at Queen Victoria Hospital in East Grinstead, he was transferred for potential facial surgery on 28 May 1945. Taylor was twenty-four years of age at this time. His injuries were classified as facial shrapnel wounds inflicted by splinters of red-hot metal from exploding enemy flak shells. His injuries required the skills of Archibald McIndoe, the surgeon who had instigated the Guinea Pig Club at East Grinstead in 1940.

Taylor required a pedicle skin graft. The pedicle created a skin tube with a blood supply that grew skin tissue and allowed it to be utilised in reconstruction surgery. Tube pedicles were often used by McIndoe to recreate an airman's nose, forehead or lips. A pedicle grew healthy skin between the two points of connection, often the facial area to a shoulder, these often restricting the patient's head movements until they were harvested for grafting. Taylor underwent eight operations to reconstruct his facial injuries. He was enrolled as a member of the Guinea Pig Club and became a stalwart member, supporting the club for the rest of his life. That support also existed to the Goldfish Club, exemplified by the fact that he voluntarily served as membership secretary for twenty years, only standing down in 1991. Affectionately known as 'Tubby Taylor' by his friends, Dennis Taylor died on 3 June 1995. He had served both clubs with distinction and great pride.

*Chapter 24*

# Pilot Officer William Batson DFM – Caterpillar Club, Captured

William Thomas Batson was of Irish decent, born in County Cork on 29 July 1920. During the Second World War, Ireland was a neutral country and its population joined the ranks of such countries as Switzerland, Sweden, Spain, and Portugal. Ireland's small size and its proximity to Great Britain made non-alliance appealing for several reasons, but primarily it was due to the country's history of British rule, which made neutrality a natural extension of what was and is a strongly held Irish identity. Ireland sought to forge its own foreign policy in the world of warring powers, and that made neutrality the strongest political option.

However, neutrality did not stop Ireland's people from volunteering in the British forces should they wish. William Batson was among the many who travelled to Britain and volunteered to fight for king and country, despite the fact it was not actually his country he was fighting for. The Irish government used wartime censorship to conceal Irish enlistments into the British forces. Newspapers did not publish any acknowledgement of their service, injury or deaths. An additional fact, and one possibly difficult to understand, is that the republic of Eire refused to recognise her veterans of the Second World War until 1995.

The account of Batson's war commences with this recommendation for recognition of his operational duty published on 11 June 1943:

> This non-commissioned officer Sergeant W.T. Batson 1051869 was posted to 50 Squadron with effect from 1 January 1942, and has carried out thirty-four sorties in one hundred and ninety-eight hours flying. He carried out his tour as air bomber having been trained on the squadron before air bombers became an aircrew category and did very well. He bought back many excellent photographs and at all times showed great determination. Many of his sorties were against Germany's most heavily fortified cities and on 17 October 1942, took part in the successful Le Creusot daylight raid. For his courage, determination and readiness to fly on operations on every occasion, I consider he is worthy of the non-immediate award of the Distinguished Flying Medal. 26 April 1943.

The day following the official publication of the medal being awarded, Sergeant Batson expressed the wish to continue flying, despite being entitled to be rested having complete a full tour of operations. His details appeared on the operational order to fly a heavy bomber to Germany's Ruhr that evening. His pilot, Flight Lieutenant Stone, and his crew realised that the operation to Bochum was likely to be met by ferocious anti-aircraft defences. Among all the 50 Squadron men that sat at the briefing, three entire crews would never return. Twenty-one crew lockers would be stripped and made ready for other replacement aircrew. The most sobering thought is that across all of the heavy bomber squadrons that flew to Bochum, there would be a total of nearly 170 lockers laying vacant on the morning of 13 June 1943.

Bochum is in the Ruhr area of north-western Germany where many heavy industries were situated, all reliant on energy from the available coalfield. The industrial Ruhr region had a concentration of industries producing raw materials and finished components essential for military equipment. It became a major target from 1942 onwards, coming under increasingly heavy attack from the air by Bomber Command. Sergeant Batson and his crew were allocated Lancaster ED828 for the Bochum operation. The squadron records confirmed that sixteen Lancasters departed Skellingthorpe airfield that evening. A few hours later, Lancasters ED828, ED429 and ED472 had the following individual entries typed after their departure records: 'No messages or signals were received from the aircraft which failed to return and must be presumed lost due to enemy action.' Batson was one of the men on board Lancaster ED828.

On 13 June 1943, a letter was typed to his father. The letter reported him missing and added that his son had carried out one operational trip on his second tour of operations and could be relied upon as a very efficient air bomber. It added that his son was keen on flying and his pleasant personality had made him many friends on the squadron. Mr Batson in Cobh, County Cork, Eire, had received the letter promptly. It was followed by a more formal letter from the Air Ministry Casualty Branch dated 28 June 1943.

In Ireland and upon the Cork shores the reality of war had been present for the Batson family. At least nineteen Luftwaffe airmen had landed, or their bodies had been washed up on, the Cork coast. In many cases their aircraft were damaged from combat and the crews decided to head for neutral Ireland, knowing they would be interned as opposed to being held as prisoners of war in Britain.

On 21 August 1943, Batson's father received an additional letter from 50 Squadron advising it had received information from the Air Ministry that the International Red Cross had been made aware that three members of his son's crew had been killed. The letter added that hope existed that the fate of the remainder of the crew would be a happier one. Batson's father was provided with additional information concerning his son gallantry medal:

The award was a very deserving one, and it must make you feel proud of the part your son has played towards victory and the triumph of decency over barbarism. Your son, and thousands of others like him have earned the respect and admiration of a grateful world, and for what they have done will never be forgotten.

There is a first-hand account written by Batson of the events that took place within Lancaster ED828 on 12 June 1943. This information was published after the war by Midleton College, Co. Cork, titled 'Descent by Parachute':

I remember when first I started operational flying in 1941, a rather grim jest was in use in the parachute packing centre. When signing for your chute before a trip the WAAF packer would smilingly say 'If it doesn't open, just return it and we will issue a new one free.' This was always taken well, because no flier ever believed the time would come when he would be forced to use his parachute. Such calamities only befall the other fellow.

For two years after that I was lucky enough to return safely from each operational trip without having to resort to my parachute. However, in June 1943, whilst returning from a night bombing mission, we had an exchange of words with an enemy night fighter, who suddenly appeared from nowhere, to give us the Nazi salute complete with cannon and machine gun fire. Unfortunately, we collected his present right in our gas tanks and control system and within a minute our aircraft was a mass of flames, plunging to earth, completely out of control. Our skipper, after doing all in his power to put the fire out and get his plane back on a level keel, gave the order to bale out. On receipt of this order,

I clipped my chute on and about thirty seconds later was blown clear of the aircraft by a terrific explosion caused by the gas tanks going sky high.

The next thing I remember with any clarity was floating earthwards with my parachute open. To this day I cannot remember pulling the rip cord but I must have done so subconsciously else you would never be reading this article. The descent itself was quite tame, there was little or no sensation of falling, in fact one got the impression of being suspended in space. I nearly got violently ill at one period, due to the swinging of the parachute, this induced the most unpleasant nausea, very similar to sea sickness, but is easily rectified by spilling air out of the chute. The immediate effect is to make your rate of descent momentarily more rapid, thus stopping the swing.

Many of you will perhaps wonder what one thinks about on occasions such as this. I can assure you I thought about everything it is possible to think about, relations, friends, things I had done or hoped to do, but the predominant thought which superimposed itself on all the rest, was to get down to earth safely and in one piece. This my parachute eventually accomplished for me after about ten minutes floating, and I landed with one hell of a bump, bruised and breathless in the centre of a cornfield.

My adventures from then do not enter into the scope of this article, and so dear reader, I take leave of you, trusting that Descent by Parachute has not bored you unduly. It certainly did not bore me.

Pilot Officer Batson had landed on Dutch soil. He was then fortunate to be befriended by members of the Fiat Libertas line. The group had also located and befriended Flying Officer Glenn, the only other survivor from Lancaster ED828. He was the crew's navigator, who had also experienced a lucky escape by parachute. Fiat Libertas, the Latin translation meaning 'freedom may come', assisted evading Allied airmen into Brussels. This line was under the command of Jan Vanhee and the main courier of evaders into Brussels at that time was a man called Karst Smit.

Smit had been among the thousands of Dutch soldiers at Dunkirk trying to get to England. He was boarded on a French merchant ship that was bombed and strafed. The badly damaged ship was beached with little hope of reaching England. Karst made for the Netherlands, where he became actively engaged in helping Dutch Jews and had been appointed as a Marechaussee at Baarle-Nassau in March 1943. This was effectively the Royal Dutch Military Police, and his enrolment meant he could carry a gun and be out after curfew. Hitler had appointed an Austrian, Arthur Seyss-Inquart, as High Commissioner for the Netherlands and on the recommendation of Heinrich Himmler, another Austrian, Hanns Albin Rauter commanded all SS troops in the Netherlands.

Smit had enabled an estimated thirty Dutch and more than forty Allied airmen to reach Brussels. Records in the National Archives reveal that he assisted a total of fifty-five Allied aircrew to escape, in addition to his other resistance work. An agreement existed for the escapers to move from Fiat Liberta to the leader of the Belgian organisation Bravery. A guide would deliver the airmen escapers directly to an apartment, the home of Mrs Elise Chabot and her daughter Elise Ambach. Several escaping airmen were in hiding in Brussels during early July 1943. Yvon Michiels from the Comet escape line moved the location of Pilot Officer Batson and Pilot Officer Glenn in company with Sergeant Gordon-Powell, who had been shot down on 28 June 1943. Tragically, the Fiat Libertas line had been penetrated by a Belgian traitor called Prosper Dezitter. It was he who betrayed Batson to the Germans in Paris on 18 July 1943.

The evading men had fallen into the control of Dezitter, who from the start of the occupation, with his mistress and later with a man called Charles Jamart, managed to infiltrate many of the groups who were helping Allied soldiers and airmen. The Fiat Libertas escape line had been totally compromised towards the end of August 1943.

The airmen would normally be guided by Ernest van Moorleghem from the Chabot apartment across central Brussels to the fish market of Prosper Spilliaert, at 167 Avenue de la Reine in the Brussels commune of Schaerbeek. This route came to an end after one of the main Dutch contacts was arrested on 15 November 1943. This arrest heralded other arrests by the Feldpolizei, the secret military police, from the counter-intelligence service of Antwerp. Charlotte Ambach, Elise Chabot, and Ernest van Moorleghem were swept up in the arrests and later tried by a German military tribunal on 2 June 1944. They were found guilty, imprisoned and sentenced to death. Van Moorleghem and the guide Willem Schmidt were executed swiftly. Karst Smit avoided arrest by hiding in a Protestant church in the Hague and lived under cover in the city from November 1943 to January 1944.

In July and August 1943 Dezitter was running a safe house and a fake escape line in Brussels. He posed as a king's messenger as well as an English or Canadian airman and used numerous false names and alternate identities. Later in the war he pretended to be a British officer called Captain Jackson, leading numerous airmen to Gestapo traps in Brussels and Paris. Dezitter developed connections to genuine escape organisations in Holland and other parts of Belgium. He also cultivated priests and other religious officials who he knew evaders would turn to. The priests, believing Dezitter to be genuine, would contact him if they knew of an evader in hiding. Escaping airmen would be met at a Brussels station by large black American cars marked with Swiss Embassy signs driven by Dezitter or his mistress, who described herself as the captain's secretary.

Dezitter, who had lived in Canada, spoke excellent English. More than seventy escaping airmen were led to Gestapo traps from safe houses in Brussels and many Belgian helpers and agents were also betrayed. After the war, Dezitter and Dings were arrested in Würzburg, Germany, while being hidden by a German resistance movement. They were brought back to Brussels, tried and found guilty. Prosper Dezitter was executed on 17 September 1948.

Returning to Batson, having been arrested, he and the others were taken directly to Fresnes Prison in Paris. Cells were kept available for the regular arrests through Dezitter's successful captures. Batson was interrogated by the Gestapo and held in the jail until the end of August 1943. Some interrogations were heavy handed as the evading airmen were inevitably wearing civilian clothing, which was an opportunity to threaten them as being suspected of being spies as opposed to treating them as prisoners of war. National Archive records confirm that a transit from Paris to Frankfurt took place, where a second interrogation was held at the main Luftwaffe interrogation centre or Dulag Luft, of which there were several across Germany and the occupied territories.

Eventually transport took Batson to the officer camp Stalag Luft III, where he arrived on 2 September 1943. There was some comfort in the fact that his navigator from Northern Ireland who had travelled through Holland, Belgium and France with him was still with him as they entered the camp. In Batson's room was a Canadian, Vernon White, from 427 Squadron. Both had similar stories, having been shot down and parachuted to safety into Holland. However, a swifter arrest came for the Canadian, who had been transported to the Dulag Luft and then to Stalag Luft III, arriving at Sagan railway station in the early morning of 8 July. The transported prisoners entered the administrative centre for the three Sagan compounds: East, Centre and North. There were batches of men constantly arriving at the camp, the majority directly from the Luftwaffe interrogation camp.

Each individual was photographed and fingerprinted, with those details placed on to camp forms and a metal prisoner of war identity tag issued.

Unknown to Batson, he had entered a camp that contained ardent escapers and the now famous Wooden Horse escape tunnel had commenced from the East compound, which was next to his. Separated by barbed wire and a wooden barrier, nothing indicated that the escape was under way. Concealing two tunnel diggers inside a vaulting horse, a tunnel was constructed in broad daylight. Day after day men performed their gymnastic routines while the diggers below were busily filling bags with sand. Later in the day the horse with the tunnel diggers and the sand inside would be carried away. The escape plan continued for months and reached fruition with a successful escape in late October 1943. The three escapees made it to Sweden via the Baltic ports and then to England.

In January 1944, there was a significant movement of prisoners to an adjacent camp called Belaria, just 3 miles away. It was a new camp under control of the authorities at Sagan. Batson was among the men transferred there. This move disrupted an escape plan from the North compound. The Great Escape tunnelling was under way and several men involved in the plan were unexpectedly moved to Belaria.

Batson became aware of the Caterpillar Club and from the prison camp he wrote to Irvins at their factory in Letchworth, reporting his emergency escape and that his life had been saved by the staff who had manufactured his parachute. The German censors accepted the letter and entered it into the postal system. Irvins replied on 8 March 1944, addressing the letter to Gefangenennummer 2255 M_ Stammlager Luft III Deutschland. It contained his club membership card and advised that his Caterpillar pin would be supplied as soon as they were able to do so.

On 24 March 1944, frantic German activity disclosed that something significant had occurred at Sagan. The guards at Belaria spoke openly of a tunnel having been found and that prisoners were missing. Eventually news came that seventy-six prisoners had escaped but seventy-three had been caught. However, fifty of those men had been shot escaping. In truth they had been executed under orders of the German high command. Three escapers made home runs back to England.

Around mid-January 1945, the Russians broke through at several points on the Eastern Front. The senior Allied officers were warned by the German commandant that the Stalag Luft III camps would be evacuated and the prisoners were to be ready to leave at a few hours' notice. Belaria was not evacuated until late January, and with snow falling the column of prisoners poured through the main gate leading to the road to Sagan. Batson carried as many Red Cross food provisions as possible, arriving at the town of Sagan and within sight of Stalag Luft III. The column headed into the countryside, it was bitterly cold and the snow and icy winds created terrible conditions. They walked day after day until they reached a railway siding with a row of cattle trucks. Crammed into the trucks, the train arrived at the town of Luckenwalde, about 30 miles south of Berlin. Once again Batson passed through barbed wire gates, this time into Stalag IIIA. The camp population was growing every day as prisoners from other evacuated camps arrived. The conditions were deplorable and food was scarce. The enormous numbers of men in Luckenwalde created huge demands and conditions worsened almost daily.

On the afternoon of 21 April, without explanation, the sentry towers were vacated by the guards and they left the camp unguarded. Liberation by Russian forces was just a few hours away. Batson took it upon himself to search the administration offices to locate his Stalag Luft personal file. He kept the documents for the remainder of his life and the photograph of himself looking gaunt and thin from the deprivations experienced in the Paris jail became a lifelong reminder of his time as a prisoner of war.

Batson presented his Stalag Luft personal file to the IS9 intelligence officer during his debriefing. The card still bears the authority stamp from that unit. The prisoner of war questionnaire document composed by the intelligence officer was signed by Batson on 22 May 1945. That document now features in the National Archives and was accessed for reference.

*Chapter 25*

# Sergeant Cecil Room – Goldfish Club, Adrift for Three Days, Rescued by the Luftwaffe

Cecil Room was born on 15 February 1920 and lived in Witney, Oxfordshire. After school he initially gained employment as a sorting clerk and telegraphist. Not long after his twentieth birthday, he enlisted in the RAF, volunteering for flying duties. The training and aircrew assessment process saw Room selected for navigator duties. His academic ability had prepared him well for the tasks required in aerial navigation. His ambition to fly had been foremost in his mind and it was realised by him being posted to fly in the Bristol Beaufighter at the North Coates Strike Wing in Coastal Command in 1942.

Anti-shipping sorties always carried the jeopardy of survival should anything go wrong with the aircraft or if it sustained battle damage in a low-level attack. Inhospitable sea conditions and the vast expanses of water covered stacked the odds of survival against any crew who ditched. The strike wing had three Beaufighter squadrons: 254, primarily equipped with torpedoes; 236, which deployed rocket-fired bombs; and 143 Squadron, which specialised in 20mm nose cannon and wing guns. These three squadrons formed a formidable trio of combined firepower, capable of deployment in a melee of acrobatic flying at low height.

Sergeant Cecil Room was posted to 143 Squadron with Warrant Officer Victor Bain as his pilot. They became fully operational towards the end of 1942. In November they flew five operational sorties along the Dutch coastline, hunting for shipping targets, often covering miles of open water without success. The reality of flying such a powerful aircraft like the Beaufighter struck the pair on 7 December when their aircraft, T3446, swung critically on taking off at North Coates. They struck a parked Lysander and a car but suffered no injuries. No doubt, a rather traumatic set of events that necessitated an explanation by Warrant Officer Bain.

The fuselage of the Beaufighter was restricted in width. The observer/radar operator sat to the rear of the pilot and above his head was a small Perspex bubble canopy. Both crew members had their own hatch in the floor of the aircraft, with the front one behind the pilot's seat. As there was no room to climb around the seat, the back collapsed to allow the pilot to escape in an emergency. The pilot could operate a lever that remotely released the hatch. He would then grasp two steel overhead tubes and lift himself out of his seat, swing his legs over the open hatchway, then let go to drop through. Evacuating the aircraft was easier for the navigator as the rear hatch was in front of his position and unobstructed.

Six further sorties were flown by the pair before the anti-shipping wing of squadrons pooled together on 18 April 1943 for the first full wing attack. By coincidence, it was Hitler's fifty-fourth birthday. The target was a moderately large and well-defended convoy off the Hook of Holland. No. 254 Squadron was to target the merchant vessels with nine aircraft carrying torpedoes. Nos 143 and 236 Squadrons, with six aircraft each, were ordered to engage the enemy anti-aircraft escort vessels. All twenty-one Beaufighters took off and closed into rough formation before dropping down to sea level as they made for the target area. The navigators closed the aircrafts' armoured doors, which effectively divided the cockpit and protected the pilot from ordnance fired from the rear.

Flying above the strike wing aircraft, a fighter escort protected them from any surprise attack. The attacking aircraft sighted the enemy convoy ahead of them off Den Helder. It was an imposing sight of eight merchant ships with large, tethered balloons to deter attacking aircraft, eight heavily armed escorts, four minesweepers and four flak ships. The Beaufighters attacked the convoy in unison. Sergeant Room and Warrant Officer Bain, having gained height to select their target, attacked from 1,500ft, while below at just 150ft the torpedo-carrying aircraft selected their targets. Within four minutes, the ferocious attack had finished and the largest ship, the *Hoegh Carrier*, which was nearly 400ft long, had exploded with debris rising hundreds of feet into the air. The huge hold of coal was destined to sink and would deprive Germany of a valuable commodity of war. Other targets were damaged and, incredibly, only two Beaufighters suffered damage. The attack was regarded as a significant success.

The dangers for Beaufighter crews are typified by the account of events that took place on 1 May 1943. Thirty-one aircraft from the strike wing participated in an operation off the Norwegian coast. One 143 Squadron Beaufighter, JL945, flew back to base with the observer dead in his seat behind his pilot. The pilot, Flight Sergeant Wilson Ceybird, had been intercepted and fought off two enemy aircraft with great daring. Ceybird's observer was killed during the action and although deprived of navigational assistance, he was able to fly the Beaufighter more than 300 miles over the sea to reach England. Flight Sergeant Jack Baker's body was extracted from the aircraft and was later laid to rest in Blackburn Cemetery. Baker and Cecil Room had sat in the same operational briefing that day when the target, the German light cruiser *Nürnberg* escorted by four destroyers, was disclosed. The targets were out of range of fighter protection, which would leave the Beaufighters unprotected. Thirty-one aircraft from the strike wing squadrons set off to hunt down the *Nürnberg*. Flying along the coast of Norway the Luftwaffe fighters found the strike wing and immediately attacked in strength. The Beaufighters were highly vulnerable as predicted. The pilots jettisoned their torpedoes and bombs as they tried desperately to fight for survival. Two 254 Squadron aircraft were immediately shot down and two 143 Squadron anti-flak Beaufighters likewise dropped into the sea below them. Ceybird narrowly escaped a similar fate but at 2130 hours Beaufighter JL945, flown by Bains and Room, also crashed into the sea. What followed was a remarkable story of survival adrift in a dinghy.

Room created a transcript shortly before his death in 2004 that presents his story of survival in detail and reveals the events that saw him becoming a member of the Goldfish Club. It expanded thereafter with a detailed account of life as a prisoner of war, an attempted escape and the forced march endured to move prisoners in the harshest conditions through central Germany. It is remarkable that this account was preserved. Extracts from the transcript that follow have been reproduced with the permission of Cecil's son, David:

> It was a sunny Sunday afternoon in May 1943 at RAF North Coates. The officers were playing the NCOs in a rugby match and I had a date in Grimsby to look forward to. All was well with the world when the Tannoy sounded summoning all aircrew to the operations room. It must have been one of the most colourful briefings ever held with those in their normal blue battledress outnumbered by the players in rugby shirts.
>
> The station commander reported that the target for the Strike Wing of Beaufighters from 143, 256 and 254 squadrons was the German cruiser 'Nuremberg' with an escort of 4 destroyers which was reported to have left Bergen in Norway and was steaming south. This was a formidable target and there were plenty of white faces as we all left the briefing to change and have a meal. I kept my rugby kit on underneath my battledress, white sweater and flying boots. We had a huge breakfast and after another detailed briefing we headed out to our aircraft. We were scheduled to return to Wick

in Scotland as our range was insufficient to get us back to North Coates.

We took off at 7.30 p.m. and as we passed over the fence at the end of the runway, we got plenty of waves from half the population of the village. The roar of 35 Beaufighters running up was sufficient for them to down tools and run down the road to see us off. We formed up over Spurn Head with the torpedo Beaus in the front and the fighter bombers on the flanks and across the rear. All the aircraft were fully armed with 4 cannon, eight machine guns and two 250 lb bombs. Ten of them carried torpedoes.

We crossed the North Sea at 100 feet to avoid radar detection. Our destination was Kristiansand, which was the furthest point the ships could have reached if they had continued to steam south. The object was to catch the ships on the beam giving the torpedo aircraft the full length of the ships as their target. There was no sign of them at Kristiansand so we headed round the coast to Stavanger, where we spotted the convoy at anchor about a mile outside the port.

Their position prevented a beam attack due to the mountains behind the port. As soon as we were spotted, they opened fire and at 100 feet it was terrifying sight. A withering wall of fire met us and it seemed impossible for any aircraft to go through it and come out the other side intact. We were committed to the attack and we blazed through with all guns firing and dropped our bombs. Six planes were shot down immediately over the target. By some miracle we passed over the convoy unharmed but our troubles were by no means over. We were staggered to see about 20 Messerschmitt and Focke-Wulf fighters coming at us from the east. Some of the leading Beaufighters having completed their attack were hotfooting it back to Wick and it was those of us left at the rear of the formation who took the full brunt of the attack from the fighters. We too headed for Wick but were followed by three Messerschmitts. We had no rear firing armament so we were in serious trouble. No matter which way we turned they stuck with us. A hail of cannon fire ripped into our engines and within seconds we were reduced to a very heavy glider. My pilot Vic yelled the ominous word 'ditching'. We were about 40 miles from the coast when we struck the water hard.

At 10 tons, a Beaufighter wasn't designed to float for very long and we had less than a minute to get out. We soon found out that practising ditching on dry land was far removed from the real thing. The heavy and cumbersome survival pack was stowed behind my navigator's seat but it had been smashed in the attack and twisted metal prevented me from extricating it so it had to be abandoned. Vic and I climbed out through the cupola on the roof and down onto the wing. The dinghy had been released automatically and was sitting on the water waiting for us. Vic had cut his leg and head in the rush to get out and in spite of being firmly strapped in I had lost six teeth although I hadn't realised it at the time.

We cut the rope attaching the dinghy to the aircraft and paddled away furiously to avoid being sucked under when the Beau sank, which she did after about a minute. When the bubbles and foam had subsided, the silence was unbearable. I had never felt as lonely in my whole life as I did at that moment. I looked at my watch and it had only been seven minutes from when we had first sighted the convoy.

We took stock of our assets and as the survival kit had been lost that job didn't take very long. We had forty cigarettes, a box of matches and 12 Horlicks tablets. The outlook was to say the least grim. Vic was groggy from the bang to his head and his leg was bleeding. We could see the mountains behind Stavanger and decided to try to keep the dinghy in the same position we had been in when we ditched. The sea was choppy and after an hour we were both soaked to the skin. We were afraid to go to sleep but we eventually dozed off for a couple of hours. When we woke the dinghy was half full of water, which meant a long session of baling out.

That first night was the longest of my life. We slept fitfully and woke at dawn to find the sea had calmed down but we were surrounded by a thick blanket of fog. We had a Horlicks tablet for breakfast and started to think about the effect of the dreaded telegrams which would by now have been dispatched to Vic's wife and my parents. All it would say was 'missing in action'.

Monday passed very slowly. The sea became choppy again but the little dinghy rode it well. We blessed the chap who had designed it. Our legs, feet and hands were frozen and the effects of exposure were creeping up on us quickly. We reckoned another day would see us finished but we tried to keep up our hopes.

We spent another terrible night, hardly sleeping at all. We woke totally drained and still very wet. Mercifully the sun was shining and the sea was flat calm. We had another Horlicks tablet and a smoke and started to feel a little better. Our clothes had become very heavy with the salt water and we were developing sores where the rough cloth had chafed on our skin. The day dragged on and by nightfall our spirits had sunk again. We were desperately thirsty and all we had eaten since breakfast on Sunday were four Horlicks tablets each.

We slept soundly and woke at 8 a.m. on Wednesday morning to the sound of aircraft engines. We stood up (not a good idea in a dinghy) and blew our whistles as loudly as we could, God knows why because no one could hear us. The aircraft came nearer until at last we could see it. I got out the pad of fluorescent dye and threw it in the water and within seconds we were surrounded by a deep yellow stain. I got the two flares from the pack on the side of the dinghy and released the ring pulls, which with my frozen weak fingers was easier said than done. Red and green flares shot up into the sky and after an agonizing wait the aircraft turned towards us and we raised a pitiful cheer. The plane passed over us and a silver object came hurtling towards us. It looked like a bomb! It hit the sea about ten yards away and we were quickly enveloped in a thick cloud of red smoke. By the time it had dispersed the plane, a Heinkel 159 [in fact a He 59], was almost on top of us. A hatch opened and our rescue had begun. Our prayers had been answered.

A ladder was lowered but we were both so weak we couldn't climb up it. Two of the crew came down and dragged us up with boat hooks. We must have looked a mess, wet and covered in red dust. The Germans stripped us of all our clothing and they were somewhat bemused to see that I was wearing my blue and white rugby kit underneath my battledress. They poured a complete bottle of schnapps over each of us and began to rub us down with towels which felt like sandpaper. They knew what they were doing and we soon began to feel the circulation returning to our frozen limbs. They dressed us in tracksuits with the Luftwaffe Eagle and Swastika on the front and tended to Vic's cuts and bruises as best they could. The crew had said nothing until one of them blurted out the familiar 'for you der var is over'. I would have thought that was pretty bloody obvious.

We landed at the seaplane base in Sola near Stavanger and on leaving the aircraft we were each held up by two hefty Germans to have our photographs taken. An ambulance took us to the base hospital, where we were both checked over and treated with great kindness and compassion. That was followed by a huge meal of meat and vegetable soup followed by cake and as much coffee as we could drink. They even took our black leather flying boots away, which came back dried and polished. We were put to bed and we slept soundly for twelve hours.

We woke refreshed and had a huge breakfast. We were recovering rapidly but Vic was still suffering with his leg. After breakfast, a Luftwaffe officer interviewed us. A prisoner was only required to give name, rank and serial number so the captain didn't get very far with either of us. I did however give my home address and as a result my name was read out on German radio by the wretched Lord Haw Haw. The news was picked up in England and my mum and dad were told that I was a PoW but to be cautious as similar broadcasts had been made using information obtained from the identity tags of airmen killed in action.

I was then moved to a detention block and Vic remained in hospital for treatment to his leg. In the afternoon I was sitting on my bed feeling pretty miserable as the realisation that I had lost my freedom was sinking in fast. I was however alive and well and I had a lot to be thankful for because as I found out much later, we were the only two survivors from the 14 crew members shot down during the attack.

I was lost in my thoughts when the door opened and the guard introduced me to two Luftwaffe officers in immaculate uniforms. I could tell by their decorations that they were obviously very experienced pilots. They told me in perfect English that they were two of the three pilots who had shot us down and that they were very pleased to see that we had survived. They had radioed their base with our position and this explained how the seaplane had managed to locate us but it didn't shed much light on why it had taken so long. Anyway, I thanked them for their help. They then asked me if I would like to go for a ride in the sunshine and I soon found myself sitting in the sidecar of a BMW motorcycle. They drove me all round the airfield and I got a good look at just about every type of plane the Luftwaffe had.

From the airfield they took me to the officers' mess and I had a feeling that this was where the interrogation would begin. I was wrong. They bought me a plate of sandwiches and a very large bottle of beer which we shared. They asked me where I came from and I saw no harm in telling them that I was from Witney in Oxfordshire. One of them looked very surprised and told me that he had learned to fly at Witney civil airfield. He rattled off the names of most of the well-known pubs in the area, the brewery and I suspected that he was well acquainted with several members of the fairer sex as he was a strikingly handsome chap. I was able to check out his story when I returned to England in 1945. After a very pleasant two hours I was taken back to the far less salubrious surroundings of my cell.

The next morning, we were moved to the prison in Stavanger, where we spent a couple of days. We had all the food we wanted and the governor even arranged for us to have a haircut. Generally, our treatment at the hands of the Germans in Norway had been excellent and we certainly had no cause for complaint. Eventually we were taken to Stavanger station for the trip to Oslo. The platform was crowded with German sailors and our two guards immediately turned us around and took us back to the prison, where the governor explained that the sailors were from the convoy we had attacked. All 5 ships had been seriously damaged and the casualties had been heavy. We would not have been at all popular on that train. We tried again the following morning and this time Vic, myself and the two guards had a carriage to ourselves.

Three days later we were walking around the exercise yard of Oslo prison accompanied by a middle-aged guard with a rifle. He didn't quite look the part as he had a kindly face and he was smoking an old briar pipe. We had noticed a group of German workmen who were repairing the prison wall which had ladders up against it. After a few minutes the workmen disappeared for a coffee break. Our guard retreated behind a buttress in the wall to light his pipe and at that second we saw our chance and haired up the ladder and over the wall, which was about eight feet high. Suddenly there we were in the main street surrounded by people. We ran, or rather I ran and Vic limped down the street and into what appeared to be a deserted timber yard. We hid behind a pile of wood under a tarpaulin to get our breath back.

We had to venture out sometime and later in darkness we crept out into the street with not too many ideas about what to do or where to go. We hadn't walked far when we felt something in our backs and up went our hands in surrender but the voices we heard were unmistakably Norwegian. The two men bundled us into the back of a car and covered us with a couple of blankets. After a short journey lasting about ten minutes we pulled up outside a house with a drive in front of it. We got out and went inside, where a lady and her daughter welcomed us and assured us that we were in safe hands. Our two rescuers remained out of sight. Our training back in England had taught us that what we hadn't seen or heard would ensure that we could give nothing away if we were recaptured.

For the next three days we lived in the attic and did exactly what we were told by the lady of the house. She told us that as soon as we had a dark night to help us we would be taken to the Swedish/Norwegian border. Sure enough, after three days our two friends turned up and we were put in the car and covered with the blankets again. We drove off into the night and after an hour or so we pulled up in a forest. We were told to walk three hundred yards where we would find a barbed wire fence. We thanked them profusely and said we were aware of the risks they were taking. They wished us luck and we were gone. We trudged through the pine forest and suddenly there was a terrifying scream. A light came on and for a few minutes there was mayhem. German voices were all around us and when they lit a storm lantern, we saw what had happened. Vic had walked into the side of a bell tent in which six border guards were sleeping. He had stepped on the head of one of the soldiers who had a boot mark on his face. For this Vic received a swingeing blow to the side of his head from a rifle butt. They tied us both to a tree, where we stayed for several hours until dawn broke. At first light the sergeant and his merry men untied us and walked us the few yards to the Swedish border. So near yet so far. We were both close to tears. We learned later that guards were placed every ten miles along the border and for Vic to step on one was bad luck to say the least.

We were marched back through the forest, placed in a truck and taken to Fornebu airport and placed in cells reserved for illegal immigrants and the like. On the second or third morning the rain was pouring down and the guard asked me if I would like some exercise. Sitting in a cell with nothing to do or read was pretty boring so I gratefully accepted his offer. He brought me a Luftwaffe greatcoat, which was far too big for me and which reached down to my ankles. I plodded round the circuit which was a roundabout outside the main airport building. Vic had his exercise separately. In no time I was very wet and bedraggled but I was enjoying the fresh air. The rain eventually stopped and the sun broke through. I was suddenly conscious of a very large car alongside me and I jumped onto the grass. It was by far the largest car I had ever seen, an open-topped Mercedes. I froze in my boots when I looked in the back of the car and saw Field Marshal Hermann Goring, the deputy Fuhrer. With him was Vidkun Quisling, the puppet Prime Minister of Norway. Goring signalled the guard to come over and they were obviously discussing me. I learned later that Goring had thought I was a German airman who was being punished for some misdemeanour. When he found out that I was a British airman he stood up in the back of the car and raised his jewel-encrusted baton. He shouted 'murderer, luftgangster, terrorbomber' and a few other epithets I couldn't understand but I was getting the message. After his ranting he slumped back in his seat and drove off. So ended my brief one-sided interview with the deputy Fuhrer. Back in the cell block the young guard was elated at the fact that he had actually spoken to Goring but I am afraid I was unable to share his enthusiasm.

The next morning the guard told us we were going to Oslo and I guessed we were at last on our way south. Not so. We drove into the city and Vic and I finished up in a very large building near the Palace. Once inside it became very clear that we were in the Gestapo headquarters. We were terrified. We were ushered into a large plain room and seated at a bare table. We sat there in silence for about half an hour and eventually a tall ugly man came in dressed in a leather greatcoat and highly polished jackboots. He knew that we had been helped by the Resistance and he wanted to know who they were and where we had been taken for shelter. We couldn't tell him because we had never seen the men in the light and we hadn't a clue where they had taken us. Every time we said 'no' or 'we don't know' he hit us across the side of the head with a large black gauntlet which had a metal buckle on the back. One particularly savage blow sent me sprawling to the ground. This went on for at least an hour and we lost count of the times he hit us. We were both dazed and in considerable pain. At last, he gave up and stormed out of the room and to our surprise and immense relief we were taken back to the airport. Our young German guard, having been with us during the interrogation and seeing the state we were in, was very sympathetic.

The following morning the guards came into the cells with a couple of 'Mae Wests' – life jackets of a German pattern – and we were marched out to a Junkers 52 transport. We sat in the back handcuffed to two guards. I wondered what we were supposed to do in an emergency. We flew to Aarhus in Denmark for fuel and to pick up more passengers. We were taken to the airport restaurant for a meal and our young guard (who we both liked a lot) suggested that we should make the most of it as the food where we were going was not very good. That turned out to be the understatement of the year. We took his advice and filled a paper bag with cakes to eat on the plane. Our final destination was Templehof airport in Berlin. We were lodged in Spandau jail, which is where Rudolf Hess was to spend many years in isolation.

Spandau was a truly awful place, dark and foreboding. After two days we were walked to the railway station. Unfortunately for us, Berlin had just been well and truly flattened by British bombers and we encountered groups of very hostile and clearly homeless civilians brandishing large planks of wood. Our guards, who I reckon were as scared as we were, drew the bolts on their rifles and the mob backed off. We were both very relieved to get on the train and we were taken to Amsterdam and yet another grim prison where the food was simply ghastly.

After four days we were on the move again and ended up in Dulag Luft, the interrogation centre just outside Frankfurt. We were now well and truly 'in the bag' as imprisonment was euphemistically termed. We spent two weeks in the cells being grilled by interrogators who used various methods to try to get us to talk. Their favourite was to heat the cell with electric radiators to a temperature of well over 100 degrees. This lasted several hours until the heat became unbearable. If you stood up it was impossible to breathe and the metal of the bed frame became too hot to touch. The air near the floor was slightly cooler so I had to lay down close to the gap under the door to try to get a few gasps of cool air. They waited until I was barely conscious and then took me to a room where an officer demanded to know my squadron number, type of aircraft, details of the operation and the weapons we were carrying. We learned later that Vic and I were the first two prisoners to be captured from Strike Wing of Coastal Command, which had been causing havoc among shipping convoys and U Boat pens. This accounted for the depth of the questions and their technical nature.

The interrogation process went on for days but all he got was my name rank and serial number. After about two weeks he came into my cell one morning with a rather jaunty look on his face and he proceeded to tell me my squadron, station and aircraft type. The look of surprise on my face told him everything he needed to know. I can only guess that a letter or an envelope found on one of the bodies washed up on the shore at Stavanger had contained the information they wanted. Anything incriminating, such as letters and personal wallets, had to be left behind in named containers but I am sure that on occasions, not every pocket was emptied.

After that Vic and I were left alone and a few days later we were taken to the outer camp where we were put with a party of about 40 other prisoners, who told us we were about to be taken to the station and onto yet another prison. We were each given a Red Cross food parcel, a bar of chocolate and 50 cigarettes which was to last us during the very uncomfortable four-day trip in cattle trucks to Stalag Luft 1. We finally arrived at the small town of Barth up the Baltic coast. In many ways we were relieved to be 'settled' and with our comrades with whom we could exchange stories. Stalag Luft 1 was the most northerly of all the prison camps in Germany and a mere 65 miles across the Baltic from Sweden which we had so nearly reached.

Life as a prisoner of war continued until 6 February 1945, when news broke of the order to evacuate the camp and measures were put in place for what was to become a most enduring and arduous period of endless walking under guard westwards towards Germany before the eventual Nazi collapse.

Room was repatriated to England by aircraft, landing at Dunsfold airfield in Surrey. He was refitted for uniform at the Cosford reception centre before interview by the intelligence service. Prisoner of war debriefing processes conducted in the repatriation of men from the camps accumulated evidence of abuse and unnecessary force used while incarcerated. On 5 April 1945, Victor Bain signed an affidavit for the investigation into events at the Dulag Luft. In November 1945, Bain was additionally summonsed to give evidence to the court at College Road, Brighton, Sussex, upon the treatment he and Room had endured at the Dulag Luft. The evidence of fourteen days in solitary confinement and the intentional overheating of confined cells was presented at a war crimes trial that commenced against five defendants on 26 November 1945. Three defendants were subsequently found guilty and sentenced to imprisonment, while two men were found not guilty. The Dulag Luft, of which there were several across Germany and the occupied territories, had been a significant part of the Luftwaffen-Fuhrungsstab intelligence structure, which in 1944 employed more than sixty interrogation officers. The chief interrogation officer, Major Junge, had received a sentence of five years' imprisonment.

Room elected to remain in the RAF after the war. The Air Ministry introduced a new rank structure for non-commissioned men in 1947 and he was issued with the insignia of aircrew 1. This was a crown surmounting an eagle with three stars between encompassing split wreaths. It was a rather bulky badge of rank that was effectively the equivalent of a flight sergeant. Now serving as a navigator in 109 Squadron, the record books identify several training flights between February 1948 and July 1949 in which Room flew as a master bomber in Mosquitoes. In June 1949, at a commissioning board he was identified as suffering from an ear condition and was temporarily unfit to fly. The following year he received a commission into the regular RAF. Having risen through the commissioned ranks with an unblemished service, on 1 January 1961 he attained the rank of squadron leader. Room later served in Borneo, where the borders were being policed against northern incursions. That saw him awarded the 1962 General Service Medal, given for service in Borneo between 24 December 1962 and 11 August 1966.

It is worthy of thought that being shot down, ditching and survival in a rubber dinghy, followed by two entire years of hardship as a prisoner of war, was not deemed worthy of recognition by a medal of any description.

*Chapter 26*

# Sergeant John Lord – Caterpillar Club, Killed in Error as Prisoner of War

Born on 6 December 1918 in Burbage, Leicestershire, as a youth John Lord developed a passion for playing rugby. He represented Hinckley Rugby Football Club on a regular basis, and was employed at the Sketchley Dye Works, which dyed hosiery. The outbreak of war saw him volunteer immediately to join the RAF. After his training was completed in 1941, he was ready for operational duties. In April 1941, an Air Ministry decision was taken to form a heavy bomber squadron with a direct association to Canada. No. 405 'Vancouver' Squadron was formed, becoming the first Royal Canadian Air Force Squadron on active service. Sergeant John Lord was posted to squadron, which was based at Pocklington, East Yorkshire.

On 12 June 1941, the squadron took part in its first raid over Germany. Lord flew on the operation as part of a crew captained by Sergeant Thomas Dougall. Their aircraft, Wellington W5535, was flown to Bremen without incident and Lord made his first operational entry in his flying logbook. Red ink was used, denoting a night operation. Unbeknown to Sergeant Lord, he had participated in an operation that had dropped the heaviest tonnage of bombs thus far in the war, commencing a period of twenty consecutive nights of operations against the Ruhr, Rhineland and German ports.

The briefing for operations on the night of 2 August 1941 saw a large map illustrating the target of Berlin. The long trip to central Germany in a Wellington was never going to be an easy or uneventful occasion. Crews engaged with Bf 110 night fighters on this operation, and three nights later the crew flew to Karlsruhe in central Germany. It was another heavily defended target. Again, Bf 110 night fighters were active. Berlin appeared again on the Pocklington Operational Orders on 12 August, with nine Wellington crews involved. Five 405 Squadron aircraft were successful in bombing the area around Friedrichstrasse Station, including Lord's crew. Once again, this operation was notable by virtue of the fact that it recorded the largest tonnage of bombs dropped upon Berlin in the war so far. On their return to base Lord's aircraft brushed a treetop on the edge of the Yorkshire Wolds as they commenced their landing approach at Pocklington in the early hours of the morning. The aircraft suffered minor damage and it was later found that the altimeter had inadvertently been adjusted incorrectly. It was fortunate the accident did not have greater consequences. Kiel was the target on 19 August, quite possibly regarded as a softer target to attack but every operation was fraught with danger, especially in the Wellington.

On the night of 28 August 1941, 405 Squadron sent up eleven aircraft to bomb Duisburg. Lord's aircraft took off at just past midnight and while over the target area the aircraft was held in searchlights. It was holed by flak and one crew member sustained a leg injury from a flak splinter. The pilot was able to make a safe return to Pocklington, landing approximately six hours later, but this would have been a very unsettling experience for the crew. Flak splinters had the capability to kill or maim indiscriminately. Likewise, a flak splinter striking an engine, fuel or oil line inevitably meant potential disaster and a failure to return.

Hamburg beckoned on 15 September and Stettin on 19 September. These were primary targets and well defended. Wellington Z8344 was allocated to the crew for Stettin. The target was identified, and the wireless operator, Sergeant Clayden, signalled that the bombs had been dropped as the Wellington commenced to leave the target area.

Sergeants Dougall, Lord, Clayden, Emsley and Forman were by now a trusted and experienced crew with a dozen operations under their belts, and would no doubt be hoping for an uneventful return to base. Much of that responsibility fell on Lord's shoulders. The calculations and numerous influences of wind speeds and directions required him to be precisely accurate with the navigation and bearings. Wellington Z8344 was an aircraft that had served them well previously. Lord's flight routes were not prescriptive but he would try and avoid well-defended areas on any return routes. Bomber Command squadrons composed daily records of operations and on many occasions the statement 'failed to return' was typed against a crew who never made it home. Seventy-two aircraft were sent to Stettin by Bomber Command on 19 September, predominantly Wellingtons. Only one record book typed up the words 'failed to return' when Wellington Z8344 never arrived home, next to the names of Lord's crew. The intelligence officers who debriefed the returning crews discovered nothing about what had happened to the missing bomber.

What is known is that Lord parachuted out and landed safely after whatever it was that sealed the fate of Wellington Z8344. That evidence originates from the Caterpillar pin awarded to him by Irvin chutes sometime after his inevitable capture and during time spent as a prisoner of war. It was not an uncommon practice for airmen to write to Irvins from camps celebrating their survival by parachutes. In most cases the next of kin received the Caterpillar Club pins after issue for safe keeping. Another crewman that also escaped by parachute and had a long friendship with Lord behind the barbed wire was Sergeant Douglas Jobson Clayden. They were together at Stalag VIIIB, a large German prisoner of war camp near the small town of Lamsdorf. The camp was renumbered Stalag 344 at the end of 1943. Sergeant Clayden was PoW number 9669 and Sergeant Lord was number 9659.

Four years behind barbed wire would have taken its toll on those two men. Aware of the Russian advances on the Eastern Front in 1945, hopes would have been high of liberation. In April 1945, Sergeants Lord and Clayden were among many hundreds of prisoners of war, force-marched between prisoner of war camps and overnight transit shelter towards central Germany. Large columns of prisoners were on the move. One column reached the little village of Gresse, east of Hamburg, on 19 April 1945. The men were moving in a westerly direction towards the front line when they were sighted by an Allied aircraft. Not knowing the column of men were Allied prisoners of war, the aircraft attacked as the pilot assumed they were German troops moving towards the front lines. The column of prisoners was strafed by Allied fighters in what later became known as the Gresse incident. Among the many casualties were Sergeants Lord and Clayden. Clayden died on 19 April, followed by Lord on 22 April from injuries sustained. Both men were at that time technically warrant officers, having been promoted while in the prison camp, and both were still young men in their mid-twenties.

On 5 July 1945 an Air Ministry letter dropped through the door of Highview, Coventry Road, Burbage, Hinkley. Lord's father, Ernest, read the following:

> I am commanded by the Air Council to refer to the letter addressed to you on 21 May, and to express to you the great regret with which they learned that it has now been confirmed that your son, Warrant Officer John Lord, Royal Air Force, died on 22 April 1945, whilst a prisoner of war.
>
> Since the letter of 21 May was dispatched, information has been received from two other repatriated prisoners of war. One of whom, it is understood, has also passed it direct to you, that your son was admitted to Boizenburg Hospital Germany, after being wounded on 19 April, and that he died

of gangrene, following an operation. He was buried by the local minister, the service being attended by a number of fellow prisoners of war who were only lightly wounded.

The Air Council desires me to express their profound sympathy with you in your bereavement.

Having cross-referenced details from several operational record books, it appears that the unit responsible for the attack on the column of men at Gresse was 247 Squadron. Eight Typhoons from the squadron, led by Squadron Leader J. H. Bryant, RCAF, were sent on an armed reconnaissance to an area around Boizenburg and Bengerstorf, which is just east of Gresse. They reported attacking a column of transports and men, but after the initial attack, they identified the column as possible Allied prisoners of war and no further attacks were made. This information was extracted from the 247 Squadron operational record book from April 1945.

Post-war excerpts from a report dated 16 July 1947 by Flight Lieutenant C. W. Dufresne, No. 4 Missing Research Enquiries Service, Germany, to the Air Ministry:

> An investigation at Greese [Gresse] reveals that twenty-nine British (Army and Air Force) and one American were buried in the local cemetery. These victims had been P.O.W.s on the march and were shot up by British planes, just outside Greese on 19 April 1945. They were buried in a collective grave, without coffins. Some on the 19 April, and the rest on the 20 April.
>
> A copy of the list of those airmen buried there provided by Pastor Stube of Greese, who officiated at the burial. Although there are thirty British listed, in exhumation we found only twenty-nine British and one American. The numbers of this list which are ticked off in red are those which were identified

for certain, mostly by their Stalag tags. It was almost impossible to tell which service some of them belonged to, by the different pieces of clothing they were wearing.

Naturally the reports contain distressing detail and the efforts to identify the casualties were detailed but it had been two years since the incident took place. On 2 July 1947 the exhumation from the collective grave recorded body eight was that of Warrant Officer Clayden. He had been wearing an Army greatcoat, service dress tunic and white sweater. Sergeant chevrons and crown and wireless badge on right arm. Stalag tag 9669.

Your observations that it was almost impossible to tell which of the Services some of them belonged owing to the many different types of clothing worn would suggest that the above names should be subjective to collective registration together with those of the other Services whose bodies, unfortunately, could not be identified.

The Gresse casualty list included details of those who died of wounds sustained including their rank, service number, date of incident and squadron, with prisoner of war numbers including the date of death due to wounds if relevant. Clayden and Lord were on the list:

Sergeant Douglas J Clayden 901682 20.9.1941 Wellington Z8344 – 405 Squadron Pow Nr 9669. Sergeant John Lord 955266 20.9.1941 Wellington Z8344 – 405 Squadron Pow Nr 9659 (Dow 22.4.1945).

Both men along with the majority of victims from that tragedy are now buried in the Berlin War Cemetery. The Air Ministry advised Lord's father on 2 November 1948 that his son's bodily remains had been removed to the British Military Cemetery at Berlin Heerstrasse, grave seven, row N, plot eleven. The family paid for a personal inscription upon the headstone that identifies his grave, which reads: 'Worthy of everlasting remembrance rest in peace'. Douglas Clayden rests on the opposite side of the large cemetery. Both of these young men had experienced so much service together, both in the air and as prisoners of war.

The sadness in this account is that John Lord survived the traumatic leap into darkness falling by parachute to unknown circumstances. He endured years of impoverished existence behind barbed wire yet lost his life to a tragic accident caused by the RAF, which he had served so diligently.

The family kept the Caterpillar Club pin finely engraved with his name and, having applied for his medal entitlement, pinned it to the trio of medal ribbons that were awarded to him.

*Chapter 27*

# The Importance of the Written Word

Members of the flying services engaged on active duty were required to keep a personal record of the flights undertaken. Flying logbooks were issued to all pilots and aircrew personnel who flew as part of the RAF or the Commonwealth Air Forces during the Second World War. The young aspiring aviators who were handed the card-covered and simply bound books accepted that they were required to keep a detailed record of their progression during training and subsequent operational flying. Each book was regarded as the property of His Majesty's Government and was required to be maintained with an accurate and frequently scrutinised record of all flights undertaken in any service aircraft. The rear pages provided for a record to be maintained of every aircraft type flown and the engine type, while the adjacent page recorded the unit or squadron served and the dates of arrival and departure. If compiled, this page provides an accurate record of service throughout the years of training and flying. It was not, however, a compulsory requirement to complete so logbooks can frequently be found with partial entries. The prior pages of Link Trainer practices were, however, a requirement to be fulfilled. The Link Trainer was a safe, ground-based way to teach new pilots how to fly by instrumentation. A system of pumps, bellows and valves created a flight simulator that responded to the flying controls and gave an accurate reading to the instructors. Assessment stamps are often seen in the logbooks signed by the instructors and, thereafter multiple short training sessions are recorded in detail of each exercise undertaken throughout operational service.

Proficiency assessments were required to be completed annually, and additionally commanding officers or their deputies were tasked with inspecting and signing logbooks on a monthly basis. Form 414 recorded the summary of flying assessments on a posting or within a year of operational duty and were signed by a commanding officer. Logbooks were of utmost importance to the individual airman or pilot as they gave evidence of their qualifications and accumulative hours spent flying operationally, and in the case of Bomber Command the number of operational raids undertaken. The regularity of submission for inspection and endorsement meant that they were handled frequently, with the card covering all too often becoming exposed on the corners and the spines worn, telltale signs that the airman had been in service for some time. The books usually had the owner's name and service number written on the page edges in order that he could quickly locate his particular book in a large stack after assessment or monthly inspection. Promotion through the ranks was evidenced in the front pages, with many books commencing with the rank of aircraftsman and then with lines drawn through the lower ranks as they progressed towards a commission and subsequent officer status.

Pilot flying logbooks were larger in dimension than the observer and air gunner logbooks as they required more detail to be recorded. These books were identified by unique reference numbers of 'Form 1767' for observers and 'Form 414' for pilots. Other differentials existed within the basic format of these flying logbooks. Those issued in South Africa had a covering of red for observers and green for pilots, which made them instantly recognisable. Those issued in India were issued with a cream-coloured cloth covering and in the Far East it was not uncommon to see any type of logbook covered in leather binding, which was created to preserve the book's integrity. Men who flew longer periods of service frequently bound additional logbooks together.

Flying logbooks were not to be carried in the air. Those young men who failed to return from operations were initially regarded as missing in action, and their logbooks would be endorsed and dispatched to an Air Ministry central depository. In the summer of 1944, Air Ministry Order A795/43 was quoted when returning a log from France to England. The instructions for compliance stated that the package was to be enclosed in a sealed and weighted bag when carried by the Air Despatch Letter Service. It must be assumed this was standard procedure. Should any of these men survive and return to their squadron, the logbooks in those instances were always accessible. The logbooks returned from the depository became recognisable by a small registration sticker applied to the outside cover, showing the depository's unique registration number. In cases where pilots or aircrew were confirmed as killed in action or lost their lives during training accidents, their flying logbooks were frequently sent to their next of kin and a small, printed slip would often be included in the book, although, there appears to be little continuity to this matter for bereaved families, so it was possibly a situation influenced by individuals and certainly not by policy.

The vast majority of flying logbooks were recovered by the Air Ministry on completion of the recipient's service and subsequently placed into storage as official documents. The accumulation of logbooks was substantial and due to the fact that storage became a problem, the Air Ministry later let it become known that the books could be returned to the individuals that had compiled them. By 1959, in spite of announcements in the press, the vast majority of logbooks remained unclaimed. Placed on shelving, the collection of logbooks stretched for some 6,500ft. Additional flying logbooks from the Admiralty and War Office added to the storage concerns of the Air Ministry and the problem was placed before the 'Paper Committee'. Subsequently, the committee recommended the destruction of the stored logbooks, bar a few selected specimens. This decision induced further press announcements, and in addition the BBC broadcast that logbooks not claimed by 15 September 1960 would be destroyed.

Less than 100ft of shelving was reclaimed as a result of the announcements. The Air Ministry therefore still faced a significant storage problem. Following the advised deadline, the decision of the committee was put into effect. Historically important flying logbooks were selected from the remaining logbooks. These included examples of foreign nationals flying with the RAF, pilots with exceptional experience and members from distinguished squadrons, a selection restricted to no more than a 20ft run of space.

As a result the nation lost thousands upon thousands of flying logbooks, irreplaceable historical records that were simply destroyed. Those that were claimed or retained by the men who served in the air during the Second World War represent valuable time capsules of operational duty, without distortion of fact or misinterpretation. Bomber Command crews who had penned green ink entries recording daylight operations, and red ink entries for night operations. Coastal Command crews who spent endless hours hunting the German U-Boats that threatened to cut off food to the United Kingdom. Fighter Command pilots who endorsed their successes against the German Luftwaffe with symbols or written words during the 'Battle of Britain', a period of aviation history that is now forever respected as having been of utmost importance to the outcome of the war.

The destruction of these historical documents has denied to the generations that have followed access to the personal written records of those brave men who flew in the war. For this reason alone, those flying logbooks that survive are treasured and rare possessions. This book has been composed around many such books, written by young men who would never have expected such accolades to ever exist upon the entries they made. Those survivors of emergency parachute jumps often penned comic images of them dangling from a parachute in the respective page of the book. Likewise, a yellow doughnut – the term often used for a dinghy – was illustrated for the Goldfish Club members. Some also hold what was known as a 'Green Entry', an official recognition of an event that was worthy of note but which was not felt significant enough for progression to an official mention in dispatches. Likewise, a 'Red Entry' was an entry made whereby an event was worthy of mention for neglect or negligence, such as damaging an aircraft unnecessarily. Flying accidents or forced landings not attributable to enemy action required completion of form 765(C) in quintuplicate. This recorded all relevant information, including comment by the pilot, other crew members, and the relevant unit and station commanders. This information generated a mass of statistics published on a monthly basis. In mid-1943 it was summarised that more training was required to reduce the number of negligent occurrences. The Air Ministry Form 1180, known as an accident card, now represents a valuable document for aviation research.

Only in 1948 did the Air Council abolish the practice of recording adverse endorsements in flying logbooks. It added that existing endorsements were to be expunged, therefore the removal of these created torn pages or torn sections of a page. This practice has created conjecture as to what had been recorded in the relevant books, which appear vandalised to the uninitiated.

It is worth remembering that many accidents also took the lives of groundcrew working on airfields. Corporal Alfred Hills was an engineer mechanic at Aston Down, Gloucestershire, when a Typhoon being flown by Warrant Officer Thompson on a training flight crash-landed and slewed into a building. The high-speed incident spewed over 100 gallons of aviation fuel into the building. The pilot and two ground crew were killed and eighteen others were admitted to hospital. Later, Aircraftswoman Nicholson and one other flight mechanic died of their injuries. Corporal Hills suffered significant burn injuries and was transferred to the East Grinstead Hospital after he was selected by Archibald McIndoe for reconstructive surgery.

A total of twenty operations were undertaken by McIndoe. Hills later became his personal assistant driver and despite the requirement to have been a member of aircrew, the Guinea Pig Club, as a rare exception, elected him as a full member.

There is a disturbing endorsement that also appears in some logbooks: 'Withdrawn from aircrew duties'. A heavy bold stamp would be placed upon the last page of entries. The author has found this was applied in the cases where a member of aircrew was removed from flying duties and ceased to be based on a squadron or aerodrome, often associated with an incidence of a psychological disorder that was referred to as 'a lack of moral fibre'. The medical term was 'Neurosis Lacking in Confidence'. One investigation into psychological disorder in flying personnel, in file AIR2/6252 at the National Archives, details the scale of the number of psychiatric casualties that occurred in the RAF. The medical planners mistakenly assumed that the level and quality of selected volunteers would be virtually immune from psychological breakdown. In reality of course, this was not the case.

When it became clear that some aircrew members were breaking down with stress in combat, in February 1941 service chiefs set up a committee under the chairmanship of Air Vice-Marshal H. E. Whittingham with the intention to investigate flying stress in aircrew. An initial report concluded that pilots with an average or better capacity for sustaining effort could be expected to undertake fifteen to twenty sorties but thereafter there was a possibility of fatigue that could ultimately end in evident flying stress. The formal tour of duty required thirty sorties, or in the case of single-seat aircraft, 200 hours operational flying before crews were given a six-month rest from operations at a flying training establishment. By 1942, fewer than half of all bomber crews survived their first tour. These figures got worse in 1943, when only one in six were expected to survive their first tour, while only one in forty would survive two tours.

Among such disastrous statistics of survival, strong bonds between squadron members or individual crews evolved and served to protect against breakdown. The reliance on each other and growing confidence in engines, airframes and armaments all served to assist in supporting each and every individual. For those who struggled against their fears, there was often sympathy and support from colleagues, but inevitably in some instances it was not sufficient.

The Royal Air Force Medical Services publication in 1954 makes it clear that every physical trauma as a result of flying in the face of the enemy produced some degree of psychological injury and these were often referred to a neuropsychiatrist. The lack of moral fibre title was a stigma to be applied to anyone. Senior officers believed that without heavy-handed control, it could escalate through entire stations. Any man adjudged to be classified as lacking in moral fibre was removed from their unit immediately. Punishments were severe. An officer's commission was terminated and the individual was refused any further service employment. Non-commissioned officer aircrew were reduced in rank to airman and if they had a ground trade, they were re-mustered to that trade without promotion prospects. If no ground trade was pertinent, they were reduced to the lowest rank of airman. In all cases, all aircrew flying badges were forfeited. This immediate and harsh, intimidating process was limited to men in the first operational tour of duty. From 1942, aircrew on their second tour were excluded from that indignation and processed with more compassion. The term 'lacking moral fibre' was not a medical diagnosis, and it appears the statement was not used openly on personnel records. The rubber stamp wording of 'Withdrawn from aircrew duties', which can be seen in an airman's flying logbook, must be regarded as an open statement to cover many circumstances that may have precluded continued operational flying.

Flying logbooks are sometimes annotated expressively, while others are exceptionally bland with just basic detail. This possibly reflects upon the person who composed the content. Regardless, each man required equal amounts of bravery to face the unique terror of enduring operational flying relentlessly. Bomber Command in particular only recently received official recognition for the enduring role it undertook over occupied Europe with a memorial in London and the official government issue of the Bomber Command Clasp in 2012 and 2013. A dedicated campaign medal was never awarded. The Air Crew Europe campaign star was the only recognisable medal issued to operational crews until June 1944, following which the France and Germany Star was received until the war was won.

Medal ribbons became available on units from late July 1945. With the exception of the 1939–1945 War Medal, all other medal entitlements had formally been announced by May 1945. A significantly large Air Ministry Order dated 23 July 1945 was published that set out the procedure for medal entitlement. The claim form (F.2825) had to be completed for each officer and airman. It was emphasised that this was a provisional assessment and the detachable major part of the document was sent to the Air Ministry for officers and the Royal Air Force Records Office, Gloucester, for airmen/airwomen. The smaller part was retained by the individual and either kept by the officer or pasted into the airman's pay book. These were then used as the authority to get a personal issue of ribbon. These forms were notoriously inaccurate as many of the clerks completing them were unable to interpret the complicated Air Ministry Order. The decision made to not award Second World War campaign medals engraved or named to recipients was, in the author's opinion, a travesty. The justification to not do so appears to be based upon the cost and the time taken to administer the process, a shallow reflection upon the people who did their duty. The cost of lives during that war had been monumental.

Unlike medal recipients from the First World War, where medals reveal every recipient's identity impressed upon each individual medal, the medals awarded to the Second World War participants in general are devoid of any identity. As family memories fade, acts of bravery, dedication and commitment are likely to be lost altogether. In many cases, it is the documentation and in particular the flying logbooks of the aircrew and pilots that evidences the remarkable achievements undertaken by those young men. This book details just a few of the many who survived against the odds in circumstances that were repeated on endless occasions, often with fatal consequences.

Finally, mention must be made of the many thousands of relatives who dealt with the sadness of being informed officially that their loved ones had been lost in unknown circumstances. The Missing Research Enquiry Service had been established to locate and identify all missing RAF personnel. The Public Records Act of 1958 ensured the safe keeping of records, which included in this instance detailed exhumation reports and the efforts to locate and identify the lost casualties. These records were considered closed documents for many years until legislation changed and they were transferred to the National Archives. Known as casualty packs, access is now possible to view approximately 20,500 files in total. Each file relates to an aircraft and all casualties associated with the aircraft loss are recorded within that file. The records include the report of initial loss, correspondence to the next of kin and information received on the incident through investigation. Time will fade war memories but the written word secured in personal notes and official documents must be preserved and shared in order that the bravery and determination of the participants in the Second World War is remembered.

On 14 July 1940 Winston Churchill broadcast to the nation:

> This is no war of chieftains or of princes, of dynasties or national ambition, it is a war of peoples and of causes. There are vast numbers not only in this island but in every land, who will render faithful service in this War, but whose names

will never be known, whose deeds will never be recorded. This is a War of the Unknown Warriors but let all strive without failing in faith or in duty and the dark curse of Hitler will be lifted from our age.

Lest we forget.

# References

Air Ministry Files., AIR. 20/9305. Report of RAF and dominions Air Forces Missing Research and Enquiry Service National Archives 1944–1949.

Air Ministry Files., AIR. 2/6252C. P. Symonds and Denis Williams, Investigation into Psychological Disorder in Flying Personnel, The National Archives.

Air Ministry Files., AIR. 2/8591/S.7.C(1) Memorandum on the disposal of members of Aircrews who Forfeit the Confidence of their Commanding Officers, 1941, National Archives.

Air Ministry, Casualty procedure in war. Air publications no. 1922 Imperial War Museum. 1943 Department of Documents. K00 /242.

Air Force Public Record files., AIR 10/206, 10/2288, 10/4018, 10/4048, 10/4165, 10,4701, 10/4942, 14/2911, 20/1446, 20/1454-1459, 20/1461-1462, 20/1492, 20/1532, 20/1565, 20/1566,20/1568, 20/5800, 20/5810, 25/777-788, 27/287-288, 27/705-706, 27/970-971, 27/1046, 27/1094, 27/1456, 27/1981 and 27/1375-1376

Aders, G., *History of the German Night Fighter Force 1917–1945* (Macdonald & Jane's, 1979)

Bond, S., Forder, R., S*pecial Ops. Liberators 223 Bomber Support Squadron, 100 Group and the Electronic War* (Grub Street, 2011)

Bowman, M., *Mosquito Fighter/Fighter-Bomber Units of World War II* (Osprey Publishing, 1998)

Bowman, M. W. & Cushing, T., *Confounding the Reich: the Operational History of 100 Group Bomber Support* (Patrick Stephens, 1996)

Bowman, M., *100 Group (Bomber Support) RAF Bomber Command in World War II* (Pen and Sword, 2006)

Bowman, M., Cushing, T., *Confounding the Reich: The RAF's Secret War of Electronic Countermeasures in WWII* (Pen and Sword, 2004)

Brettingham, L., *Even When the Sparrows are Walking. The Origin and Effect of 100 Bomber Support Group, 1943–1945* (Librario, 2002)

Carter N. and C., *The DFC and How it Was Won* (Savannah, 1998)

Chorley, W. R., *Bomber Command Losses* (Midland Counties, 1997)

Cooper, A., *Air Battle of the Ruhr* (Airlife Publishing, Shrewsbury, 1992)

Cordingly, N., *From a Cat's Whisker Beginning* (Merlin Books, 1988)

Cummings, C., *The Price of Peace. A Catalogue of RAF Aircraft Losses between VE-Day and End of 1945* (Nimbus)

Dennis, R., *Farnborough's Caterpillars* (Footmark, 1996)

Docherty, T., *Dinghy Drop* (Pen and Sword, 2007)

Gibson, E. & Kingsley Ward, G., *Courage Remembered* (HMSO, 1989)

Grehan, J. & Martin, M., *Far East Air Operations* (London, 2014)

Halley, J., *Squadrons of the RAF & Commonwealth* (Air Britain, 1988)

Hendrie, A., *Canadian Squadrons in Coastal Command* (Vanwell, 2004)

Hering, P., *Customs and Traditions of the Royal Air Force* (Gale & Polden, 1961)

Houghton, G., *They Flew Through Sand* (Jarrolds, London, 1942)

Jefford, C. G., *Observers and Navigators; non-pilot aircrew in RFC, RNAS & RAF* (Airlife, 2001)

Jennings, P., *Dunlopera, The Works and Workings of the Dunlop Rubber Company* (Privately published, 1961)

Jones, S., *Fallen Flyers: Tragedy in the skies over war time Gower* (Bryngold, 2005)

Maton, M., *Honour Those Mentioned in Dispatches* (Token Publishing, 2013)

Maton, M., *Honour the Air Forces* (Token Publishing, 2004)

McCarthy, J., *Aircrew and the Lack of Moral Fibre in the Second World War* (War and Society Vol. 2, 1984)

Middlebrook, M. & K. Everitt., *The Bomber Command War Diaries* (London: Viking, 1985–

Middlebrook, M., *The Battle of Berlin* (Penguin, 1980)

Middlebrook, M., *The Berlin Raids* (Viking, 1988)

Middlebrook, M., *The Peenemunde Raid* (Allen Lane, 1982)
National Archives recommendations for honours and awards, under the terms of the Open Government Licence.
Clutton-Brock, O., *RAF Evaders* (Grub Street, 2009)
Clutton-Brock, O., *Footprints on the Sands of Time* (Grub Street, 2003)
Payne, L., *Air Dates* (Heinemann, 1957)
Perquin, J., *British Parachutes* (Histoire Collections, 2015)
Price, A., *The Instruments of Darkness* (Macdonald & Janes, 1979)
Rawlings, J., *Coastal Support and Special Squadrons* (Janes, 1982)
Reid, D. D., 'The Historical Background to Wartime research in Psychology in the RAF' in Dearnley, E. J. & Warr, P. B. (Eds), *Aircrew Stress in Wartime Operations* (London, 1948)
Rexford-Welch Squadron Leader, *RAF Medical Services, Administration* (HMSO, London, 1954)
Robinson, A., *Night Fighter* (Ian Allan, 1988)
*Royal Air Force 1939–1945 Vol. I, II and III* (HMSO, 1953)
Shores, C. and Izawa Y., *Bloody Shambles Vol. 1 and 2* (Grubb Street, 1992)
Streetly, M., *The Aircraft of 100 Group* (Robert Hale, 1984)
Streetly, M., *Confound and Destroy 100 Group and The Bomber Support Campaign* (Macdonald and Jane's, 1978)
Sturtivany, R. Hamlin, J. Halley J., *RAF Flying Training and Support Units* (Air Britain, 1997)
Tavender, I., *The DFM Register for the Second World War* (Savannah, 2000)
They Shall not Grow Old Commonwealth Air Training Plan Museum (1996)
Wynn, K., *The Men of the Battle of Britain* (Gliddon, 1989)

# Index

Adams, Sgt Michael E., 102, 104–105
Ahrens, Sqn Ldr, 4
Aitken, WO, 19
Anderson, Flt Lt, 82
Andrews, Sqn Ldr L.V., 26, 29

Babbington-Smith, Plt Off
    Constance, 93–4
Bailes, Flt Sgt, 19, 21, 24
Bain, WO Victor, 216–18
Baker, Flt Sgt Jack, 218
Barcroft, Sgt, 55
Barker-Read, AC, 17
Batson, Plt Off William, 205–207,
    209–10
Beecroft, Sgt Brian Dennis, 92–3,
    98–9, 101
Bellaby, Sgt, 70
Bellingan, Flt Sgt Leslie, 24
Bennett, Wg Cdr, 94
Bevan, Sgt, 176
Black, Plt Off Alexander, 49
Blackman, Plt Off F.H., 21
Board, Sgt Kenneth, 33, 37, 40,
    44–6
Bradley, Sqn Ldr, 23
Braham, Gp Cpt John Randall
    Daniel, 75–6
Brown, Sgt Alexander, 87, 91

Brown, Sgt J. L., 29
Bryant, Sqn Ldr J.H., 238
Bull, Sgt N.J., 29
Burness, Sgt James, 123–26
Burt, Sgt Richard, 174
Buttling, Sgt A., 165

Campbell, Flt Sgt C., 164–5
Ceybird, Flt Sgt Wilson, 218
Chandler, Sgt Roy, 95–6
Cheshire, Sgt, 17
Clark, LAC, 114
Clayden, Sgt, 235–7, 239
Clegg, Flt Sgt, 17
Clubs:
    British Parachute Company,
        19, 24
    Caterpillar Club, 9–13, 16, 18,
        29, 33, 37, 44, 46–7, 51, 54, 62,
        64, 121, 123–4, 127, 144, 173,
        179, 205, 213, 234, 236, 240
    Dominion Parachute Company,
        14–15
    Elliot Parachute Company, 24
    Goldfish Club, 65–8, 71–3, 85,
        91–2, 102, 109, 122, 124, 126,
        128, 134, 136–7, 143, 147, 153,
        197, 201, 203–204, 216, 219, 245
    GQ Parachute Company, 125

Guinea Pig Club, 190, 192–4, 196–7, 204, 246
Late Arrivals Club, 157–61, 163, 173, 179–80, 185, 188–9
Pioneer Parachute Company, 10
Roo Club, 14
Switlik Parachute Company, 10–13
Collins, Sgt, 17
Connor, LAC, 133
Constable, Flt Sgt P., 165
Corrie, Sgt, 17
Cross, Sgt Donald, 130
Currie, Sgt, 202

Day, Sgt John, 98–9
Deacon, Sgt, 70
Dexter, Sgt P. H., 21–2
Dixon, Plt Off Patrick Leslie, 102, 104–105, 108
Docherty, Flt Sgt Thomas, 173–6, 178
Douglas, Sgt Thomas, 234, 236
Drake, Sgt D.J., 21
Drysdale, Flt Lt, 114
Du Pont, 2
Dudeney, Plt Off, 114
Dufresne, Flt Lt C.W., 238
Dunlop, Sgt, 17
Dunmall, Flt Sgt, 30
Dunsmore, Plt Off William, 87, 89, 91
Durie, Sgt, 176

Elliott, Flt Lt H.P., 93–4, 96–7
Elliotte, Flt Lt Jack MacGregor, 38, 44

Evans, Sgt, 96
Ewen, Flt Sgt, 4

Falk, Wg Cdr Roland, 121
Ferguson, Flt Lt Ronald William, 75, 80, 85
Fleming, Sgt, 17
Fletcher, Sgt, 79
Folly, Plt Off, 82
Forrest, Sgt Malcolm, 131
Forshaw, Sqn Ldr, 82
Forster, Sgt Thomas, 49–50
Frost, Flt Sgt W., 10

Gibson, Sgt, 55
Glenn, Plt Off, 210
Goddard, Sgt G., 165
Gordon-Powell, Sgt, 210
Goug, Flt Sgt, 119
Grace, Sgt J.N., 102
Granbois, Sgt, 164–5
Gray, Flt Lt P.J., 21
Green, Flt Sgt A., 165
Green, WO, 21
Guymer, Sgt Haydn Neil, 98

Hall, Sgt Thomas John, 39, 44
Hammett, Sgt, 176–8
Hare, Sgt William, 174
Harris, Lt Harold, 9, 12
Harrison, Flt Sgt J., 165
Harrison, Sqn Ldr, 63
Hart, Sgt E.G.A., 80
Hayler, Sgt Edward John, 39, 44
Hayward, Sgt S., 165
Henderson, Flt Lt, 141

Hind, Flt Sgt W.T., 19, 21
Hobdey, Sgt, 50
Holman, Plt Off Richard, 49–50
Hood, Sqn Ldr, 121
Houghton, Wg Cdr, 158–60, 163, 185
Hudson, Flt Sgt, 164–5, 171
Hughes, Flt Sgt, 17
Hunt, Plt Off, 117

Irvin, Leslie (Parachutes), 1, 3, 6, 9–14, 16–18, 36–8, 44, 127, 144, 213, 236

Jacobs, Flt Lt, 75
James, Sqn Ldr, 104
Jarvis, Flt Sgt Victor, 111–16
Jones, Flt Sgt G., 165, 168

Keegan, Wg Cdr, 17
Kelly, Sgt H.A., 58
Kelsall, Sgt R., 21
King, Plt Off Martyn, 3
Kirkpatrick, Flt Sgt P., 165
Knowles, Plt Off, 176–8
Knowles, Sgt, 132

Lacey, Sgt Ginger, 15
Lawson, Sgt A., 102
Leboutte, Flt Lt Lucien, 81
Lees, Sgt, 31
Lewenden, Plt Off, 119
Lewis, Flt Sgt L.J., 21
Lockwood, Flt Sgt Cecil Harry, 54, 58–9, 61–2, 64
Lord, Sgt John, 234, 236–7, 239

Mahaddie, Gp Cpt Hamish, 97
Markham, Sqn Ldr, 58
Marshall, Flt Sgt, 70
Martin, Ft Lt, 121
McHugh, Sgt, 70
McKern, Wg Cdr, 56
Miller, Sgt Percival, 47–8, 50–3
Mitchell, Flt Lt, 55
Motts, Sgt George, 4
Murrel, Sgt, 132

Nash, Sgt F., 165, 171
Nethercote, Sgt, 162–3
Neville Duke, Sqn Ldr, 141
Nicholls, Wg Cdr, 63
Nicholson, Sgt, 131
Nightingale, Sgt, 16
Norris, Sgt R., 165
Norton, Flt Sgt, 70

O'Connor, William, 9
Ogilvie, Sqn Ldr, 95–6
Osborne, Flt Lt Roger, 73, 83, 85

Parrish, Flt Lt Charles Woodbine, 25–6, 28–9, 30–2
Payne, Sgt D.M., 29
Peck, Flt Sgt G.B., 58, 60
Penfold, Plt Off, 10
Pertus, Sgt, 127
Pike, Wg Cdr, 49–50
Price, Sgt Frederick, 100, 102, 104

RAF Squadrons:
  2 Squadron, 112–14, 181
  4 Squadron, 181

Index    257

5 Squadron, 181–3, 185–6
7 Squadron, 25, 30
10 Squadron, 69
12 Squadron, 202
15 Squadron, 97–8
21 Squadron, 66
25 Squadron, 111
26 Squadron, 112, 114
27 Squadron, 60
35 Squadron, 125
36 Squadron, 54–6, 58, 62
38 Squadron, 176–7
39 Squadron, 87
41 Squadron, 146
43 Squadron, 144
50 Squadron, 206–207
51 Squadron, 69
57 Squadron, 198
58 Squadron, 69
59 Squadron, 112
62 Squadron, 60
75 Squadron, 30, 39, 92–3
80 Squadron, 159
86 Squadron, 87
99 Squadron, 93
100 Squadron, 55, 57–8, 60, 62
103 Squadron, 34
109 Squadron, 128–32, 232
111 Squadron, 144–5
113 Squadron, 19
122 Squadron, 145–6
141 Squadron, 76, 79–83, 85
143 Squadron, 216–19
145 Squadron, 138–42
148 Squadron, 161–2, 174
149 Squadron, 26, 93, 102–103

159 Squadron, 16, 23
162 Squadron, 132
172 Squadron, 69
211 Squadron, 23
214 Squadron, 92
217 Squadron, 87–8
218 Squadron, 198
219 Squadron, 49–50
236 Squadron, 217
247 Squadron, 238
254 Squadron, 217, 219
256 Squadron, 75
268 Squadron, 114
275 Squadron, 116
276 Squadron, 116
277 Squadron, 76, 116, 118–19
278 Squadron, 116
279 Squadron, 116, 123–5, 127
280 Squadron, 116
294 Squadron, 68
355 Squadron, 21, 24
356 Squadron, 21, 24
405 Squadron, 234–5, 239
427 Squadron, 212
486 Squadron, 76, 79
501 Squadron, 15
514 Squadron, 164–5, 167
578 Squadron, 169
600 Squadron, 51–3
601 Squadron, 141
609 Squadron, 117
613 Squadron, 113
825 Squadron, 152, 154
836 Squadron, 148–9, 151, 154
Rawlins, Sgt Robert, 128–33, 136
Reid, Sqn Ldr, 166

Richmond, Sgt, 126
Ricketts, Sgt Albert, 66
Robertson, Charles, Goldfish
    Club, 65–7, 71, 91, 201–203
Rockett, Sgt, 16
Rolph, WO Henry, 161, 164–6,
    168–9, 171
Room, Sgt Cecil, 216, 218, 232

Sadler, Sgt P., 165
Scott, Wg Cdr, 79
Searles, Plt Off W.G., 29
Singer, Gp Cpt, 20
Smith, Sgt Donald, 31
Smith, Sgt Frank, 98
Snelling, Flt Sgt Robert James,
    24
Spence, Flt Sgt John Alexander,
    118–19
Steanes, Flt Sgt H., 10
Stephens, WO R.W., 21–2
Stephens, Sgt W.G., 80
Stone, Flt Lt, 206
Sutherland, Flt Sgt Alexander,
    137–40, 142, 145

Tayler, Flt Lt Thomas Henry
    Brian, 98
Taylor, Sgt Dennis, 197–9,
    201–204
Tetley, Sgt D., 165
Thompson, Flt Lt Frank, 98–9

Thompson, Sgt Ron, 66
Thompson, WO, 245
Thomson, Flt Sgt, 138, 141
Titterton, Sgt Lawrence, 98
Tregenza, Sgt Robert, 132–3
Twidale, Sgt Harry, 49–50

Vardy, Sgt, 70
Virgo, Flt Sgt, 70

Waddington, Sgt, 117
Waddy, Sqn Ldr J.D., 79
Waring, Gp Cpt E.F., 124
Warren, Sgt L., 164
Watson, Sgt Harling Walter, 48,
    51, 53
Watts, Fg Off Frederick, 4
White, Sgt, 176–8
White, Sqn Ldr, 85
Wilde, Flt Sgt E., 165
Wilkins, Sqn Ldr J.T., 62
Wilkinson, Sgt John, 87, 90–1
Williams, Plt Off Eric, 30
Wills, Flt Lt, 131
Wilson, LAC, 17
Wilson, Sgt W., 165
Wolf, Flt Sgt Herbert, 130
Woodage, Flt Sgt John Derek, 24
Woodbridge, Flt Sgt Stanley
    James, 23
Woodhall, Gp Cpt, 50
Woods, Sgt F.J., 102